HOME LANDSCAPES

HOME LANDSCAPES
Planting Design and
Management

Edward C. Martin, Jr., FASLA
Pete Melby, ASLA

TIMBER PRESS
Portland, Oregon

Line drawings are by Pete Melby.
Photographs are by Edward C. Martin, Jr. and Pete Melby.

ISBN 0-88192-282-X
Printed in Singapore

TIMBER PRESS, INC.
The Haseltine Building
133 S.W. Second Ave., Suite 450
Portland, Oregon 97204-3527, U.S.A.

Library of Congress Cataloging-in-Publication Data

Martin, Edward C. (Edward Curtis), 1928-
    Home landscapes : planting design and management / Edward C.
  Martin, Jr., Pete Melby.
        p. cm.
    Includes bibliographical references and index.
    ISBN 0-88192-282-X
    1. Gardens--Design. 2. Landscape gardening. 3. Gardens--Design-
  -Pictorial works. 4. Landscape gardening--Pictorial works.
  I. Melby, Pete, 1947- . II. Title.
  SB473.M295 1994   93-39302
  712'.6--dc20   CIP

Contents

Color photographs precede page 97

DEDICATION

To those who are intent on improving the quality and usefulness of private gardens and public landscapes, and to those who accept that we have not always conducted our activities to be in harmony with the earth—to all who desire to begin the process of living and gardening in a balanced manner with our environment, we dedicate this book.

Preface

For years, as practicing landscape architects and educators of landscape architecture students, we have longed for a publication that combines planting design with landscape management in an illustrated format. We decided to put our years of professional experience to good use and create the book we sought.

Our goal has been to produce a photographic guide with written commentary on the various components of design and management. The photographs illustrate why certain planting designs work and how plants can be used productively, such as by blocking afternoon sun to reduce heat gain and thus energy bills. The management or maintenance of these productive planting designs follows the design explanations.

The thrust of landscape architectural design is to create an overall design scheme that is in harmony with the land, and whose spaces convey personalities compatible with the needs of the user. The first chapter offers basic insights into the specific design process used by professionals to create designs. It also explains the basic elements and principles of design. Here readers learn how to begin to create spaces with personalities and moods. Chapter 1 provides a foundation for all that follows.

The next four chapters focus on creating planting designs that are both functional and aesthetically pleasing. Plants, along with building walls and fences, are the major space makers in home landscapes. Written descriptions and complementary photographs combine to explain the many functional uses of plants. Chapter 6 gives an overview of historical landscape architecture and presents garden design techniques that stand the test of time.

Section II focuses on effective landscape management—maintaining home landscapes for maximum performance and health with minimum commitment of time and resources. Detailed information covers the techniques and considerations necessary for effective management of one's garden. A monthly management calendar briefly summarizes what to do and when to do it, as well as estimating the time required to complete specific tasks.

This functional planting design and landscape management book will be of value to homeowners who want to enhance the design, use, enjoyment, and value of their property. It can also assist students in a design studio and serve professionals in the landscape industry. By understanding the principles of planting design and landscape management, all gardeners can gain the inspiration and knowledge necessary to create effective planting designs, reducing the time spent working in the garden, and increasing the time spent enjoying the garden. With this book we sincerely hope we help readers toward this pleasant end.

Edward C. Martin, Jr., FASLA
Pete Melby, ASLA

Acknowledgments

This was a very challenging and exciting book to write and pull together. At times we thought this exciting three-year endeavor was a limitless journey of refinement. Our editor Micheline Ronningen labored along with us to make the material concise and logically presented. We thank her for her gentle assistance.

A host of designers and scientists shared their knowledge and ideas in creating a book that embraces design, science, and management. Noted floral designer Ralph Null, AIFD, and former president of ASLA Cameron R. J. Man, FASLA, helped us to better understand the design elements and principles and improved our presentation. Art teacher Christine Codling generously gave of her insights on teaching methodology and art resources. Guiding us on tours to photograph gardens and/or providing useful information were landscape architects Richard C. Griffin, Clifton B. Egger, Neil G. Odenwald, Ben G. Page, René J. L. Fransen, Sam Hogue, Charles E. Parks, and Stuart M. Mertz.

We are also grateful for the scientists and educators of Mississippi State University, the Mississippi Cooperative Extension Service, the Mississippi Agricultural and Forestry Experiment Station, and the United States Department of Agriculture, each providing a wealth of useful information. Specific thanks to Dr. Charles Wax, geographer and State Climatologist, for his knowledge of climatic conditions and sun path regimes. Dr. Karl Riggs contributed his knowledge about rock and soil genesis.

That the gardener be able to comprehend the physical nature of soils and their absolute importance to garden management is paramount to our efforts. Supporting this effort, agronomy professors Dr. David E. Pettry and Dr. Jac Varco, and horticulturists Dr. Freddie Raspberry and Dr. Milo Burnham, all shared their expert knowledge. Extension agronomist Dr. Wayne Houston helped in clarifying soil pH manipulation and the use of wood ash as a potassium source. Entomologist Dr. James H. Jarrett helped in categorizing and organizing information on insects in chapter 16, "Regarding Pests and Diseases." Extension plant pathologists Dr. Frank J. Killebrew, Dr. William F. Moore, and Dr. Donald J. Blasingame were extremely helpful to us with identification of plant disease symptoms and in categorizing diseases. Biologists Dr. Jerry Jackson and Dr. Walter J. Diehl offered practical viewpoints about the biological consequences of managing landscapes and information on soil microorganisms and insects.

Turfgrass specialist and agronomist Dr. Jeff Krans met with us many times to educate about turfgrasses, their growth habits, and management. Agronomy professor Dr. Mike Goatley worked with us to be sure both the scientific and practical aspects of using fertilizers would be clearly communicated.

The management section (II) is composed not only from years of practical experience, but also from lectures by guest landscape managers and landscape contractors at our university. Experts who shared their experiences include those from the Brickman Company, Teas Nursery, Greenscape, North Haven Gardens, Lamberts, and Environmental Care. Landscape contractors Bob Callaway and Charles Scoggins eagerly shared their knowledge and provided constructive criticism. Assistance with specific management techniques regarding garden pools, wetland and aquatic plants, root pruning, and tree transplanting came from horticulturists Mr. Boyce Tankersley and Mr. Ben Chu, of the Missouri Botanical Garden, and Dr. Lester Estes, of Mississippi State University. Mississippi State commerical nursery specialist Dr. David Tatum provided bulb planting depth information. Expert *Caladium* gardener Mrs. Marilyn Epperson shared caladium growing and managing knowledge. Mississippi State plant pathologist and rose researcher Dr. James Spencer provided rose management information. Ecologist and forester Dr. Victor Rudis imparted an understanding of management techniques for natural prairie and wildflower meadows.

There were other special people whose assistance was fundamental. Lou Melby and Roberta P. Martin reviewed this book as it was being written, working tirelessly through text and guiding us toward idea clarity. We deeply appreciate their efforts. Thanks to Mr. Jack Brunt for reviewing passages and serving as our model gardener, spiritedly discussing ideas and techniques. John Davis, garden center operator, explained the use of regular and slow-release fertilizer and contributing current information on organic mulches for home gardeners. We value writer and editor Etta Wilson for sharing points about writing gained from her years of experience and awareness. Mrs. Owen Palmer, Jr. provided the excellent photograph of her espaliered *Camellia sasanqua*. Arboriculturist Robert T. Buckelew reinforced the chapter on the care of trees and shrubs. Jim Harfst, computer specialist, helped us through several near computer catastrophes. Dr. H. Graham Purchase and Jo B. McKenzie also helped provide computer assistance. Thanks to typist Jeanise Lane who typed and retyped without one audible complaint.

To all these people we are enduringly grateful. We never cease to be amazed by people who give so generously of their time and knowledge. Their individual contributions enhance the detail and effectiveness of this publication while enriching our experience.

SECTION I: Design

1

Process

Thoughtful landscape design aims toward creating a landscape that is orderly as opposed to chaotic. Orderly landscape compositions are pleasing to see and experience. Chaotic designs look and feel unorganized and are not generally pleasing to experience. To create a design with a sense of order it is necessary to start with order. We do this by following the landscape architectural design process and employing the elements and principles of design.

The design process landscape architects use is to establish a program, make a program analysis diagram, do a site analysis, develop a concept plan, and finish with the design or master plan. This process ensures a design created in harmony with its environs that is reflective of the client's needs. Each of these process steps will be discussed. By applying this step-by-step sequence, the designer gradually creates a logical and appropriate design solution.

Once the landscape architectural project evolves to the design plan phase of the design process, it is time to apply the elements and principles of design. The elements and principles give a design feelings and expression; some call it personality. The elements are the building blocks of a design and the principles are the ways to arrange and use the elements. Elements and principles vary with different designers but the result of using the design process and the elements and principles is a pleasing composition.

The program for the site—the beginning point for design—starts with listing the types of land uses, facilities, and feelings desired in the landscape. For example, a person might include a reflective, quiet patio space, an active swimming pool area, and an arrival-entry space that conveys a feeling of strength and security. These desired use areas, facilities, and feelings comprise the program development part of the design process.

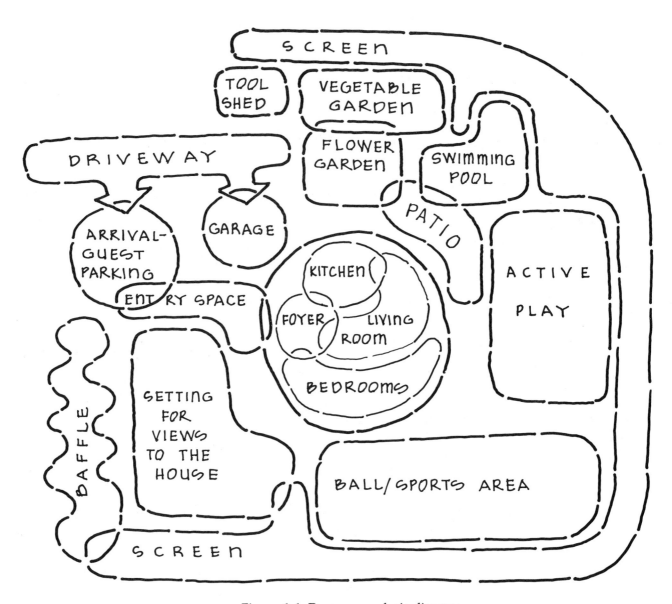

Figure 1-1. Program analysis diagram.

Designers analyze the ideal use interrelationships of a proposed site program by drawing bubbles or diagrams (Fig. 1-1). This is a program analysis. By working quickly through different relationship diagrams, the ideal location and interrelationships of uses eventually evolve. When developing a program analysis, do not relate the land uses and facilities to the site. Relate uses only to one another at this stage. The ideal use relationships are applied to the site at the concept plan stage.

Site analysis is an intensive look at the site and its surroundings to determine assets and liabilities. The site analysis includes factors such as seasonal sun angles, prevailing winds, site history, slopes, vegetation, existing spaces, soil characteristics, utilities, and views. Understanding a site through such an analysis helps ensure a harmonious relationship between the design and the existing site.

The concept plan involves defining proposed land use areas on the site according to the ideal interrelationships found in the program analysis, moderated by any constraints noted in the site analysis. The location of land uses on the site in the concept plan must be determined before moving into the design plan phase. Land uses can be represented as diagrams or bubbles on the site.

From the land use areas of the concept plan, the actual site design or master plan is developed by applying the elements and principles of design. The master plan is translated as a finished drawing of the dream or vision for the landscape. It includes the forms and materials of all site facilities and spaces.

Design elements are line, shape or form, space, texture, and color. They are the parts or building blocks of design. The elements of design appeal to the senses of sight and touch. Through understanding and knowing how to use the elements, a holistic design is assured.

Two- and three-dimensional materials and objects create lines in the landscape, conveying feelings to the viewer. Examples of lines in the landscape include a straight line in a row planting of trees or shrubs, the meandering edge of a bed of ground cover, and the angular edges of a wall. Lines can express movement and establish mood (Fig. 1-2).

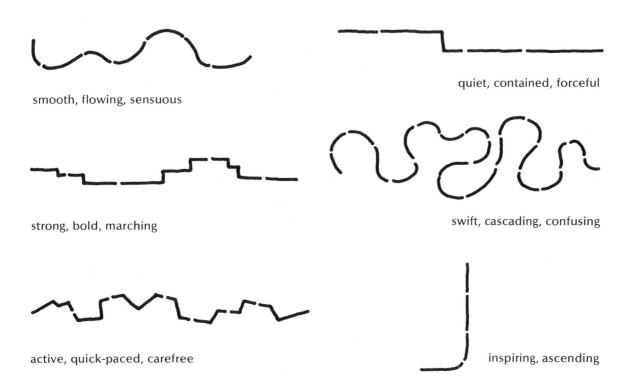

smooth, flowing, sensuous

quiet, contained, forceful

strong, bold, marching

swift, cascading, confusing

active, quick-paced, carefree

inspiring, ascending

Figure 1-2. Types of line effects and resulting feelings.

Shape refers to a two-dimensional outline. When a third dimension is added, a shape becomes a form. A circle is a shape while a sphere is a form. Forms can be tagged geometric or organic. For example, a pyramid is a geometric form and a tree is an organic form. Every three-dimensional object has form. Three-dimensional objects can give the impression of being light or heavy, and of being active or stable, depending on their form and position in a space. A pyramid is a stable form while a human figure leaning forward is active and implies movement.

Space is defined by three-dimensional objects like buildings, walls, and plants. Large spaces can feel free and open, overwhelming or sometimes intimidating while small spaces can be intimate and comfortable for visiting. When spaces are too small they generate a feeling of claustrophobia among users. The size of a space needs to relate to the activity being accommodated and the feeling the designer wants to express in the space.

Texture is surface quality and it is perceived through the tactile and/or visual senses on a tangent from rough to smooth. Somewhat rough, coarse textures are perceived as warm, active, friendly, and informal. Smooth textures lend a cool, undemanding, tranquil, and more formal sense to the overall feeling being created in a design. All plants and materials have texture and evoke a sensual response.

The color wheel is one organized way for selecting color. The primary colors on the wheel (Fig. 1-3) are yellow, red, and blue, and the secondary colors are orange, green, and purple. Two primary colors produce the secondary colors: yellow and red mixed together make orange, yellow and blue make green, red and blue make purple. Colors bordering one another on the wheel are called analogous. They will usually look good when used together because they have a single color in common. Colors opposite one another are called complementary colors and when used together provide a maximum color contrast that is very noticeable.

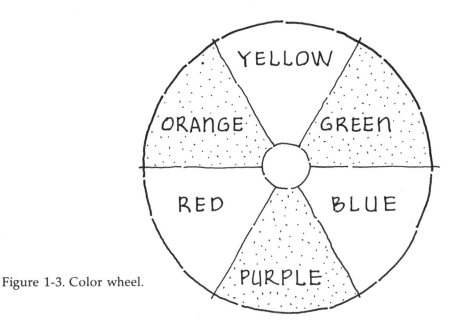

Figure 1-3. Color wheel.

Color value is the lightness or darkness of a color. Through color value a flat surface can appear to be three-dimensional. Paintings with depth are examples of color value creating a three-dimensional sense. Colors are selected for predictable psychological responses. Only people are recognized as being psychologically responsive in this manner. Warm colors (fire) like yellow, red, and orange are active, happy, and festive. Cool colors (ice) like blue, green, and purple are restful, tranquil, and peaceful. Black, white, and gray are neutral colors. They tend to evoke calm, peaceful psychological responses and feelings of formality.

People respond positively to designs with order and harmonious composition. Utilizing design principles can help to evoke that sense of order and composition by unifying and organizing a design. The principles enable one to arrange the design elements to work effectively in the overall composition. Principles are used together in a design in concert rather than separately, although one principle might be more evident in the composition than others. Principles include balance, unity, variety, proportion, emphasis and contrast, and transition.

When something is balanced, its components or masses have equal visual or actual weight about an axis or point. When both sides are equally balanced in actual weight, that is, when one side is a mirror image of the other, there is symmetrical balance. Symmetry can lend dignity, formality, and stateliness. It is poised or static rather than dynamic. Asymmetrical balance is when one side is not a mirror image of the other side, yet the composition or feature still maintains balance. Asymmetrical balance is created by grouping forms or shapes on either side of an axis so the visual weight is equal. Things that have asymmetrical balance usually appear more active or dynamic and interesting. Viewers tend to ponder asymmetry because figuring out what gives the balance is visually demanding.

A design with unity is defined as yielding a sense of completeness and harmony, and it will attract and hold attention. Unity in a design is achieved by one or more of the following methods:

1. Having both dominant and subordinate components.

2. Repeating features such as color, texture, line, shape, or form.

3. Limiting the number of objects, forms, colors, textures, and lines.

4. Surrounding an object or area with an enclosure.

Repetition is the easiest way to achieve unity in a design composition. Through repetition of components rhythms are created. Without repetition, there would be no rhythm. Rhythm is the related visual movement of components in a design that demands attention. Figure 1-4 illustrates three examples. Rhythm can also be illustrated through the example of playing a piano. Pressing only one key one time does not yield rhythm. Repeatedly playing the same key for the same duration gives rhythm, though such can get annoying. Actual rhythm is achieved by playing a combination of notes of long and short duration. Alternating long and short notes is not a complex rhythm and is not very exhilarating. In design the simpler the rhythm, the calmer the design; the more complex or varied the rhythm, the more exhilarating the design. Creating unity and an interesting rhythm in a landscape could be accomplished through repetition of a line of three shrubs and a tree throughout the length of a border planting.

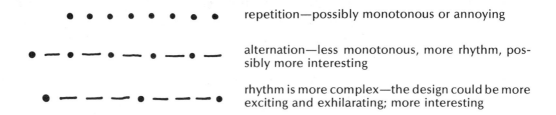

repetition—possibly monotonous or annoying

alternation—less monotonous, more rhythm, possibly more interesting

rhythm is more complex—the design could be more exciting and exhilarating; more interesting

Figure 1-4. Rhythm examples.

A courtyard with concrete paving, concrete benches, and concrete planters has unity through repetition of material. Repetition carried to extremes though creates monotony. A successful design also has variety, providing richness and excitement in a unified design. Variety is attained through a diversity of materials, forms, spaces, colors, lines, and textures in a design composition. Too much variety produces chaos, which is discomforting to most. Generally, three different building materials can work together in a composition without producing chaos. If more than three building materials are used, the composition may have too much variety and chaos will result.

Since many plants are similar in color, texture, line, and form, a larger number of different plants can be used together in a composition without necessarily resulting in chaos. However, chaos threatens when an excessive amount of colors, textures, lines, and forms of plants mix together into one composition.

Proportion is the relationship of components to each other. By having components in proportion to one another there is a pleasing relationship between sizes and shapes or parts. For example, accent plants at the entry space to a residence should relate to both the size of the space and to the size of people. All components of the entry space, including paving, sculpture, plants, and even the space itself, should relate to the size of a person. Plants that are too small would be out of proportion with the entry space and human scale, and entering would not feel comfortable.

Consider the proportion of a sculpture in a landscape: the sculpture is in proportion within its space if it does not appear huge or tiny. A large space dwarfs a small sculpture and makes it seem insignificant. A large sculpture in a small space cannot be viewed from far enough away. The large sculpture could make being in the space overpowering, uncomfortable, and dwarfing for the viewer.

Emphasis differentiates between the most important and the least important in a design composition. A person can achieve emphasis in a design composition through contrast. To get contrast one has to select and arrange both visually dominant and subordinate garden components to emphasize some feature. Such an arrangement can reinforce what should be visually prominent in a composition. Contrast can be established by locating a visually dominant color, texture, or form against a larger mass of a visually subordinate color, texture or form. Color photograph 41 illustrates contrast through emphasis particularly well.

Features that command attention and are visually attractive are dominant and emphasized in garden design. Those features that are visually recessive and do not require attention are subordinate and de-emphasized in the composition. In order for a design to be pleasing to see and to use, both dominant and subordinate components are necessary.

Effective transition establishes a logical and pleasing movement from one color, texture, line, form, or space to another. For example, cool, calm colors like green, blue, and gray along with fine-textured plant and paving materials could be used at the arrival and entry space to a residence. These colors and textures would give a sense of tranquillity and formality. As guests move to the active, festive outdoor entertaining space, colors could begin a transition from green to yellow-green. Upon arrival at the entertainment patio, yellow, orange, and red colors and a variety of fine and coarse textures could be used to create a festive, happy atmosphere. Notice on the color wheel how these colors make a transition from cool green to warm yellow, orange, and red. The textures made a transition from fine to a combination of fine and coarse textures. Locating a small, paved patio on the edge of a large lawn area is not sufficient transition from the small to the large area. Yet by introducing several small trees at the patio area and repeating the trees at several locations within the large lawn area, an adequate transition from one space to the next is established.

Theoretically, in applying these elements and principles of design, harmony, beauty, and suitability will evolve. A design with harmony is one having an interrelationship between parts that results in cohesiveness. For example, is the design surrounded by an enclosure and are enough forms and colors repeated to give unity? Does unity flee with the seasons? Is there a look of togetherness and pleasing balance in the design?

Beauty in a design simply means the design is aesthetically pleasing to the individual for whom it was created. The needs of the individual are personalized in the design. *Beauty is in the eye of the beholder* applies here. Suitability is established if the needs outlined in the initial program are met. The design forms should evolve to accommodate requisite needs and desired feelings in the space.

2

Designing Space

Plants may define space through enclosure, such as a tree providing a canopy, or they may be treated as three-dimensional forms on the ground. The result is a positive and a negative, a mass and void composition with the plants forming the masses and the spaces forming the voids. This is spatial definition, creating or defining spaces or outdoor rooms in a garden. Plants play a vital role in garden design. Properly used, plants are one of the most significant materials in outdoor space or garden design.

It is important to remember that the voids are as important as the masses, because the voids allow for people and activity. Too often, the home gardener is more concerned about the appearance of the plant or plant masses, and ignores the resulting space or void created by the plant's position. The objective of planting design is to meld these masses and voids, to create attractive, useful spaces for people while providing aesthetically pleasing plant compositions.

Desirable (or undesirable) feelings can be created by the effective use of plants in design. For example, a person alone in the middle of a huge open space might feel uncomfortable or overwhelmed by the large, undefined space. By merely adding a single sugar maple (*Acer saccharum*) tree, the tree canopy establishes a smaller space more related to the size of the human figure. Landscape architects call this "human scale." In garden design, multistoried structures can better relate to the land and the scale of people through the addition of plants nearby that reduce the feeling of vastness. In urban design, street trees creating a canopy over a street make the driving space beneath feel more comfortable psychologically, lending security and a measure of interest. In addition to providing psychological comforts, a tree canopy provides the physical comforts of shade, windbreak, and insulation.

Another way plants can define space architecturally is by creating rooms with low or high walls of plants. Plant masses are physical barriers and are used as garden walls to define a space, screen a view, and separate uses.

Plants used as a solid mass or as a baffle can enclose space. The solid may be a hedge of a single plant variety or a composition of several varieties providing seasonal effects. A mass 3 ft (1 m) high provides a psychological barrier to discourage circulation by people and animals. Physically, it usually requires more than 3 ft (1 m) to control mobility.

A baffle is a row planting. Plants can be sited in a row so one can see and walk through them yet enjoy a sense of enclosure. A row of street trees planted at equal distances is an example. Street trees serve as a baffle separating vehicular and pedestrian circulation and allowing people on a sidewalk a feeling of protection from the traffic.

The garden floor material may be a solid lawn or other materials, or it may be a lawn enclosing an area and providing contrast of color and texture. There are no set rules on how large or small a lawn floor area should be. Appropriate size depends on the surrounding masses, materials, and activities. Remember that everything is relative, and that a comfortable feeling by people who occupy the space will often depend on what encloses the lawn floor.

Plants can separate different use areas in design through the use of screens and baffles. For example, plant masses may be used to separate outdoor living spaces from the garden shed or compost area. A swimming pool area may be discreetly separated from a public area. Boundary plantings may separate different use areas of each property. Shrubs and trees may separate street parking from pedestrian entry areas to a house and yet allow easy access to both.

Plants do much to reduce the vastness of space and make people feel comfortable. As mentioned earlier, a single tree in a large space can humanize it. Plants can also make small spaces feel larger. This is especially important with high land costs resulting in high density developments. If some parts or edges of a property can be concealed from view through the use of a human-scale planting, it can make the space appear larger by tending to create curiosity about what is hidden beyond. This is referred to as establishing concealment and revealment, leaving something to the imagination and surprised delight of the viewer. Then too, few garden design compositions are created which do not include screening to hide undesirable views or to satisfy privacy. Many homes are designed with uninterrupted views of the garden spaces, and the extensive use of window glass may require planting screens for privacy.

To create interest on flat topography, low-growing forms of plants, such as small shrubs or ground covers, can be used. People can see past them while enjoying their color and texture, yet the forms also define space in much the same way as furniture in a house creates spatial interest.

Within smaller home landscapes, there is usually a need and benefit in establishing a greater feeling of depth. One way depth can be achieved is by placing trees as a foreground vertical element of interest against a solid mass background. This arrangement provides a sense of depth. Also, a baffle of trees in front of an empty space provides a feeling of potentially greater distance in the background.

When using plants to create depth, it is valuable to consider the design elements of color and texture. Dark colors create depth when used in the background if light colors are used in the foreground. Remember that cool colors recede visually and warm colors come forward.

Fine-textured plants create a feeling of depth and spaciousness when used in limited-space areas. Coarse textures in garden design stand out and demand attention while fine textures recede and appear passive. Coarse textures used near an outdoor seating area with fine textures in the background create a feeling of depth, which may be highly desirable for a small home landscape. In large or more open areas, coarse textures make the spaces feel smaller by being in proportion to the spaces.

Ground forms of plant masses provide a transition from different heights of plants and structures to the garden floor. When properly used, transition plantings can unify areas and materials. A small tree near a house serves as a transition from the roof to shrubs, ground covers, or lawn under the tree. A ground cover in front of a brick garden wall is a transition from a higher, hard construction material to a lower lawn area, the garden floor. Low or weeping plants located around the edge of water will help relate the water surface to the land, boat docks, or foot bridges.

Due to plant growth, seasonal sun angles or weather, and plant shadow patterns, the visual perception of a landscaped space is continually in flux. Perceptual changes of space are caused by many factors, including plant growth, the use of mulch, plant forms, and time, and do not exclude changes in the individual. With time, careful initial planting can transform a vast space into an area possessing human scale, resulting in a more comfortable environment.

Because plants grow and change in size, it is important to learn how fast and how large plants grow. This knowledge enables one to space plants adequately for an effective, long-term design, potentially reduce initial installation costs, and curb maintenance expense. Often, plants are spaced too closely due to a lack of knowledge of growth rate and ultimate size. By allowing sufficient space for plant growth, the perception of changing spaces can add to the enjoyment of the garden by observing the plants expanding, thus reducing the spaces between them. A reduction in long-range management expenses will also result.

To allow for plant growth when setting out plants, void spaces between plants and along the planting area edges are created. An application of organic mulch in the void areas helps unify a mass of spaced plants by providing ground level continuity. Along the edges of the planting, the mulch provides a distinct boundary of a defined space. The type of line the mulched area makes will help create a specific mood. For example, that mood could be one of relaxation (curvilinear line) or action (angular line).

Plant forms have a great influence on spatial definition and feelings of comfort. Natural forms of trees may be rounded, angular, pyramidal, oval, vase-shaped, columnar, irregular, or weeping. Shrub forms may be rounded or angular, upright, mounded, horizontal, vase-shaped, prostrate, leggy, weeping, or trailing. Different forms induce different feelings and effects, and all have a place in garden design if properly selected and placed. For example, spreading and weeping plants tend to look passive and relaxed. They also relate well to uneven topography by providing a rhythmic feeling, blending the plant form to the mounding, undulating earth form. Tall, erect plant forms provide dramatic emphasis.

Seasonal changes are to be considered as well. Spring foliage is generally light green, deepening as time passes. Flower buds give way to bursts of color and new forms, often followed by attractive fruit and seeds. With the fall season comes a rainbow of foliage colors more widespread than those of spring. Winter brings a perception of lines, patterns, textures, shadows, and a feeling of openness.

The perception of space changes from morning to night and from childhood to adulthood. A small child may feel many plants to be very large and overbearing, yet as an adult one feels more comfortable with the size of plants, though they have grown, too. Time also provides for adults a greater appreciation of the beauty, function, and management of plants and spaces.

Plants define space architecturally by enclosure, canopy, and ground forms. The perception of spaces and plants is constantly changing. It is important to consider that the spaces or voids created by the architectural use of plants are as important as the actual plant masses.

3

Engineering Considerations

Here we will discuss briefly how plants can be used to solve specific engineering problems to enhance safety and health. Plants can reduce mechanical light glare, influence pedestrian and vehicular traffic circulation, control erosion, buffer sound, and reduce dust and fumes.

Plants can help to reduce mechanical light glare from reflections on pavements, building materials, earth, and water surfaces. Outdoor lighting may enhance and extend the use of gardens, yet glare from lights is to be avoided. Property owners on a corner or cul-de-sac are typically distracted by car headlights from the street. This can be modified or eliminated by using shrub masses near the street. Glare from overhead street lights can be reduced through the use of trees. Properly used, plants can do much to control unwanted light.

Masses of ground covers and shrubs and lines of trees can serve to direct pedestrian traffic. Psychologically, a low plant mass 6 in (15 cm) in height will help direct pedestrian circulation at residential properties. Taller plant masses of 3 ft (1 m) or more are effective in controlling pedestrian circulation in public site developments, such as school and other public building grounds. Plant masses or tree baffles along the side of a raised walk or beside a walk bordered by a steep incline provide a feeling of security for people using the walk.

Plants along a drive or street can help in managing traffic. Shrubs and trees planted along a drive or road provide visual direction for drivers. If plants are located near the pavement, thus making the drive feel smaller, they can help control vehicular speeds.

The actual road space remains the same, though the proximity of the plantings makes it feel more narrow, causing drivers to slow down. For a drive curving over a hill or stopping beyond, trees planted on the other side of the hill give cues about the curve or end of the drive. A line of street trees also directs the eye ahead to the line of traffic, reducing streetside distractions and thus enhancing traffic safety. Where a street or road runs alongside a ravine, plantings will not usually stop a vehicle from running off the road, but they will serve as a warning, a demarcation, and will provide a feeling of security.

Without plant cover, sloping soil areas wash away and become hazardous to people and the site in general. For home landscape erosion control, turfgrass can be grown and easily maintained on sloping land no steeper than a ratio of three to one. This means for every 3 ft (1 m) horizontally, the vertical soil slope should be no greater than 1 ft (0.3 m). It generally becomes unsafe to use mowing equipment on slopes steeper than this. For soil slopes steeper than 3:1, living ground covers, such as English ivy (*Hedera helix*), can be maintained. Ground covers can be used to control erosion up to a 1:1 slope, a slope of 1 ft (0.3 m) horizontally to 1 ft (0.3 m) vertically. For steeper slopes it is difficult to have effective erosion control with plants. Usually it becomes necessary to use mulches, including rocks, or retaining walls.

A mixed planting of shrubs and trees of different species and heights adjoining a road helps to reduce noise, dust, and toxic fumes. For noise reduction, 25 ft (8 m) is the minimum width of planting required and wider planting widths are recommended. Deciduous shrubs and trees reduce vehicular noise by approximately 25% to 50%. Evergreen needled foliage plants, in particular low branched trees, plus earth mounding, will reduce traffic noise by over 75%. Plantings over 6 ft (2 m) high which screen views of traffic or other noise sources provide a feeling of noise reduction, even though the actual effect may be minimal. Plantings can help to reduce air pollution, but the planting width required is greater than is available in many home landscapes. For example, a planting 200 yds (2 hm) wide reduces atmospheric dust by 75%.

4

Climate Control

In all regions, plants contribute to climate control by providing shade, windbreaks, insulation, and wall cooling. A careful selection of plants can reduce outdoor summer temperatures by 10°F (5.5°C) and winter wind speed by 75%. Through proper plant selection and placement, the costs of heating and cooling a home can be reduced by approximately 30%.

When designing a planting plan for effective climate control it is important to acknowledge the cardinal points, particularly the north and south orientation of a site. It is also important to have basic knowledge of the sun's position at various seasons. For example, the hot noon sun is high in the sky in the summer (Fig. 4-1). It is best to plant large deciduous or evergreen trees on the west and northwest side of a structure or outdoor living area to provide shade from the hot afternoon sun. In the winter, the sun is low in the southern sky. Any shade trees planted on the southern exposure should be deciduous, so that warming sun rays are not blocked by foliage in the winter. For the same reason, a deciduous vine on an overhead south-facing structure or wall of a house is a climate effective planting.

Plants can increase the efficiency of a mechanical heat pump air conditioning system in the summer. Providing shade from small trees for this equipment will help reduce the cost of its operation.

In addition to knowing the location of the sun and the orientation of the site, consider whether a plant is evergreen (plants that do not lose their leaves in winter) or deciduous (plants that do lose their leaves in winter). A few deciduous trees, such as beeches (*Fagus*) and red oaks (*Quercus*), retain their dried foliage through the winter.

Figure 4-1. Sun angles. Seasonal extremes, at noon on the summer and winter solstice.

These are undesirable for a southern exposure because they cause winter shade. Evergreen trees, shrubs, and vines are highly desirable on a northern exposure for deflecting winter winds. Windbreaks are usually located away from a structure (Fig. 4-2).

Unlike windbreaks, insulation plantings are adjacent to a structure. Evergreen shrubs and small trees used against a northern wall help conserve energy by providing a dead air space or insulation. Evergreen trees such as hemlocks (*Tsuga*) and broad-leaved evergreen shrubs are suitable insulating plants because of their density and sturdy branch system, which will not break easily in icy conditions. Some pine (*Pinus*) trees are to be avoided due to brittle wood which can be damaged by ice and high winds.

In spaces too small to grow trees and shrubs, vines are ideal to control sun rays and provide insulation and they will grow in areas with limited soil. Space limitation is the primary difference in selecting an insulating plant (trees and shrubs) and a wall cooler (vines). For walls exposed to the north, evergreen vines, such as English ivy (*Hedera helix*), will shade the wall and help to insulate it against winter winds. The use of deciduous vines, such as Boston ivy (*Parthenocissus tricuspidata*), on a southern exposed wall permits the flow of the sun's heat rays to the wall surface in the winter.

In addition to considering the general climate, one needs to be aware of the small climate zones known as microclimates. A microclimate varies somewhat from the general, overall climate because of specific environmental factors. For example, the soil area under house eaves is a microclimate. Such areas, particularly on the north side of the house, have less light and moisture than the open area of the garden. The top of a planted earth mound, a berm, is another example of a microclimate, as the area usually has less moisture than the natural ground grade. What will grow in the natural climate may not survive in a microclimate due to the reduced moisture or light in the area. A larger scale microclimate is the bottom of a hill where frost will settle. A disregard of microclimate growing conditions for plants can be very costly. It is as important to make careful plant selection for microclimate planting areas as it is for other planting areas.

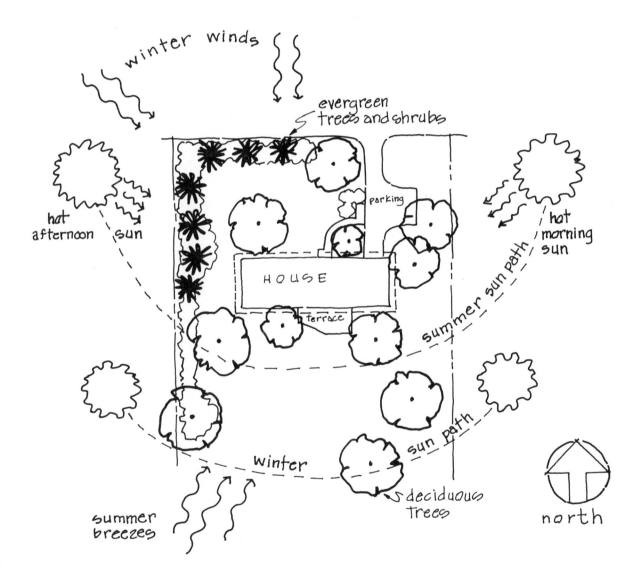

Figure 4-2. Locating plants for climate control.

5

Aesthetics

Aesthetics is the study and theory of beauty. As a planting design function it is considered here last, not to imply least importance, but to allow the emphasis that trees, shrubs, vines, and ground covers are used in design for many reasons in addition to beauty. Too often, a homeowner places major emphasis on attractive flowers, giving little or no consideration to the functional use of plants in design—energy conservation, screens, circulation direction, erosion control, and more. When aesthetics are considered, desirable effects can be obtained not only from flowers, but from plant foliage, fruit, seed, and bark. Careful tree, shrub, vine, and ground cover plant selections can result in both aesthetically pleasing and functional planting designs.

For aesthetical value to evolve from planting design, one must consider all the design elements and principles needed to produce a total composition. Plantings in the landscape produce order or chaos. In a designed composition, the end product is always order. Landscape design may also entertain concepts surrounding enframement and backdrop, reflection, silhouette/shadow projections, pattern, living sculptures, accent or focal points, and which seasonal effects will benefit the composition.

Enframement is the framing of a view or accentuation by the use of plantings on either side. Enframement directs views and focuses the eye on accents. For example, a garden may have both a pleasant view and an unpleasant view. By using enframement, the pleasant view attracts and directs attention while the unpleasant view can be screened. The front entry of a house can be enframed with plantings so that it becomes a special accent from the street.

Backdrops are planting backgrounds. Backdrops can often highlight activity areas, plants, sculpture, furniture, or other accessories. Dark shrub backdrops highlight tree trunks with light bark or anything lighter. Colorful flowering shrubs, like azaleas (*Rhodo-dendron*), will be more effective if located in front of a taller green shrub backdrop. Backdrops can serve, too, as a screen, enclosure, or spatial definer.

Water can provide a double image of garden beauty by reflecting the garden plantings or reflecting the sky, adding blue to the garden. Today, with the extensive use of glass in construction, windows also provide attractive garden reflections. How does one determine what is worth reflecting? A growing sensitivity to art elements and principles in a designed composition can help with that decision. Looking at things discriminatingly does improve with practice.

As outdoor lighting becomes a more integral part of the home landscape, the selection and location of specific plants for silhouette and shadow projection qualities are becoming part of many design plans. When one incorporates a nighttime silhouette, only the outlines or shapes of the plants are displayed against a lighted background. To test a silhouette, place a light behind the plants in view. By washing light on a wall, the line quality of the plants will be dramatically displayed, creating the silhouette.

When projecting a shadow, place the light source in front of the plant and direct the light to a wall or fence. A low light source angled upward will project the plant many times its size, possibly establishing a textured, artful, nighttime view.

Pattern, or visual texture, is formed by solids and voids, usually in two dimensions, such as shadows and line and color compositions. Plants provide pattern naturally, in branching and leaf arrangement, or lend themselves to a prescribed pattern such as a vine trained on a wall or the pattern of an espaliered shrub. A shadow pattern may be created on a wall or floor surface by natural light shining through a planting. Trees can provide a beautiful pattern against a wall at any season, but they are especially effective in winter when their naked branches make shadow patterns against a light-colored south-facing wall. Plant patterns against walls and floors define the space by contrasting line and color.

A well-pruned tree in which the interior limbs have been expertly selected for removal enhances a garden as a living sculpture. In particular, this is true of deciduous trees. Removal of the limbs is like thinning annuals in a flower garden in order that the remaining ones can become stronger. Thinning mainly the interior secondary limbs and branches of a tree permits the remaining ones to become stronger and more sculptural. Large shrubs can receive the same treatment and are popular as accents at major door entries. When used against a solid background of shrubs or construction materials, trees having irregular branch patterns, such as a star magnolia (*Magnolia stellata*) or Japanese maple (*Acer palmatum*), naturally appear as living sculpture.

Small trees, shrubs, and vines can do much to soften the hard construction materials used in the home landscape. As an energy conservation measure, some very old and very new homes have mostly wall areas with few window openings. These walls can be defined and muted with plant materials. Garden walls and pillars can also be visually softened by using vines and small trees. Plant shadow patterns will soften hard surfaces on walls and floors. In the use of trees near walls, care must be taken not to plant close enough to cause damage to the walls or foundation by extended limbs or by the roots. Rapid-growing trees, such as green ash (*Fraxinus pennsylvanica*) and silver maple

(*Acer saccharinum*) often have brittle limbs; therefore, it is best not to use this type tree near walls and structures to avoid limb breakage and damage from high winds or ice accumulation.

Garden accent can be created by the contrast of form, line, color, or texture and position. Plants visible at the end of a walk are often an accent simply because of their position. A tree defining the vertical space at a curve or at the end of a walk is a focal point or accent. It is a vertical form contrasting the horizontal plane of the walk and garden site. Living sculpture plant lines against solid backdrops provide line accent. Using white-flowering species azaleas (*Rhododendron obtusum*) at a home entry composition with colored ones beyond but within sight will accentuate the door. Bold textures against fine textures will create textural accent, such as coarse-textured aucubas (*Aucuba japonica*) used with fine-textured boxwoods (*Buxus sempervirens*).

The unique features present in each season hold the potential to yield an aesthetically pleasing garden year-round. Sometimes it is colorful flowers, sometimes it is textured bark. As educators and designers, we teach and practice that if a garden is aesthetically pleasing in January, it will be pleasant in all other seasons. In winter, the dark pattern of lines of a deciduous tree contrasting with snow cover or a steel blue sky is beautiful. Long lasting, warm-colored plant berries can add interest and spark to the cold, bland days of winter, and they also provide bird food. Tiny buds forming on a tree, or a bulb pushing its way through the frozen earth or snow can be a sign of hope, an affirmation that life follows death and spring is coming again.

Spring signals the rebirth of plants after a hard, cold, quiescent winter. Spring greens the earth in everchanging tones and hues. Trees take on new shapes and foliage color dots the landscape. As spring gives way to summer, the new greens deepen, blossoms waiting for the warmth of summer appear, and fruit forms and ripens. As the long, hot days of summer begin shortening, seed pods appear and deciduous foliage swaps its rich greens for the vibrant tones of fall. Leaves cover the ground, exposing the varied textures of bark and limb, and plants prepare to rest again.

Each part of a plant can enhance the total garden design composition. A closer look at each part and its seasonal effect follows.

Foliage. Foliage is the element of primary importance in design because it is the plant element that usually lasts the longest. Foliage of broad-leaved evergreens and deciduous plants provide color changes from initiation to maturity. Some of the evergreens, both broad-leaved and coniferous, provide warm color tones in winter. Examples of these include Japanese cleyera (*Cleyera japonica*) and shore juniper (*Juniperus conferta*). Deciduous foliage provides major seasonal change in the fall with a range of warm to cool colors in trees such as sugar maple (*Acer saccharum*), sweet gum (*Liquidambar styraciflua*), and the ashes (*Fraxinus*). The lack of foliage in the winter allows new textures and lines from bark and limb.

Flower. The flower color of trees, shrubs, vines, and ground covers provides seasonal color for short periods of time, usually about two to four weeks. A flowering dogwood (*Cornus florida*) will produce effective spring flower color for approximately two weeks, yet a crape myrtle (*Lagerstroemia indica*) will provide extended blossom color due to its periodic flowering periods throughout the summer. Some plants flower only on new wood, such as the crape myrtle. Light tip pruning of branches at the end of a flowering period accelerates new growth and new flower buds, providing extended blossom color.

The dedicated gardener's eyes and mind enjoy the entire flower cycle from the time the bud begins to swell until full bloom and petal drop. For example, observe the beauty of the oriental magnolia (*Magnolia soulangiana*) as its buds swell from early winter to spring when they burst into full color of rose and white.

It has been said that color preference and even perception is a personal thing, and we agree. For that reason, we will not elaborate on what constitutes an effective color scheme. Usually, lighter colors are more prone to be accents, such as white-flowering kurume azaleas (*Rhododendron* 'Adonis') at a house entry with pink ones beyond but within sight. Do consider the color of the house exterior when selecting plant flower colors to avoid direct color clashes. For example, the rose-pink or magenta color of the redbud (*Cercis*) tree is difficult to blend with warm-colored living and non-living materials, and often it will clash with a wide range of red brick color variations.

Fruit. The seasonal display of fruit develops over a long time and provides a wide range of color, texture, pattern, and form. Fruit color ranges from the warm oranges, yellows, and reds to the cool blues, purples, grays, and blacks. Some fruit appears singly, such as the kumquat (*Fortunella japonica*); other fruit appears in clusters, such as on the leatherleaf mahonia (*Mahonia bealei*). The size of fruit ranges from only .25 in (1 cm) in diameter as on some nandina (*Nandina domestica*), to fruit 2–3 in (5–8 cm) in diameter or more, as with Japanese persimmon (*Diospyros kaki*). Many landscape plants' fruit becomes showy in late fall, such as the hollies (*Ilex*) and crabapples (*Malus*). Some plants wait until late winter, such as a mahonia (*Mahonia bealei*); early spring, such as the loquat (*Eriobotrya japonica*); or early summer, such as the mayhaw (*Crataegus aestivalis*).

Seed pod or capsule. The range of seed pods or capsules is about as wide as that of flowers. For the trained eye and mind, they can enhance the beauty of a garden design. A seed pod or capsule display can be particularly impressive on trees of considerable size, pattern, or color. The southern magnolia's (*Magnolia grandiflora*) rusty brown, cone-like pod is 3–4 in (7–10 cm) long and filled with bright red seeds. The common catalpa (*Catalpa bignonioides*) has 6–12 in (15–30 cm) long, bean-like pods, developing from green to brown. The tuliptree's (*Liriodendron tulipifera*) cone-shaped seed is 2–3 in (5–8 cm) long, light colored, and attractive. Some seeds, like those of an American sweet gum (*Liquidambar styraciflua*) are round, woody, dark brown, prickly balls, 1–1.5 in (2–3 cm) in diameter. The seed pods of the goldenrain tree (*Koelreuteria paniculata*) are papery, 2 in (5 cm) long, with colors developing from light green to tan. They are produced in bunches, providing an attractive pattern against the fall and winter sky for a long period of time. Some seeds are the dried remains of flowers, such as the oakleaf hydrangea (*Hydrangea quercifolia*) shrub and the sourwood (*Oxydendrum arboreum*) tree. These seeds remain on the plants for months. Learning to appreciate the value of dried fruits and seeds on plants will enrich one's garden experiences.

Bark. The aesthetic value of bark is apparent in every season, though leafless plants in winter provide a greater display of bark textures and colors. Trees with textured bark include hackberry (*Celtis*), cottonwood (*Populus*), and pine (*Pinus*). Smooth bark is found on crape myrtles (*Lagerstroemia indica*), Chinese parasol trees (*Firmiana simplex*), and beeches (*Fagus*). Bark that peels off or exfoliates annually, such as on young river birch (*Betula nigra*) or sycamore (*Platanus occidentalis*), provides additional interest in texture and pattern. The textured bark of the river birch creates a contrast against a fine-textured, smooth background of living or non-living materials. Light-colored bark is typical of the European white birch (*Betula pendula*), deciduous magnolias such as the saucer magnolia (*Magnolia × soulangiana*), and the evergreen American holly (*Ilex opaca*). The light colored barks create strong color contrasts when used against a dark backdrop. For example, a star magnolia (*Magnolia stellata*) tree against a background of yew (*Taxus*) or boxwood (*Buxus*) shrubs creates an attractive composition.

The exquisite beauty of each season beckons the attentive heart. Foliage, flower, fruit, seed, bark, and bare limb join forces in the total landscape, enriching sight and soul and bringing beauty to all seasons of life.

6

Garden Elements: Origin and Evolution

Throughout world history, garden design has been influenced by geography, topography, and climate, as well as by social, political, economic, and religious factors. With the possible exception of religion, these factors remain in the United States as influencing factors. Why consider garden design history when creating contemporary designs? It is interesting to understand not only the historical context of contemporary designs, but also the factors listed above. By incorporating historical garden design techniques into today's gardens, designs are created with historical depth and relevance.

This chapter points out various historic landscape architectural design features, techniques, and garden styles, the era or civilization of development from which they evolved, and why the designs evolved. Styles and features are arranged by geographic, topographic, climatic, social, political, economic, and religious factors. The garden design styles and features discussed are the result of conditions in the five basic periods of the historic development of landscape architecture:

> Ancient—2200 B.C. to 570 A.D.
> Medieval—570 to 1420
> Renaissance—1420 to 1750
> Informal—1715 to 1900
> Contemporary—1900 to current time.

GEOGRAPHIC INFLUENCES

Formal, symmetrical balance, and rectilinear garden design layout. In ancient Egypt, site development was formal and symmetrically balanced. This accorded with the religious rituals and funeral processions that progressed from the Nile up to the rocky cliffs and the temples and tombs of the Pharaohs. Layout shapes were rectilinear, the easiest to reconstruct, due to the annual flooding of the Nile river from July to October and the necessity of resurveying properties. The formal design in ancient Egypt was the prototype of all garden design in the West until the 18th century and the development of the English informal design.

American (USA) colonial gardens (1620–1775). As gardens developed in Colonial America the informal landscape park design was establishing itself in England. This informal design was not copied in Colonial America—mostly due to already having an abundance of undeveloped, natural environments, the geographic influence. Instead, colonial gardens adopted the formal Renaissance garden design. These early gardens were enclosed and small in scale, formally balanced, laid out according to major axial lines, and patterned after designs taken from English books about the Tudor and Dutch formal gardens. Over the southwest United States, the Spanish influence was evident in patio designs and the common use of tiles.

The urban gardens of New England were very compact and utilitarian. Also, further south the early private gardens of Williamsburg, Virginia, were small and fenced to keep out stray livestock. The homesites contained topiary, herbs, boxwood (*Buxus*) borders and patterned gardens, and brick and pea gravel walks. Many native plants were used in the gardens, including dogwood (*Cornus*), beautyberry (*Callicarpa americana*), catalpa (*Catalpa bignoniodes*), and maple (*Acer*). The garden enclosure was generally a picket fence. Gate designs show a Chinese influence, popularly adopted in England at that time and mimicked by the colonists.

In South Carolina there were large plantations with extensive gardens of formal design. The first garden, a formal one, said to have been planned by a designer was at Middleton Place (c. 1755) near Charleston, South Carolina. Here the camellia (*Camellia japonica*) and azalea (*Rhododendron indicum*) were first introduced. Other plants from the Orient that were also introduced into these gardens include banksia rose (*Rosa banksia*), mimosa (*Albizia julibrissin*), and crape myrtle (*Lagerstroemia indica*).

TOPOGRAPHIC INFLUENCES

Retaining walls. Until the Italian Renaissance (1420–1750), varying garden levels were connected with functional, not necessarily decorative, stairways. With the Italian Renaissance the use of decorative and functional steps, ramps, landings, balustrades or stone banisters, and walls was established. A prime example is found in the varying levels of the Vatican's Belvedere Court in Rome.

The construction of the 900 by 300 ft (274.3 by 91.4 m) court, as designed by Donato

Bramante, began in 1505. The level transitions were started fifty years later. The completion of the Belvedere Court on three different levels established the possibility of constructing gardens on steep hillsides with functional and attractive stairways.

Dynamic water displays. Extensive elevation changes allowed for multiple water effects in Italian Renaissance gardens. Dramatic water displays included water cascading from one level to another, water rushing down the tops of stone banisters, and water jetting skyward. The water source and pressure for these displays were most often the result of a natural river diverted through a garden and forced upward or falling from level to level.

CLIMATIC INFLUENCES

Pergolas/arbors. For the hot climate of ancient Egypt, shade was essential to outdoor comfort. Structures such as pergolas and arbors served as a support for vines grown for shade and fruit. For aesthetics, the supports displayed painted decorations, such as papyrus stems and buds. Later (200 B.C.) in Pompeii, according to frescoes, arbors took on more architectural importance, becoming garden features and not merely support for vines. In the Italian Renaissance, the arbor became a very strong structural garden feature, often with heavy masonry pillars supporting elaborate wood frames. In the Medieval Era the *berceau* served a similar purpose as the arbor, being a vaulted trellis support for greenery and a walk enclosure. Today, arbors provide shade and serve as a focal point in a garden, particularly in limited areas, such as townhouse courtyards not large enough to accommodate shade trees. They remain popular in Spain, Italy, and the southern United States and Mexico, where summer heat is intense.

Pleached allée. In England the pleached allée (braided tree walk) has been providing temporary shelter from the frequent light rain showers for hundreds of years.

A pleached allée is a walkway enclosed on the sides and above with deciduous trees which permit winter sun heat to penetrate. Branches twine, trained and forced to grow as an enclosure. The pleached allée provides shelter from showers, shade from summer sunshine, and partial protection from frost, wind, and snow. These visually dramatic garden design features are typical in the cool, moist climatic conditions of England as well as the hot, dry Mediterranean region where they provide protection for different climate influences. In the United States, a good example of a pleached allée is in the Palace gardens at Williamsburg, Virginia.

Trees planted for shade. In ancient Egypt, gardens contained trees such as the plane or sycamore (*Platanus*) tree planted especially for shade. Oftentimes trees such as the fig (*Ficus*) and date palm (*Phoenix dactylifera*) served a dual purpose in providing both shade and fruit.

In the Moorish patio or courtyard gardens of Spain, trees played a functional and aesthetic role by providing shade, shadow patterns, and a contrast of light and dark. The

Moors, Arabs from North Africa who invaded Spain in the 8th century, were the first to consider seriously the play of light. In their architectural structures varying degrees of light provided a transition from indoors to outdoors. The natural light coming into structures and patios from concealed sources varied as if in a woodland, focalizing a feature, such as water, sculpture, or a plant, against a wall.

Tree groves. Due to bright sunshine and a hot climate, the Italian Renaissance gardens had heavy tree covers for shade. Tree groves, called *bosco* (bosk in English), were planted to provide a shade canopy, to enframe an axis (enclose a major garden linear space) or walk, or to contain smaller gardens within.

Glorieta. In medieval Spain, a *glorieta* was a pavilion, arbor, or bower in the major center space of a garden at the intersection of walks or axes. As a wooden structure it is similar to today's garden gazebo. In some gardens a *glorieta* consisted of tall, sheared plants in a circle, using plants such as Italian cypress (*Cupressus sempervirens*) trees. The wooden pavilion or plant enclosure provided a space for seating and a relief from the hot sun, plus a view of the garden beyond. It is conceivable that on a hot day this space would have been an ideal place in which to sip sangria, the national drink of Spain.

Topiary. The Roman civilization was the first in the West where the art of horticulture was closely related to climate and cultural development. The climate was notably hot and dry in ancient Rome, though increased rainfall provided more plant growth than in other areas of the Mediterranean region. In and around Rome, large palace and garden complexes developed on the hills and the seashore. In the first century, the Romans perfected the art of topiary—the trimming of shrubs into fanciful balls, boxes, pyramids, animal shapes, and almost anything other than the natural shapes of the plants themselves. The art of topiary spread from Italy throughout Europe and into England.

Plant walls. Spanish garden walls, usually high, were either stuccoed structures or pruned plants. Usually Italian cypress (*Cupressus sempervirens*) trees were used to enclose space and provide needed shade. The Spanish Arabs or Moors displayed a love for enclosing small spaces yet retaining a view of the world beyond. This tradition continues in various means employed to establish an indoor/outdoor relationship desired in today's garden design.

In Italian Renaissance gardens, sheared trees and shrubs served as architectural extensions of buildings by defining and enclosing spaces. The evergreen Italian cypress (*Cupressus sempervirens*) and holly (*Ilex*) trees provided spatial enclosure and served as backgrounds, often contrasting the lighter color of a sculpture placed against it. Boxwood (*Buxus*) shrubs were severely pruned as walls or hedges, too. Lawns were limited to small rectilinear spaces due to the maintenance difficulties caused by a hot, dry climate.

Potted plants. Although the ancient Greeks appreciated flowers, their hot, dry climate was not suitable for extensive flower cultivation. Gardening was basically limited to temple tree groves, orchards, kitchen gardens, and potted plants. Pot gardening originated as a tribute to the young Greek god Adonis, who died in his youth. To commemorate his short life, the Greeks planted quick-sprouting seeds in pots. Lettuce (*Lactuca*) and fennel (*Foeniculum vulgare*) plants grew rapidly, blossomed, then died an early death, like Adonis. The potted plants were referred to as an Adonis garden. In urban areas today, where soil is limited or the climate severe, gardening in pots is useful and attractive for growing flowers and herbs and for defining garden floor space.

Glazed pottery and tiles. In medieval Spain, with its hot climate and limited rainfall, decorative glazed pottery containers added color to gardens and patios and defined the floor space. Often pots without plants were used for decorative effect, as is done in Mexico today. Green, blue, pale yellow, and white were most often used for their psychologically cool color effect.

In the 8th century, the invading Moors introduced into Spain the *azulejo*, from the Arabic *zulejo*, meaning "burnt stone." This is a tile made of sand and water with a glaze that was oven-baked or hardened in the intense sun. Islamic law limited the tile design to arabesque or geometric. The colors were lemon-yellow, turquoise, sage-green, and white. They were separated by a black ridge line. By the 12th century an *azulejo* industry had developed in Seville. Though the Moors were driven from Spain in 1248, the *azulejo* remained a decorative garden feature in a climate where colorful flowers are difficult to grow. The tiles were used as a veneer on walls, benches, and steps. The same art expression prevails today worldwide in most warm climates.

Stone pavements. The climate and limited rainfall made growing lawns and ground covers difficult in medieval Spain. As a result, small pebbles, stones, mosaics, and stone pavers were used to surface outdoor spaces in interesting patterns. The idea of using stone to surface outdoor areas spread to Mexico and even today remains popular there and in the southwest United States, California, and Florida, and in the Middle East.

Building orientation. Being sensitive to the ideal solar orientation at his Virginia home, Monticello, Thomas Jefferson located his most frequently used rooms—bedroom, study, and kitchen—on the south side of the house to receive the heat from the winter sun. This orientation provided protection from winter winds yet the rooms still received southerly summer breezes. Unlike other plantation houses of the 18th century, which have outbuildings visible from the main house, Jefferson constructed his outbuildings with a major part of the structures below the ground surface to reduce their visual impact. These buildings, including a kitchen, storehouse, and stables, extend out from the south and north sides of the main house and turn at right angles westward toward the rear gardens. At the far west end of the outbuildings on each side was a brick guest room constructed above grade at the ground level of the main house. Because the roofs of the outbuildings were at the floor level of the main house, they served as walkways to the guest rooms. The connected and recessed outbuildings provided all-weather access from the main house while enclosing the rear garden near the house.

Although Thomas Jefferson made much of solar orientation, the ancient Greeks were the first to orient building windows toward the south to profit from summer breezes and winter sunshine. Rooms of a home were opened to a court or peristyle. A peristyle is a porch-like roofed and paved court that abuts the house and is enclosed on the other sides by columns.

Later, the ancient Romans developed the Greek peristyle into a garden oasis with plants in raised planters and depicted in frescoes painted on the walls. Stone walks divided planting areas in the soil floor. This outdoor garden space, enclosed by a colonnade, contained sculpture, fountains, stone walks, and irrigation lines. The Roman peristyle was a family space onto which all the private rooms of the home opened.

Small-scale water effects. Pools of water in the gardens of ancient Egypt provided a cooling effect and a place to grow water plants and to raise fowl for eating. Garden irrigation was necessary due to the hot, dry climate. Water was lifted from irrigation canals by a container strapped to a pole that pivoted on a post in the garden. This watering device is called a *shaduf*.

The Moorish or Islamic garden highlighted water for its cooling sight and sound and because water played a part in religious rituals held in the garden. In Spanish gardens, water as a decorative effect was limited to small channels (runnels) carrying water across a flat area or down a stair-step stone banister. Water was often featured as a small, slender jet spouting from the center of a delicately carved stone lotus bud or blossom. Water was also used for irrigation in Spanish gardens and mosque (house of worship) courts planted with citrus trees.

Always a garden accessory of the highest value, water is commonly used today for its cooling effect in hot, dry climates, such as the Mediterranean and the southwestern United States. Still water has frequently been used simply for cloud reflections in areas with cool, moist climates, such as England.

SOCIAL INFLUENCES

A discussion of social influences in garden design necessarily includes wide-ranging cultural factors. What may have originated in ancient Greece is picked up thousands of years later in Chicago, Illinois. As such, this discussion is arranged by design feature: how the Greeks started the planting of street trees and park development, how the Roman atrium evolved into a patio, how asymmetry in garden design layout was unknown in the Western world before 18th-century England, and how the perennial garden superseded bedding out.

Street trees and parks. The ancient Greeks are credited with being the first to plant street trees in Athens. Being very democratic and sociable people, they enjoyed congregating outdoors in the *agora* (marketplace), the academy, and in parks. Although used for indoor and outdoor sports events, the parks were a place for philosophers—Plato's Academy and Aristotle's Lyceum. The philosophers taught and walked along paths lined with plane trees (*Platanus*), sculptures, benches, and shrubs (c. 370–286 B.C.). The trees provided a respite from the hot sun and created comfortable spaces for conversing and debating. Such walkways became known as "Philosopher's Walks." These park-like walkways for discussion and learning are defined by some as the first college campuses.

In the United States, interest in civic beautification was sparked by the Columbian Exposition in Chicago in 1893. There were two positive results from the exposition and one somewhat discouraging one. For the first time an interprofessional group designed a site and structures, the exposition's "White City." It aroused much civic interest in design. As a result, plantings were made of trees along streets and around public buildings throughout the United States.

Called "The White City" because it highlighted white-colored classical design, the exposition stimulated a wave of eclecticism that penetrated all parts of the nation. In landscape architecture and architecture there was much interest in developing large residential estates designed in the classical and other styles. Some consider this eclectic design a discouraging result in that it may have retarded design progress. Such estate design was a display of wealth and was primarily intended to be viewed, rather than enjoyed as garden space.

Frederick Law Olmsted, one of the collaborating "White City" designers, is considered the father of landscape architecture in the United States. In 1863, he originated the term *landscape architect* in a letter written about his design of Central Park in New York City. In addition to designing Central Park, he also designed the classic Riverside subdivision near Chicago in 1869. Riverside reflected its natural environment with curving streets coordinated to the topography. This was a major breakthrough from the grid system of streets, the conventional street pattern in use since its origin by Hippodamus in ancient Greece.

Olmsted's major landscape architectural design contributions were to public works: Prospect Park, Brooklyn, New York, the United States capitol grounds, Washington, District of Columbia, Stanford University campus, Palo Alto, California, and numerous other sites. His last major design project is the eclectic design of George W. Vanderbilt's Biltmore Estate, Asheville, North Carolina begun in 1888 and completed in 1895.

Atrium/patio. The ancient Romans developed the atrium, a reception room at the front of the house. Originally, the atrium was the kitchen and had a recessed fire pit centered under a hole in the roof. As the smoke from the fire pit caused the walls to blacken, the room was referred to as *atrium* from the Latin *ater*, meaning charcoal.

After the kitchen was removed from the house to an outside location due to the fire hazard, the atrium served as a vestibule for guests. The fire pit became a pool containing water plants. Plants were also used in pots and illustrated in frescoes on the atrium walls.

The Spanish patio evolved from the Roman atrium via the influence of the medieval cloister (church courtyard). Each Spanish patio had a focal point, usually a small water feature. Plants were used for their individual merit, often informally espaliered against light-colored stucco walls to contrast colors and textures. Patio paving patterns and textures continue as important design characteristics of the Spanish or Islamic patio, originating from the Arab influence in the 8th century. Also, pots are used to define space in paved patios and provide color.

The Arabs brought to Spain a high respect of nature and the individual. Arabian garden design style combined considerations of the enclosure of space, the distant view, and the use of water. It is interesting to compare their high value for distant views and open space with their love for enclosing space.

Informal, asymmetrical garden design layout. Informal design in Europe originated in England in the 18th century. Its formation was influenced by English writers, painters, and Jesuit missionaries. The writers Joseph Addison, Horace Walpole, and Alexander Pope, the news reporters of the day, made fun of the prevailing severely clipped shrubs and topiary, referring to them as vegetable sculpture. The painters Claude Lorrain, Nicolas Poussin, and Salvator Rosa had painted rugged Italian landscapes and ruins of classical structures, which were then copied in informal garden design. Jesuit missionaries, returning from the East, brought back romantic concepts of asymmetrically designed Oriental gardens. A major reaction against formalism or formal design resulted. The origins of informal design were due more to an effort to destroy the prevailing formal style of design rather than a wish to create new interpretations of beauty.

One part of the informal romantic landscape experience was to allow the observation of grazing livestock beyond the garden. Charles Bridgeman developed the *haha*, a fence in a ditch used to control the grazing stock and to accommodate uninterrupted views of the pastoral scene from the house. He used the haha in his plan (c. 1720) for the garden at Stowe, Buckinghamshire, England. A good example of an historic haha in the United States can be seen at Mt. Vernon, Virginia. Its use there provides a view from the house porch of grazing stock and wildlife, yet keeps the animals away from the house and gardens. The Mt. Vernon haha is typical of the ultimate design of those in England— a masonry retaining wall on one side of a depression with a sloped side on the other.

In addition to the use of the haha, the design characteristics of this 18th-century informal style include asymmetrical, large-scale sites, informal mass and void compositions of tree groupings, rolling land forms and pasture, and water (reflective and cascading). This was the era of the palatial English country house surrounded by acres of pastures. The pastures were defined by tree groupings and water and usually contained grazing sheep and deer.

The three major English garden designers of this informal style were William Kent, Lancelot "Capability" Brown, and Sir Humphrey Repton. Sir Repton influenced the 19th-century American landscape architect Frederick Law Olmsted. Repton felt the landscape around the residence should be somewhat formal, becoming less formal as it progresses away. That historic design concept is immensely practical today for large-scale sites as intensive, detailed landscape management is minimized.

An example of the English landscape park style can be seen today at Monticello near Charlottesville, Virginia, the home of Thomas Jefferson for fifty-six years. In 1768, at the age of twenty-five, Jefferson began the development of Monticello and it became a lifetime project. Jefferson, a diplomat to France from 1784 to 1789, had been influenced by what he saw of English gardens and by the classical architecture of the Italian Renaissance architect Andrea Palladio. The rear garden at Monticello is curvilinear with a large, asymmetrically designed lawn area enclosed by a pea gravel walk, referred to as the "roundabout walk." Originally, the flower beds bordered the walk but they were later divided into 10 ft (3 m) sections paralleling the walk. Beyond the walk, the hilltop property exemplifies the English informal style with trees creating a mass and void pattern in the extensive, sloping lawn. The area immediately in front of the house is formally designed, with a center walk leading to the door dividing the front area in two equal halves and establishing its symmetrical balance.

Another exception in early America to the use of formal garden design is in South Carolina. Magnolia Gardens (c. 1750) was an informal or naturalistically designed site where native live oak (*Quercus virginiana*) and cypress trees (*Taxodium*) were arranged around natural water bodies and swamps.

The late 19th-century eclectic garden design of Biltmore House (1888–1895) in Asheville, North Carolina, included the English landscape park style. The palatial French chateau of Biltmore House, designed by architect Richard M. Hunt, forms one end of the major axis of an Italian Renaissance design and is surrounded by an English landscape park design, complete with a classically designed bridge on the approach drive. The garden itself was designed by landscape architect Frederick Law Olmsted. Noted contemporary Californian landscape architect Thomas Church used the idea of the English park and haha design for several country homes in California. Near Starkville, Mississippi, Pete Melby also found success using this style, complete with a haha, for a client's rural residence.

Perennial garden. About 1875, the English garden designer William Robinson began to denounce the Victorian style of bedding-out plants. In the mid-1800s in England, bedding out emphasized brilliant color contrasts and involved planting separate areas or beds with seasonal annuals. Additionally, isolating flower groupings in the open for seasonal effects of only two or three months typified Victorian bedding out. In the late 1860s, foliage plants became valued for providing more subtle color, plus a display of textures. Yet often these beds lacked unity and design composition, a concern to Robinson.

In 1883, Robinson published *The English Flower Garden,* which emphasized using perennials and shrubs in an informal garden border composition. William Robinson's design philosophy for perennial border composition encompassed plant heights, sizes, shapes, textures and colors of foliage and flower, time of bloom, fragrance, and repetition, in order to unify a garden design composition. That philosophy remains suitable and useful today. Robinson promoted perennial borders 12–15 ft (4–5 m) wide with hedges, fences, and walls as backdrops to provide eight months of seasonal effects.

Other Robinson contributions were in the development of English rock gardens in which native plants were used in a natural setting. Also, he advocated relating garden design to the existing site topography, vegetation, and water bodies. To reduce or eliminate maintenance, he advocated using hardy, exotic (cultivated) plants suitable for existing site conditions. One of his books, *The Wild Garden,* first published in 1870, emphasized this use of plants in design. The fact that the book was reprinted in 1977 and in 1983 proves that William Robinson's philosophy remains of value in contemporary garden design.

A contemporary of Robinson was Gertrude Jekyll, painter, garden designer, and authority on the use of color in perennial borders. Her philosophy was that no color stands alone, it always exists in relationship to other colors. Jekyll authored several books, including *Colour Schemes for the Flower Border* (1908). This and several other of her books have been reprinted in recent years and remain valuable. With Robinson's design guidelines for borders and Jekyll's creativity with color, the English perennial herbaceous border or "cottage garden" has become world-renowned.

POLITICAL INFLUENCES

Espalier. During medieval times, wars forced people to live in limited spaces in walled cities and enclosed castles for protection. To conform to the small outdoor spaces, fruit trees were trained to grow flat against walls to conserve space and yet still produce fruit. This form of training, pruning, and patterning is called *espalier.* Though it provides a method to grow fruit trees in a limited space, today its most popular use is for its aesthetic value. Espaliered shrubs and trees are often used decoratively on walls or fences to provide foliage and branch pattern as well as flower, fruit, and seasonal color.

Herb gardens. Herb plantings have been incorporated throughout Western history for their cooking and medicinal uses. In the warring medieval era, herbs were used as much for treating the wounded and ill as for seasoning foods. In some monasteries during the Dark Ages, herbs were planted in rows and patterns—such plantings developing into the famous pattern gardens of the Renaissance era. Examples of Renaissance pattern gardens include the knot garden in England and the parterre in France. The knot garden was made of low, clipped herbaceous plants in curvilinear patterns or knots. Herbs and flowers were planted in the resulting spaces between the low, clipped hedges.

The pattern garden was modified and developed into the famous French *parterre de broderie* seen at Vaux-le-Vicomte, Seine-et-Marne, and Versailles, Yvelines, France, and throughout Europe. The French Renaissance parterre garden was located where it could be overviewed from raised walks and/or from the chateau. These gardens consisted of a curvilinear pattern of low, clipped shrubs, such as boxwoods (*Buxus*), with a ground cover of brick chips, pea gravel, colored soil, and iron filings. The clipped shrub pattern outlines often were filled with flowers. The famous French Renaissance garden designer of Louis XIV, André Le Nôtre, however, seldom used blooming plants in his parterre gardens. Le Nôtre used perennial ground covers, bands of turfgrass, and the stated non-living materials referred to as ground covers.

Mount or mound. During the medieval period, particularly in England, a mount was built within the walled gardens. This made it possible for people to walk up and view the surrounding countryside while remaining protected behind the walls. As garden designs progressed, the mount developed into a raised terrace featuring turfgrass or fine sand and enclosed with a stone balustrade. Located at the back of English Renaissance houses it allowed an overlook of the garden.

Tree-framed axis. The design technique of planting tree groves to frame the garden axis (the major linear space of a garden) was first used in Italian Renaissance garden design and was called *bosco*. A smaller garden within the tall, evergreen holly (*Ilex*) trees, the *giardino segreto* (secret garden) was enclosed with plant hedges and, having seats, provided an intimate space for people. Later, the tree grove adaptation into French Renaissance gardens became known as *bosquet*. The bosquets were planted with deciduous trees, and contained various garden features such as fountains and sculptures within the tree groves. Some bosquets were of geometric designs like a medieval labyrinth.

The Grand Style. France is now world-renowned for the Grand Style developed in the 17th century by André Le Nôtre. Le Nôtre had learned gardening from his father, superintendent of the Tuileries Gardens in Paris, and he had visited Italy to study the Renaissance garden designs originating from religious influence and the wealthy strata of society. Unlike France, where political leaders supported the arts, in Italy the church and merchants were the patrons of the arts, architecture, and landscape architecture. Religious expression was ritualistic and formal; the life of the wealthy was formal. Cathedrals were rectilinear and symmetrical in design. Garden design was formal, rectilinear, symmetrical, and also highly influenced by the geographic conditions of climate and topography.

The major design traits of Le Nôtre were symmetry, the bosquet-framed grand axis and cross axes, massive scale, a terminal feature on the major axis, such as the Grand Canal at the Versailles Palace gardens, and vistas and allées cut through the surrounding woods. The château looked down upon open parterre gardens, which displayed a prominent use of water in pools and fountains. Fine sculpture was located against pollarded trees for background. Grand stairs, often sculptural in effect, were incorporated into the large-scale garden designs.

In large-scale gardens in the early United States, the garden axis was enframed with tree allées or bosks. An example of the allée can be seen at the Palace at Williamsburg, Virginia, an example of the bosk at the Palace at New Bern, North Carolina. In the late 19th century, during a major eclectic design period in the United States, the tree-lined garden axis found expression at Biltmore House in Asheville, North Carolina. The yellow poplar or tuliptree (*Liriodendron tulipifera*) plantings remain. Today, planted tree bosks can be seen in large commercial landscape developments, such as on the approach drive to Dulles International Airport near Washington, District of Columbia. Bosks are also used in historic restorations of antebellum gardens in the South.

Pollarding. Pollarding is a grand-scale form of topiary featuring trees pruned into geometric forms. It was perfected in France during the Renaissance to effectively frame garden axes with large-growing sycamore or plane (*Platanus*) trees. Pollarded trees bordered or enclosed major linear central or diagonal spaces of a formal garden and provided a dense green background for the display of sculpture. An example of pollarding with the small-scale hornbeam tree (*Carpinus caroliniana*) can be seen at Dumbarton Oaks Garden, Washington, District of Columbia, originally designed between 1921 and 1947 by landscape architect Beatrix Farrand Jones.

ECONOMIC INFLUENCES

Plant introductions. Late 18th-century England witnessed much travel abroad and a great deal of interest developed around finding new plant materials. Exotic plants were introduced from the Orient and the United States into Europe. Interest in naturalistic design began to be replaced by the use of new ornamental shrubs, trees, and annuals and perennials in the open spaces of informal design.

The Industrial Revolution created radical economic and social changes in the late 18th century, bringing a temporary end to craftsmanship and setting limits on individual creativity. The trend subsequently infused garden design; plants were often located randomly in open spaces and the garden spaces lacked design composition. Gardens previously designed with interesting, open spaces were now crowded by exotic new plant types. Lacking repetition, there was little design unity. For example, in Stourhead, Wiltshire, England, originally designed as an informal garden of tree-covered rolling hills and lakes, large masses of *Rhododendron* occupied the open spaces. Also, additions of low growing annuals and perennials were planted in patterns of brilliant color contrasts (the "bedding-out" phenomenon). The result of all this furor of planting was plant groupings lacking compositional unity. This typified the Victorian era style (1850–1900) originally featuring annuals in patterns of color, and later using foliage plants for more subtlety. Also included in this style was the placement of unrelated decorative objects: metal fences and benches, iron deer and Great Danes, urns, and bird baths. Generally, such garden designs are not perceived as well coordinated. Although it was an era of economic growth and exotic plant introductions, the Victorian era can be seen as a low point in garden design because of the general lack of composed garden designs.

RELIGIOUS INFLUENCES

Human scale spatial enclosure. Though Spain belonged to and was influenced by the Roman Empire from the 1st to the 3rd centuries, it is the Islamic garden design beginning in the 8th century for which Spain is most highly regarded. The Mohammedan Moors brought the culture of the East to Spain, yielding stuccoed, high walls enclosing small, partitioned, rectilinear gardens with a central, usually small-scale, water feature.

The proportion of these enclosed courts related to the size of a person, individuals being highly esteemed by the religion. Few garden designs today equal this unique human-scale element of the Moorish garden. The Moors did much to enclose space, yet space always opened to include a view beyond. This visual union of indoors and outdoors is a major concept employed in landscape architecture.

Labyrinth/maze. Though the medieval period (570–1420) is referred to as the Dark Ages, several interesting garden practices developed. One of these is the maze or labyrinth. References to a labyrinth date back to the palace of Minos at Crete (c. 2200 B.C.). It was a structure with many rooms that was difficult to exit without guidance. The term also refers to a circle or hexagon design with crisscrossing lines leading in and out of the total composition. In the medieval era the labyrinth was a mosaic floor design in cathedrals used by penitents. Later, the design was used as a feature in gardens.

As a garden feature, original labyrinths consisted of 8 ft (2.5 m) high clipped hedges bordering an irregular walk pattern that proved challenging to people wishing to exit the labyrinth. The purpose was entertainment for those seated on a higher elevation, sometimes a mound overlooking the labyrinth. No doubt, those on the mound may have been sipping on spirits which made the increasingly desperate flight of those in the labyrinth more humorous than otherwise. (In that era, with all its political wars, it probably did not require much distraction to find humor). Large labyrinths remain at Hampton Court, London, and in the Palace Gardens at Williamsburg, Virginia. The one at Williamsburg is made of clipped American holly trees (*Ilex opaca*) and can be viewed from a mound as in medieval European gardens.

Specimen plants. The Moslem religion greatly respects all living things—such as plants, animals, and people. This respect was manifested in Spain with plants featured individually against walls, providing pleasant contrasting colors, textures, and patterns. Climate also influenced planting against walls. The coolness of the soil against the wall provides a more desirable place for roots to develop than warmer sites in full sun away from structures.

THE ORIGIN OF CONTEMPORARY AMERICAN GARDEN DESIGN STYLE

About 1930, garden design in the United States changed from large-scale gardens, created primarily for the display of wealth, to smaller-scale gardens that were both attractive and functional. This change was influenced by the Bauhaus School (political), the Great Depression (economic), and the California School (social).

Bauhaus was a school founded by Walter Gropius in 1919 in Weimar, Germany. Its artists, architects, engineers, industrial designers, and others began designing buildings using contemporary materials such as plastics, chrome, and concrete in a more fluid manner. By 1933 the school was closed due to Adolph Hitler and his Nazi activities. Most of the group fled Germany for the United States. They continued developing what is known as the Bauhaus Style, creating new fluid designs with contemporary materials, first in public buildings, later in private ones. This work had an immediate influence on structure and design throughout the United States.

About the same time, the Great Depression brought a temporary end to grandiose estate planning and development. Landscape architects became engaged in public works projects that were federally funded, one result of the government's nationwide attempt to curtail unemployment. Such work programs were originated by the Civic Works Administration (CWA), Public Works Administration (PWA), and Works Progress Administration (WPA). The programs resulted in the development of a wide cross-section of public improvements. City, county, and state parks, roadside parks and overlooks, slum clearances, greenbelt towns, and high density housing all got new life. The works projects also provided incentives for painters and other artists who experimented with the use of space in freer, more flexible ways and relationships. Eventually, these works influenced the design of houses and gardens.

About 1936, a group of three graduates of the Harvard Graduate School of Design—Garrett Eckbo, Daniel Kiley, and James Rose—spearheaded a new style of West Coast, free-form garden design. They were later joined by Thomas Church. Meeting people's needs for beauty and activity and relating to the natural landscape form became priorities. Spatial design principles were expressed as a series of outdoor related spaces designed for human use and enjoyment. The concept behind their space theory was that everything in the landscape should be developed as three-dimensional; the space is occupied and enjoyed by people and not merely viewed as a two-dimensional painting. This concept brought about new ideas of enclosure, shelter, and surfacing, using materials such as concrete in new asymmetrical, free-form designs. Gardens became spaces to be lived in, not just a series of views on axial lines.

This new informal, free-form design concept began on the West Coast and spread throughout the nation. It was highly publicized in periodicals and other contemporary publications, and today this design style is referred to as the California School.

People cannot improve on nature, but they can make improvements to harmonize with nature. With this theme, since 1930, significant progress has been made in landscape architecture. Contemporary American designs reflect people's needs to relate to factors influencing historic garden design and harmonizing with the natural landscape and ecological systems.

SECTION II: Management

7

Management Strategy

What can be discouraging about one's gardens and landscape is the overwhelming amount of time required even to make them look just average. The first part of this book dealt with ways to make a landscape design look better than good, not just average. It also dealt with creating productive landscape designs that perform various tasks. This section will explain how to work a garden in harmony with nature, utilizing the least amount of resources, while keeping the time required for maintenance and improvements within bounds.

When creating a garden design, create a landscape that is balanced. We consider this to mean working with the forces of nature so that the landscape is designed equally for the easiest maintenance possible, the most attractive look, and the least management cost. A balanced landscape also results in the healthiest landscape possible, without the need for excessive supplemental fertilizer or the use of chemicals.

Creating a good-looking design and a balanced landscape involves considering the time and resource commitment necessary for maintaining the landscape. Landscape contractors usually estimate professional maintenance costs at about 20% of the installed cost of a landscape. For example, if $20,000 were spent for a landscape, it would cost about $4,000 a year to be maintained by a landscape contracting firm. Management of a landscape is too costly to ignore, both in terms of time expended and material costs, when creating the home landscape design.

Another way to state this is that a balanced landscape is one that requires the absolute least amount of attention in order to perform well and look its best. A balanced landscape is created when attention is given to the:

soil conditions,

geographic conditions, such as sun, shade, slopes, land forms, and prevailing wind,

selection of plants that matches soils and geographic conditions,

selection of plants with their mature sizes in mind; relating plants to the sizes of the spaces in which they will be located,

design and regular management tasks for reduced landscape maintenance.

Many people first experience trying to create a balanced environment with an aquarium, striving to get that perfect balance of aquarium components. Once the right amount of catfish, snails, aquatic plants and other fish is determined, the water quality remains sparkling, the bottom clean, and algae is continuously removed from the sides of the tank glass. A balanced fish tank requires very little upkeep to be healthy and look its best. By contrast, an unbalanced aquarium would keep one busy cleaning the tank and medicating the fish. The same principle of balance versus unbalance applies to a home landscape.

It is necessary to know the soil of one's landscape, and chapter 8 will help with this task. Understanding how long soil will hold moisture and how well it drains affects plant selection and irrigation requirements. How much air space the soil has for root growth is critical with most plants. Know the available nutrient value and pH of one's soil. The pH will measure how alkaline or acidic a soil is. Many plants have a preferred pH and will not grow well outside a specific pH range.

Amend soils to satisfy the needs of the plants chosen. Regularly enrich soils just as enrichment occurs in the meadow or forest, by mulching with composted organic matter in the spring and fall. Knowledge of the existing soils, creation of ideal soil conditions for certain kinds of plants that require it, and creation of a soil health program will help to create a balanced landscape.

Certain plants flourish in the shade, some in sun, some in dry soil and others may need the continually moist conditions of stream bottom soil. Knowledge of what conditions plants need will help in selecting plants that will grow best. Know the site's geography, including where it is windy, sunny, shady, wet or moist, and where the slopes drain quickly and dry fast. The geography of a site affects the availability of water to plants. Being knowledgeable of site soil and geography helps in selecting plants and designing for reduced maintenance.

In observing plants in a natural landscape, one finds each species flourishing where the soil, light, and moisture levels are best suited. The same species may be languishing nearby because one or more of these factors differs. It is ideal, therefore, to select plants that will adapt to specific soil and geographic conditions. If one is insistent on having plants unrelated to a site's conditions, a suitable soil environment will have to be created and one will have to depend on a sustained higher maintenance level for the plants to survive.

A recent planting of a river birch tree (*Betula nigra*) on a hillside, in view from a kitchen window for its beauty and sculptural effect, lacked any consideration of its maintenance needs. Because hillside soils dry out fast, the tree had to be watered constantly to get it established and keep it alive. If a tree native to hillside conditions had been selected, not only would maintenance demands have been reduced, but the tree would have been healthier. Despite heroic effort, the hillside birch died. A tree, money, a lot of effort, time, and water were wasted.

Besides selecting an inappropriate location, a common mistake is to put a plant that likes an acid soil, like an azalea (*Rhododendron*), directly in alkaline soil. It only takes a few stressful years for acid-loving plants in alkaline soil to die. Even selecting a lovely pink-flowered hydrangea (*Hydrangea macrophylla*) and planting it in acid soil can surprise most. Acid soil usually makes hydrangeas develop blue flowers. Successful plant selection does not begin at the nursery or plant catalogue. It begins with site conditions, followed by familiarity with plant habitat and needs.

Ease of maintenance will be a year-round joy. The following pointers can direct a person toward designing a landscape requiring the least amount of energy to look great.

Minimize lawn areas. Lawns are high-maintenance elements.

Locate lawn grasses in sunny areas where grass can be healthiest.

Design lawn areas so they can be mowed quickly and without a lot of pushing and pulling of the mower. If using a riding mower, design the edges of the lawn in smooth, sweeping lines to accommodate the equipment. Create plant beds with a large enough radius to accommodate mowing.

Avoid creating lawn areas on steep slopes that are difficult and hazardous to mow.

Avoid placing objects on the lawn area that have to be moved before mowing. Picking up and moving birdbaths and gazing globes twenty times a growing season adds a lot of effort.

Use appropriate ground covers and mulch beds in shady areas and on hard-to-access steep slopes.

Minimize the need for trimming along the lawn edges. Create mowing strips between lawn areas and ground cover, flower, and shrub beds to reduce trimming and to keep grass from creeping into planting beds. Even with mowing strips one will still need to trim bed lines after every third or fourth mowing.

Avoid creating acute angles in planting areas. These are difficult to mow and most plant forms will not relate well visually without intensive pruning.

Mulch all beds with an organic mulch to reduce watering needs during dry periods and to aid weed control.

Create loose, airy soils by amending heavily with organic matter in order to easily dig or lift out weeds and reduce incidence of root disorders.

Install sprinkler and/or drip irrigation for efficient watering during droughts. Develop an irrigation system to water areas automatically by setting a timer or turning a manual valve.

Wait to water lawn areas until just before they become stressed in order to reduce the need for mowing and to conserve water. A lack of resiliency in grass can be the first warning signal of imminent stress, indicating the need to water.

Select plants to provide diversity yet still maintain a visually unified design. Through diversity, insect and disease problems will be lowered. There is a law of ecology that states that through diversity there is strength.

Select plants to relate to the site's geographic conditions, thus ensuring healthier plants with lower maintenance needs.

Reduce the need for pruning through selecting plants whose mature sizes relate to the spaces in which they will be planted. Locate large-growing plants in areas where they will not need frequent pruning.

Avoid planting trees that will grow into utility lines and need to be frequently pruned.

A favored resource we employ is a landscape management plan. Its purpose is to give an overall look at how to maintain a landscape over an entire year. A sample plan appears as Appendix C. The usefulness of a landscape management plan is in knowing what happens when, and what equipment, supplies, and labor will be needed to most effectively accomplish the job. By matching maintenance chores with seasons and dates, one can more efficiently manage time—for labor, equipment usage, and general resources.

Effective and practical management aims to obtain maximum performance with a definable amount of time and money. In a garden, productive time is maximized by organizing tasks, having the right equipment and supplies, scheduling people, and anticipating events based on seasonal trends. With practical landscape management, one can have a healthy and attractive landscape for lower overall management costs both in terms of time and money.

Before developing a management plan, let us consider a task-time study for a landscape. This will determine which tasks require the greatest time expenditures during particular seasons of the year.

Table 7-1 shows typical tasks and time expenditure for the Melby 0.5 acre (0.2 hectare) residential landscape before it was redesigned to be balanced. In this landscape, a 2000 ft² (186 m²) home is situated in the center of a square lot. The hours required to accomplish the tasks reflect the hours spent managing this landscape, which is not properly balanced. Table 7-2 gives monthly and seasonal breakdowns.

Table 7-3 shows task and time requirements after converting this unbalanced garden into a balanced landscape. Additional tasks actually reduced expenditures.

Compared to the requirements of the unbalanced landscape, there is now a 38% savings in hours required for landscape maintenance. Table 7-4 is the accompanying task-time monthly and seasonal chart. It illustrates that in a balanced landscape one can reduce some of the time spent in the garden in summer and distribute chores to the fall and winter months.

Through converting to a balanced landscape, total annual maintenance hours were cut by 38%. Additionally, by charting chores and when they need doing, a gardener can distribute tasks more evenly throughout the seasons. By creating and following a landscape management plan, a person can reduce the time spent in the garden in the busy and all too brief summertime.

Table 7-2 shows fifty-seven and a half hours spent in the unbalanced landscape maintaining the garden in spring. Spending nearly five hours each weekend for the twelve springtime weeks working at routine chores in the landscape can take the fun out of gardening. By contrast, the balanced landscape and landscape management plan (Table 7-4) illustrates that only twenty-nine hours need be spent maintaining a garden in spring.

To begin developing a landscape management plan, start by listing what is routinely required, when it has to be done, and how much time it takes to get the job done. See Table 7-4 for some common tasks. Be sure to carry the listing throughout an entire calendar year. Once the list is complete, estimate the hours spent accomplishing the tasks and relate them to the months of the year. Note that some tasks, such as weeding, vary in the time needed at different seasons. The landscape management plan in Table 7-5 appends climate information as well. This allows one to anticipate some of the landscape needs throughout a typical year. For example, the need for irrigation usually becomes quite pronounced from May to October, and is not solely based on rainfall. As the first frost is usually in mid-November, pruning and planting times are pre-determined.

The result of these efforts will yield a broad-brush look at managing one's landscape. The management plan helps plan chores, schedule any extra people to assist, and anticipate needed gardening supplies. The plan will also show where the most tedious hours are spent and maybe where modifications might be in order to make the landscape more balanced and reduce tedium.

Maintaining a home landscape well is complex. Creating a landscape management plan as a guide throughout the year will allow a person to maintain the garden more logically and with more enjoyment.

Table 7-1. Task and time expenditure: 0.5 acre (0.2 hectare) unbalanced landscape.

Task	Frequency	Time in hours	Total hours per year
Mow, summer	20 times a year	2.0	40.0
Edge	10 times a year	1.5	15.0
Weed	April–May	20.0	
	June–July	9.0	
	September	3.0	32.0
Prune	February	8.0	
	June	3.0	11.0
Plant			
tree, shrubs	December	2.0	2.0
annuals, perennials	March–May	10.0	10.0
Fertilize			
lawn	spring, fall	3.0	6.0
flowers, shrubs, trees	March–July	5.0	5.0
Watering, by hand and movable sprinkler	June–September	12.0	12.0
Rake leaves	October–November	5.0	10.0
Cleanup	December–January	1.0	2.0
		Total	145.0

Table 7-2. Annual time expenditure: 0.5 acre (0.2 hectare) unbalanced landscape.

Task	Jan.	Feb.	Mar.	Apr.	May	Jun.	Jul.	Aug.	Sep.	Oct.	Nov.	Dec.	Hours
Mow	—	—	—	6.0	8.0	8.0	8.0	6.0	4.0	—	—	—	40.0
Edge	—	—	—	1.5	4.5	4.5	1.5	1.5	1.5	—	—	—	15.0
Weed	—	—	—	12.0	8.0	6.0	3.0	—	3.0	—	—	—	32.0
Prune	—	8.0	—	—	—	3.0	—	—	—	—	—	—	11.0
Plant	—	—	6.0	2.0	2.0	—	—	—	—	—	—	2.0	12.0
Fertilize (lawn)	—	—	—	3.0	—	—	—	—	3.0	—	—	—	6.0
Fertilize (other)	—	—	1.0	1.0	1.0	1.0	1.0	—	—	—	—	—	5.0
Watering	—	—	—	—	1.5	4.5	4.5	1.5	—	—	—	—	12.0
Raking	—	—	—	—	—	—	—	—	—	5.0	5.0	—	10.0
Cleanup	1.0	—	—	—	—	—	—	—	—	—	—	1.0	2.0
Total hours:	1.0	8.0	7.0	25.5	25.0	27.0	18.0	9.0	11.5	5.0	5.0	3.0	145.0

	Spring	Summer	Fall	Winter
Percent effort by season:	40%	37%	15%	8%
Total hours by season:	57.5	54.0	21.5	12

Table 7-3. Task and time expenditure: 0.5 acre (0.2 hectare) balanced landscape.

Task	Frequency	Time in hours	Total hours per year
Mow			
summer	20 times	1.0	20.0
winter	5 times	0.5	2.5
Edge	6 times a year	1.0	6.0
Weed	April–May	6.0	
	June–July	2.0	
	September	2.0	10.0
Prune	February	4.0	
	June	2.0	6.0
Plant			
trees, shrubs	December	2.0	2.0
annuals, perennials	March–May	7.0	
	October	1.0	8.0
Fertilize			
lawn	March	2.0	2.0
flowers, shrubs, trees, with compost	February, June, September	2.0	6.0
Watering, automatic drip and sprinkler irrigation	June–September	0.25	1.0
Irrigation system maintenance	March, July, November	1.0	3.0
Rake leaves	October	4.0	
	November	3.0	7.0
Compost, turn weekly	April–September	1.0	
	October–November	2.0	10.0
Test soil			
nutrients	October	0.5	0.5
pH	January	0.5	0.5
Mulch	March	1.0	
	November	2.0	3.0
Winter overseed	October	1.0	1.0
Cleanup	January, December	1.0	2.0
		Total	90.5

Table 7-4. Time expenditure: 0.5 acre (0.2 hectare) balanced landscape.

Task	Jan.	Feb.	Mar.	Apr.	May	Jun.	Jul.	Aug.	Sep.	Oct.	Nov.	Dec.	Ho
Mow													
summer	—	—	1.00	3.00	4.00	4.00	4.00	3.00	1.00	—	—	—	20.
winter	0.50	0.50	—	—	—	—	—	—	—	—	0.50	1.00	2.
Edge	—	—	—	1.00	1.00	2.00	1.00	1.00	—	—	—	—	6
Weed	—	—	—	3.00	3.00	1.00	1.00	—	2.00	—	—	—	10
Prune	—	4.00	—	—	—	2.00	—	—	—	—	—	—	6.
Plant													
trees, shrubs	—	—	—	—	—	—	—	—	—	—	—	2.00	2.
annuals, perennials	—	—	2.00	3.00	2.00	—	—	—	—	1.00	—	—	8.
Fertilize													
lawn	—	—	2.00	—	—	—	—	—	—	—	—	—	2.
flowers, shrubs, trees, with compost	—	2.00	—	—	—	2.00	—	—	2.00	—	—	—	6.
Watering	—	—	—	—	—	0.25	0.25	0.25	0.25	—	—	—	1.
Irrigation system maintenance	—	—	1.00	—	—	—	1.00	—	—	—	1.00	—	3.
Rake leaves	—	—	—	—	—	—	—	—	—	4.00	3.00	—	7.
Compost	—	—	—	1.00	1.00	1.00	1.00	1.00	1.00	2.00	2.00	—	10
Test soil													
nutrients	—	—	—	—	—	—	—	—	—	0.50	—	—	0.
pH	0.50	—	—	—	—	—	—	—	—	—	—	—	0.
Mulch	—	—	1.00	—	—	—	—	—	—	—	2.00	—	3.
Winter overseed	—	—	—	—	—	—	—	—	—	1.0	—	—	1.
Cleanup	1.00	—	—	—	—	—	—	—	—	—	—	1.00	2
Total hours:	2.00	6.50	7.00	11.00	11.00	12.25	8.25	5.25	6.25	8.50	8.50	4.00	90

			Spring			Summer			Fall			Winter	
Percent effort by season:			32%			28%			26%			14%	
Total hours by season:			29.00			25.75			23.25			12.50	

le 7-5. Landscape management plan for the Pete Melby family, Starkville, Mississippi: yearly summary.

ivity	Jan.	Feb.	Mar.	Apr.	May	Jun.	Jul.	Aug.	Sep.	Oct.	Nov.	Dec.
v lawn as ...led.	—	—	Mow once. 1 hour	Mow three times. 3 hours	Mow four times. 4 hours	Mow four times. 4 hours	Mow four times. 4 hours	Mow three times. 3 hours	Mow once. 1 hour	—	—	—
v rye grass ...ted in ...scape.	Mow once. ½ hour	Mow once. ½ hour	—	—	—	—	—	—	—	—	Mow once. ½ hour	Mow once. ½ hour
e and trim ...s from ...s and ...g plant ...s. Remove ...around ...s.	—	—	—	Trim grass from edges. 1 hour	Trim grass from edges. 1 hour	Trim grass from edges. 2 hours	Trim grass from edges. 1 hour	Trim grass from edges. 1 hour	—	—	—	—
d garden, ...bs and ...nd cover ...by hand ...oe.	—	—	—	Remove weeds. 3 hours	Remove weeds. 3 hours	Remove weeds. 1 hour	Remove weeds. 1 hour	—	Remove weeds. 2 hours	—	—	—
he trees, ...bs, and ...nd ...ers.	—	Prune trees, shrubs, and ground covers. 4 hours	—	—	—	Prune trees and shrubs for form if needed. 2 hours	—	—	—	—	—	—
t trees ...shrubs.	—	—	—	—	—	—	—	—	—	—	—	Plant trees and shrubs. 2 hours
t annuals, ...nnials.	—	—	Divide perennials and replant. 2 hours	Add bedding plants. 3 hours	Add bedding plants. 2 hours	—	—	—	Plant spring-blooming bulbs. 1 hour	—	—	—
ilize lawn.	—	—	Spread fertilizer if needed at beginning of month. 2 hours	—	—	—	—	—	—	—	—	—
ilize ...ers, ...bs, and ...s in plant ...s with ...post.	—	Apply 2 in (5 cm) of compost. 2 hours	—	—	—	Apply 2 in (5 cm) of compost. 2 hours	—	—	Apply 2 in (5 cm) of compost. 2 hours	—	—	—

continued

Table 7-5. Continued.

Activity	Jan.	Feb.	Mar.	Apr.	May	Jun.	Jul.	Aug.	Sep.	Oct.	Nov.	Dec.
Water—use drip irrigation, water manually as needed. Set lawn sprinklers for automatic control.	—	—	—	—	—	Check for soil moisture. Turn on drip when needed. 15 min.	Check for soil moisture. Turn on drip when needed. 15 min.	Check for soil moisture. Turn on drip when needed. 15 min.	Check for soil moisture. Turn on drip when needed. 15 min.	—	—	—
Check irrigation—sprinkler coverage, pressure, clogging.	—	—	Check system for operation and coverage. Run manually through each circuit. Flag inoperable heads. 1 hour	—	—	—	Check system for operation and coverage. 1 hour	—	—	Winterize—sprinkler system. 1 hour	
Rake leaves from turf areas, compost leaves.	—	—	—	—	—	—	—	—	—	Rake leaves. 4 hours	Rake leaves. 3 hours	—
Attend to compost. Add organic matter, turn as needed, check moisture.	—	—	—	Attend compost. 1 hour	Attend compost. 1 hour	Attend compost. 1 hour	Attend compost. 1 hour	Attend compost. 1 hour	Attend compost. 1 hour	Begin new pile. 2 hours	Attend compost. 2 hours	
Test soil nutrient levels from lawn, flower, and vegetable garden areas.	—	—	—	—	—	—	—	—	—	Test soil sample or deliver to testing lab. ½ hour	—	—
Test soil pH of lawn, garden beds, and shrubs (azaleas).	—	Use test kit to check soil pH. ½ hour	—	—	—	—	—	—	—	—	—	—
Adjust soil pH if needed.	—	Spread material on lawn; use cultivator, work into garden soil.	—	—	—	—	—	—	—	—	—	—

le 7-5. Continued.

vity	Jan.	Feb.	Mar.	Apr.	May	Jun.	Jul.	Aug.	Sep.	Oct.	Nov.	Dec.
ly mulch redded , leaves, straw, or r organic erial.	—	—	Apply mulch. 1 hour	—	—	—	—	—	—	—	Apply mulch. 2 hours	—
ter seeding ant rye s over nant n-season s.	—	—	—	—	—	—	—	—	—	Over-seed with rye grass. 1 hour	—	—
nup	Cut back spent stalks of annuals and perennials. Pick up fallen limbs, trash. 1 hour	—	—	—	—	—	—	—	—	—	—	Cut back stalks of annuals and perennials. Pick up fallen limbs, trash. 1 hour
ck for pest and ase damage.					Throughout year as needed.							

prical climatic data: Starkville, Mississippi

	Jan.	Feb.	Mar.	Apr.	May	Jun.	Jul.	Aug.	Sep.	Oct.	Nov.	Dec.	Total
fall (inches)	5.55	5.52	5.93	4.47	3.76	3.48	5.27	3.20	3.16	2.54	3.93	4.48	51.48
ootranspiration[1]	0.79	1.03	2.15	3.78	5.85	7.43	8.04	7.49	5.50	3.33	1.52	0.89	47.80
	4.65	4.49	3.78	0.69	−2.09	−3.95	−2.77	−4.29	−2.40	−0.79	2.41	3.95	

erature (degrees F)

nal high	58	67	72	81	87	92	94	93	92	83	72	63
aximum	81	84	89	93	99	105	111	108	103	96	88	82
nal low	29	31	37	46	54	62	67	66	56	43	32	30
inimum	−6	−1	14	28	38	41	53	52	40	28	10	−8

t expectancy: last frost March 27, first frost October 29.

potranspiration (EVT) is the amount of water evaporating from the soil and transpiring from leaves and twigs. Note that EVT rates are st in January and highest in July for this section of Mississippi. Local EVT rates are available from irrigation equipment suppliers and Experiment Stations at Land Grant Universities.

8

Soils

The most critical ingredient in the recipe for a flourishing landscape is well-conditioned, healthy soil. By understanding that there are various soil types, differing in structure and fertility, one can begin to understand the landscape. Be aware what characterizes the ideal garden soil that seasoned gardeners are constantly striving to create and maintain. Keep up with changing pH levels and know how soil sweetness or sourness affects the availability of nutrients for landscape plants.

Soil is composed of weathered minerals, organic matter, air, and water. The ideal garden soil can be described as having 50% pore space, for air and water movement, about 5% organic matter, and 45% mineral content. The weathered minerals are possible plant nutrients and can contribute to plant health and growth. The minerals derive from rock, volcanic matter, and coral which has broken down over time. Ideal soils are also teaming with microflora and microfauna—the fungi, bacteria, and tiny animals that break down and balance matter into states beneficial and usable to plants.

Clay soils have evolved from primary rock minerals such as feldspar and mica. Clay soil is made up of the finest sized particles. Due to the fine size of the particles and their chemical arrangement, clay soils have a large amount of microscopic air spaces and the resulting capacity to hold large amounts of water. The hazard of most clay soils is that the air spaces are so small that plant roots are smothered or obstructed. Clay soils tend to have low porosity. Air and water do not move easily through clay. Its fine particle size makes clay soil more fragile than other soil types. If its surface is compacted, through rain or foot traffic, the microscopic conduits for air and water movement through the clay are sealed. Also, if clay soil dries out it takes a long time to recharge with water.

The next smallest soil particle size is found in silt. Silt can be generated from a variety of minerals, commonly silica or feldspar. Silt is somewhat mobile and can be transported to new locations by water or wind. Silt transported by water creates alluvial soils. Silt transported by wind creates loess soils.

Referring to particle sizes, sand contains the next biggest particles after silt and clay. Like silt, sand can be any mineral, although it is often quartz. Sandy soils are defined as having 85% or more sand and not more than 10% clay.

Loam soils are of a mixture of sand, silt, and clay. The desirability of loam soils for gardening comes from the fact that their internal structure is open and conducive to air and water movement. The composition of loam may or may not include organic matter.

The following U.S. Department of Agriculture soil type definitions and field methods of determining soil types is useful for the home gardener:

Sand. Loose and single grained, the individual grains of sand can be seen or felt. When squeezed in the hand, and pressure is released, sandy soil will fall apart when dry and form a molded shape that will crumble when moist.

Sandy loam. Containing mostly sand, this soil type has enough silt and clay to make it stick together. When squeezed, it will form a molded shape that will fall apart when dry and barely hold together if handled carefully when moist.

Loam. This soil has a mixture of sand, silt, and clay in such proportion that no one component is predominant. If squeezed when dry, a molded shape will form that will hold together if handled carefully. Squeezing moist soil will form a more durable shape.

Silt loam. Over half the soil particles are silt-sized with the remainder being sand and a small amount of clay. When soil is squeezed either dry or moist, it will form molded shapes that can be freely handled without breaking.

Clay loam. The majority of the particles are fine-textured with generally lesser amounts of sand and silt-sized particles in the soil. When dry, the soil forms clods. When moist, soil pinched between the thumb and finger forms a ribbon that will break, barely sustaining its own weight. Moist clay loam is plastic, that is, it will change in shape under a steady force. When kneaded in the hand, moist clay loam does not crumble easily. The moist soil will form a molded shape that will bear much handling.

Clay. This fine-textured soil forms clods when dry and is usually plastic and sticky when wet. When moist soil is pinched, a long, flexible ribbon is formed.

By referring to a county soil survey, a person can usually determine the soil type with which to begin (or continue) gardening. The soils in nearly every county in the United States have been evaluated by the Soil Conservation Service and the Agricultural Experiment Stations. These soil survey reports are available through the U.S. Government Soil Conservation Service offices and local libraries.

Organic matter helps to provide the mineral nutrient needs of plants that are often supplied by commercial fertilizers. As plant and animal matter decays, humus is formed. Humus is that dark, moist, great smelling, decayed matter found on the forest floor and

Table 8-1. Soil characteristics.

Soil type	Permeability	Erodability	Reservoir of available water	Drainage (porosity)	Nutrient holding capacity
	high	high	low	high	low
Sand					
Sandy loam					
Loam					
Silt loam					
Clay loam					
Clay					
	low	low	high	low	high

comprising finished compost. Leaves and twigs become humus when they are rotted beyond recognition. Microorganisms, the microscopic bacteria and fungi, decay the plant and animal matter and transform it so that plant roots can use it. A rich soil is alive with these microorganisms, which are constantly breaking down organic matter into fertilizer for plants. A soil with a good humus content might not need supplemental fertilizer. The humus or composted organic material will supply plant nutrients similar to a slow-release fertilizer. Soils with a high humus content are very fertile and are wonderful growing mediums for plant roots.

When the microorganisms break down organic matter, they release minerals such as nitrogen, phosphorus, and potassium contained within the decaying plants. Additionally, some microorganisms in the humus help reduce plant disease by attacking the diseases or pathogens. Pathogens are disease-causing organisms. Plants grown in soil rich in composted matter have fewer disease and insect problems. A high humus content enhances the physical condition of a soil by creating large pores that conduct air or water.

Air is a must in garden soil. Plant roots need it to take up the nutrients in the soil, and many microorganisms will die without it. Air is abundant in the top 8–12 in (20–30 cm) of an ideal garden soil. In forests almost all of a tree's feeder roots are in this upper soil area.

Water is essential to life. An ideal soil acts like a sponge to hold water for plants and support microorganisms in the soil. While clay soils will hold water the longest, sometimes water is held overly long for plant root health. Clay soils usually have to be amended to create more macropores, or large pore spaces, to increase water and air movement. Sandy soils, at the other extreme, have too many macropores. Its few small pores cannot hold onto enough water. Water drains through quickly and leaves the area dry. Ideally, a soil has lots of humus in it to hold water in a sponge-like manner and slowly release the water to plants. Humus can hold up to 200 times its weight in water.

A great garden soil becomes the basis of a flourishing environment for annuals, perennials, shrubs, and ornamental trees. Its composition reflects a balanced mixture of air, water, organic matter, and minerals, along with a healthy population of microflora and microfauna.

Since most annuals and perennials need an ideal garden soil to do their best, experienced gardeners know to modify or amend existing soils in planting beds before planting. Remember, tight clay soils with slow permeability do not allow adequate drainage. Conversely, the abundant macropores in sandy soils let water pass through so quickly that usually plants need frequent watering to avoid drying out. Additionally, if large amounts of water are allowed to pass through soils, the valuable plant nutrients wash out or leach beyond the top 12 in (30 cm) plant feeder root zone. Nearly every garden soil needs improving to best accommodate garden plants.

At the Melby home garden, the importance of creating and maintaining good soils was learned the hard way. For twelve years annuals and perennials, azaleas, ferns, and hostas were acquired and planted in areas that had only been cleared and the soil tilled. The plants maintained a "hanging on" look as long as possible. Nothing was robust or exuberant. Finally, after learning about the relationship of soils to plant health, the suffering garden was slowly dismantled and ideal soils were belatedly created one bed at a time.

Ideal garden soil requires that composted materials are added about three times a year. The first application should be three to four weeks before the growing season. The organic matter will then be mellow and incorporated enough not to compete for available nitrogen for decomposition. The second application can be in the summer during active plant growth, and the third application can be in the fall. If applying compost during the growing season, remember to consider the carbon to nitrogen ratio (C:N). If the C:N of the compost is not 10:1, microorganisms will take any available nitrogen for their own energy and growth and create a nitrogen deficiency for plants. Placing fresh manure or green (unfinished) compost matter in the soil can actually kill plants. Such materials create a nitrogen deficiency and the hot temperatures generated from increased microbial action can burn roots.

At the Shaw Botanical Garden, St. Louis, Missouri, gardeners add 1.5 in (4 cm) of composted leaves and grass to their flower beds three times a year. They found that after only three years of treatment the soil in the plant beds increased by a 6 in (15 cm) depth. The gardening supervisor also noted that the compost acts to hold more water and improves soil drainage.

If the ideal garden soil has been prepared yet organic matter is never added, soil can be depleted of nutrients and the macropores in its physical structure deteriorate. Soil structure is maintained by particles binding together to create stable clusters. Silt, clay, and organic matter all help particles stick together to create this structure. A soil with a significant amount of organic matter will have the beneficial macropores or voids in it which allow air and water to move. Since soil structure is constantly modified as organic matter breaks down, the voids eventually fill through compaction and water percolating through soil. Voids must be maintained.

Beneficial live additions, such as worms, are attracted to soils with an open, porous structure containing an abundance of organic matter. As the organic matter becomes depleted, the soil environment no longer meets the food, air, or even pH demands of fauna which help in aerating soil.

To retain soil structure and reduce unwanted compaction, cover soil with an organic mulch to cushion pressure from feet and pounding rain. This protective cover for the ever fragile soil structure breaks the impact of raindrops and protects soil particles from the eroding effects of flowing water or wind. Add composted material regularly and keep gardening soil ideal.

Since it is performing such a valuable, even essential service for garden plants, soil warrants regular monitoring. At the least it is holding water for times of drought and providing nutrients on a slow-release basis. Check the nutrient availability level and soil pH in the fall. Know the amount of nitrogen, potassium, and phosphorus available to plants. The pH and fertility of soil can be determined by either collecting and delivering samples to a soil testing lab, or by conducting tests with a commercial test kit. Agricultural extension agents assist the public with soil sampling, or soil testing kits can be purchased at garden centers and through gardening catalogues.

Performing a soil pH test is somewhat like taking a person's temperature; the test indicates general health or ill-health. Yet pH is always readily correctable. It is common to conduct separate pH tests for each planting bed because soils may be of two or three types even on a 0.5 acre (0.2 hectare) landscape. Beds might have different histories and levels of soil amendments which affect pH, and different plant types require certain pH levels for best performance. When a pH test indicates soil is too acidic, it is saying that the soil is locking up many plant nutrients. Needed minerals are not readily available for plant growth and health in highly acidic soil conditions. At a pH below 5.5, populations of microorganisms and earthworms that convert organic matter into available plant nutrients are greatly reduced.

At a neutral pH of around 6.5–7, needed plant nutrients again become available. A neutral pH also indicates that microorganisms and earthworms are thriving and consuming organic matter, breaking it down into plant food. Most compost has a neutral pH (pH 7), depending somewhat upon the type and variety of material composted. Hardwood tree leaves have more calcium and create a sweeter, more alkaline, compost. Pine needles are acidic.

If soils are too alkaline, nutrients are once again locked up. Microorganisms and earthworms also depopulate in highly alkaline conditions. See Figure 8-1 for a detail on how soil pH affects the availability of some specific soil nutrients.

Some plants have specific pH needs. Some plants are pH indifferent. Magnolias (*Magnolia grandiflora*) prefer an acid soil with a pH of 5–6, although they will grow without obvious distress in chalky soils that have a pH of 8. The majority of plants grow best within a specific pH range, and around pH 6.5 is considered nearly ideal for most, but not all garden plants.

Acid-loving plants, such as rhododendrons and blueberries, do poorly in alkaline soils. They yellow, nearly stop growing, and become stressed and open to disease. The same occurs in plants needing neutral to alkaline situations if they are planted in acid soil. Appendix B lists selected trees, shrubs, flowers, vines, and vegetables with their pH preferences.

If a pH test indicates that soils around azaleas are too alkaline, add chelated iron or iron sulfate powder, according to package instructions. This will help to build an acceptable acid level in the soil. Azaleas (*Rhododendron*) need a soil pH around 4.5–6 for even adequate growth and bloom. After creating acid soil, begin adding composted organic matter every month or two to help in developing a more beneficial soil environment for the plants.

If soils are too acidic, add lime and work it into the soil to reduce the acidity. Additionally, adding composted organic matter three times a year will help the soil adjust toward a neutral pH.

Generally, pH tests are taken in the spring. If gardening in an area of high rainfall, such as east of the Rocky Mountains, it is best to do pH testing and any adjustments in early spring. Rainfall creates acid soil conditions and leaching could wash out any lime placed on soil in the fall.

The two commonly available forms of lime that can be used in garden soil pH adjusting are calcite and dolomite. Calcite lime is calcium carbonate and is a chief component of chalk, marble, and limestone. Calcite is also known as agricultural lime and it is available in bags or by the truckload.

Dolomite lime is magnesium carbonate. It also provides the nutrient magnesium for use in soils where magnesium is not available, such as in chalky, limestone areas. Most dolomite is so similar to calcite that chemical tests have to be made to tell them apart.

Both calcite and dolomite lime come from finely ground rock. Many limestone buildings and marble statues are actually dolomite lime. Both types of lime are slightly soluble in water. Finely ground dolomitic limestone can neutralize soil acids by direct contact. Both the calcium and magnesium in dolomitic limestone act as neutralizing materials. Calcite limestone has calcium as a neutralizing material.

The speed at which dolomitic or calcitic limestone reacts with the soil depends on how finely ground the limestone is, and how thoroughly it is mixed with the soil. Soil temperature also plays a part. Finely ground limestone mixed with soil will react with the soil acids and begin to neutralize them within a few months.

The fastest reaction of limestone with soil occurs during the warm season when soil biological activity and root growth produces carbon dioxide which enhances the effect of lime on acid soils. Create a healthy environment for microorganisms and plant roots and there will be plenty of carbon dioxide. To lime lawn areas to reduce soil acidity, place lime with a spreader in the fall in regions of low to moderate rainfall and in the spring in regions of high rainfall.

For flower and vegetable gardens, spread limestone evenly over the soil and thoroughly mix it with a rotary tiller to a 6–8 in (15–20 cm) depth. This mixing enhances contact between the lime and the soil. Generally, soils in rainy parts of the country need lime because the soils are naturally acidic. In the arid parts of the South and West, the soil is generally alkaline. Use these general trends only as a guide. Test the soil to be cultivated and follow with amendments to bring the pH within the ideal range for the plants' soil environment.

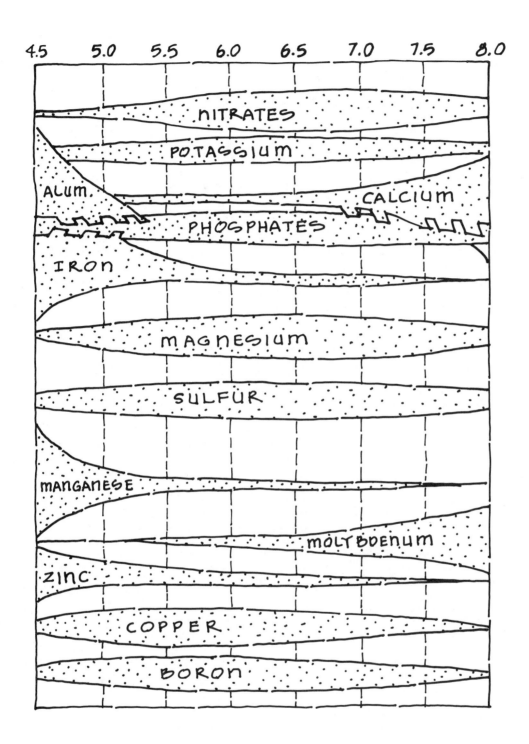

Figure 8-1. How soil pH affects availability of plant nutrients.

9

Fertilizers

Why the need to fertilize gardens when forests and meadows thrive effortlessly? Perhaps if planting beds were managed like Mother Nature manages her fields and forests, supplemental nutrients would not need adding to the soil.

First of all, in nature organic matter constantly returns to the soil through the dropping of plant and animal matter. Decomposed organic matter, also called humus, is the soil's storehouse of nutrients. Gardeners think they have to buy commercial fertilizers in order to provide nutrients for their plants. In fact, decomposed organic matter can provide nearly all the essential nutrients for plant growth. For example, the average amount of nitrogen released yearly when the top 6 in (15 cm) of soil contains 19% organic matter is 15–20 lb (7–9 kg) per acre (.16 hectare).

Nitrogen comes from other sources as well. Approximately 10 lb (4.5 kg) of nitrogen per acre (.16 hectare) is provided by certain microorganisms that can extract nitrogen from the air and bring it down into the soil. Rain and snow bring about 10 lb (4.5 kg) of nitrogen per acre (.16 hectare) from the atmosphere. The air we breathe is 79% nitrogen. Heat from lightning in the atmosphere causes the nitrogen to mix with oxygen to form nitrogen oxide.

How can reliance on fertilizers be reduced? Through regular nurturing of the soil with composted organic matter, most plant nutrient needs can be met. Fertilizers can be cautiously used to supplement the soil's ability to provide nutrients until a productive soil is built. Building that productive soil is mainly dependent on large quantities of composted organic matter. A goal of reducing the use of fertilizers will not only save money but also move toward the creation of sustainable landscapes that are in harmony with the land and nature. Sustainable landscapes rely on naturally available resources and processes for sustenance and health, much like the indefinitely sustainable natural ecosystem.

While a flower garden mulched with organic compost might get by fine being synthetic fertilizer-free, lawns and plants in shredded bark or pine straw mulch beds will need occasional fertilization to maintain health. Mulches that are not composted will yet be broken down by microorganisms. As the layer of mulch nearest the soil where moisture and air are present begins decomposition, microorganisms will be using all nitrogen available in order to multiply and carry out the decomposition process. Since most mulches are higher in carbon than in nitrogen, supplemental fertilizer is necessary to sustain plant health.

Lawns require supplemental fertilization. There is a law of ecology recognizing that diversity promotes stability. As natural diversity is reduced, such as in a lawn, certain nutrients have to be added to make up for what is lost by monoculture. Monoculture is growing only one type of plant in an area. A lawn is comprised of thousands of grass plants, all similar and with similar needs.

Stability in a landscape occurs with a diversity of flora and fauna that is matched with the environment. The plants, animals, and insects are in balance with one another and their environment, actively providing for one another's needs and creating healthy conditions. Without a diversity of flora and fauna matched with the environment, the gardener has to be on constant alert for nutrient deficiencies, or invading diseases and insects.

Supplemental lawn nutrients can be provided by a bag of commercial fertilizer. A bag of fertilizer has numbers on it telling buyers the amount of nitrogen (N), phosphorus (P) and potassium (K) in the bag. Nitrogen, phosphorus, and potassium in one fertilizer comprise a complete fertilizer containing the major nutrients (N-P-K) required for plant growth. A fertilizer bag with the numbers 8-8-8 means the sack contains 8% nitrogen, 8% phosphorus, and 8% potassium. The nutrients make up only 24% of the bag, the remaining 76% is filler, which allows for more even distribution of the nutrients onto the landscape and helps in reducing potential leaf burn. Some fertilizers will also contain micronutrients; this is usually stated in the description of bag contents. As these elements are needed in very small amounts by plants, it is easier to provide them along with the major nutrients. Micronutrients are needed when soils are low in clay and high in sand content, for example in prepared soil mixes. The problem with the sandy soils is that they leach nutrients so the nutrients have to be supplemented.

Eventually it will be necessary to compute the *actual* amount of a certain type of fertilizer needed in the landscape to correct deficiencies or maintain a healthy lawn. To do this, one can follow these simple steps.

1. Start with the recommended amount of an element, like nitrogen, needed per 1000 ft^2 (92.9 m^2). Let us say lawn grass needs 2 lbs (.9 kg) of *actual* nitrogen. The 2 lbs of nitrogen in this example does not mean 2 lbs of fertilizer but 2 lbs of *actual* fertilizer.

2. Select the fertilizer that best fits the (lawn grass) situation. Whether the

need is for a complete fertilizer (one containing all three elements, N-P-K) or a single source fertilizer, such as 34-0-0 (ammonium nitrate) or 0-20-0 (superphosphate), use the percentage for the most important element being recommended for the plants in the next calculation. Let us assume the complete fertilizer 24-4-12 is preferable for the lawn grass.

3. Divide the recommended amount of fertilizer in step one by the most important element needed in step two. The lawn needs 2 lbs (given above) of actual nitrogen per 1000 ft^2. Since 24-4-12 complete fertilizer is preferable this time, divide 2 by .24 (24% nitrogen). This results in determining that 8.33 lbs (3.78 kg) of 24-4-12 fertilizer will supply the 2 lbs of actual nitrogen needed for 1000 ft^2 (92.9 m^2) of lawn.

The following description of plant nutrients available as fertilizer explains characteristics of each needed nutrient. Having a general idea of how plants react to nutrients will help in determining any fertilizer needs. Macronutrients are elements needed in large amounts for plant growth. Micronutrients are elements needed in very small amounts. Overuse of fertilizers can stress plants and waste resources.

Nitrogen (N). Nitrogen is important for vigorous growth, the green color of leaves, protein building, and photosynthesis. Photosynthesis is the production of needed sugars through the action of light on the chlorophyll in green plant cells. All green plant cells conduct photosynthesis in the presence of light.

Nitrogen is the building block of plant life, though it is transient. It fluctuates rapidly in soil and when depleted, plants begin displaying a yellow color in the older leaves. The available nitrogen in the plant actually moves to the youngest leaves where the plant is still trying to actively grow. These young leaves remain green longer. If there is too much nitrogen, rampant shoot growth can result. Root growth, which requires almost no nitrogen, might not be able to keep up, and the plant will become stressed. Excessive, soft, succulent growth also attracts insect damage.

Nitrogen fertilizer is produced in a rapidly available or slowly available form. Over a period of months both forms of nitrogen fertilizers can contribute to making soil more acid. The rapidly available, or rapidly released nitrogen is soluble in water and plants will have a quick, but brief growth response to it.

There is a chance for leaf burn if too much quick-release fertilizer is applied. This can happen in two ways. Fertilizer burn occurs directly when concentrated N granules fall on plant leaves and literally draw the water out of the leaves. This action can be seen when fertilizer falls on paved surfaces and creates small pools of water around each granule as moisture is pulled out of the air. Fertilizer burn occurs more indirectly if N is overapplied and worked into the soil. The fertilizer will attract and hold soil water, making it unavailable to plant roots, and thus causing leaves to stress or burn from lack of water.

Examples of fast-release, water soluble nitrogen fertilizers available on the market are ammonium nitrate, ammonium sulfate, nitrate of soda, urea, and potassium nitrate.

All but the nitrate of soda and potassium nitrate slowly increase soil acidity levels with extended use. Therefore, it is essential to know the soil pH and available nutrient level before applying N fertilizers. More harm than good will be done if soil pH becomes too acidic.

With the exception of isobutylidene diurea (IBDU), none of the slow-release nitrogen sources are water soluble. Microorganisms are depended upon to release the nitrogen for plant use. In order for microorganisms to be effective, soil pH has to be above pH 6 with adequate soil moisture and warmth. Plants display a slower yet extended growth response to slow-release nitrogen fertilizers. Since leaf burn potential is limited, these fertilizers are easier for the home gardener to use. Alternative slow-release fertilizers include dried sewage sludge such as Milorganite, cottonseed meal, and blood meal. Table 9-1 lists nitrogen fertilizers and their characteristics.

Slow-release fertilizers are usually more expensive than the fast-release type, but many gardeners and agronomists say their plant value is nearly equal. Fast-release nitrogen sources do have greater potential for some of the nitrogen to wash or leach beyond plant roots before plants can use it and can even contaminate groundwater. Also, when nitrogen is available all at once, a plant experiences a growth surge which might exceed the root system's ability to provide adequate moisture. With slow-release nitrogen sources, nearly all of the nitrogen is used by the plant in a timed-release manner and it will rarely leach beyond the plant root zone.

Table 9-1. Nitrogen fertilizers.

	% N	Acidifies soil	Water soluble	Released by microorganisms
Fast release				
Ammonium nitrate	33	Yes	Yes	No
Ammonium sulfate	21	Yes	Yes	No
Sodium nitrate	16	Yes	Yes	No
Nitrate of soda	10	No	Yes	No
Urea	45	Yes	Yes	No
Potassium nitrate	13	No	Yes	No
Slow release				
Urea formaldehyde (UF)	38	No	No	Yes
Isobutylidene diurea (IBDU)	31	No	Yes	No
Dried sewage sludge	6	No	No	Yes
Cottonseed meal	6	Yes	No	Yes
Blood meal	12	Yes	No	Yes

Phosphorus (P). Phosphorus is important for root growth, fruit ripening, and winter hardiness. It also needs to be applied directly into the soil when planting, as it is important for early plant development. This macronutrient is highly immobile in the soil. Often it is not available to plants because it is tied up chemically with other soil materials, especially clay particles. A phosphorus deficiency in plants can usually be identified by stunting and a change in leaf color. Normally green leaves turn bluish green with a purple tint. Weak plant structure, undeveloped root systems, and small leaves are other deficiency symptoms.

A soil test might show adequate phosphorous, yet there is a possibility it remains unavailable to plant roots. More phosphorus remains available for plant use at a pH of 6.5–7.5. At pH extremes, when soils are strongly acid or alkaline, less phosphorus is available for plant use. A phosphorus deficiency in the soil may simply reflect pH extremes.

If a soil test indicates inadequate levels of phosphorus, it is available as bone meal, rock phosphate that has been chemically treated to be water soluble, superphosphate, and concentrated or triple superphosphate. Sources of phosphorus and their concentrations are given in Table 9-2.

Table 9-2. P-K sources and concentrations.

Source	Percent concentration	Additional elements
Phosphorus (P)		
bone meal	13–34	1–4% nitrogen
rock phosphate	$^-2$	
superphosphate	15–22	11% sulfur
concentrated	37–53	
Potassium (K)		
potassium chloride (muriate of potash)	58–62	
potassium sulfate	48–53	17% sulfur
potassium nitrate	44	13% nitrogen
wood ashes	gen. 10	

Potassium (K). Potassium is the third essential mineral element involved in plant growth. This macronutrient directly affects the production of specific sugars in leaves and speeds the seed ripening process. It could be said that potassium is necessary to plant maturation: it helps in stiffening plant stalks, developing green wood into brown, and in developing viable seed. Since it serves as a regulating element in cell moisture levels, it is often used in the South as an antifreeze or coolant treatment to help plants survive extreme winter and summer temperatures.

A lack of available potassium is generally hard to spot but will often result in poorly colored and flavored fruit. Plant leaves will curl and spot at the edges and look scorched.

In the soil, especially in sandy soils, potassium is subject to leaching. While clay and high-organic content soils contain large amounts of potassium, generally less than 2% is available for plant use. This is because potassium usually binds with other insoluble soil minerals.

While ashes from a wood stove or fireplace have a concentration of 10% potassium, they also cause soils to become more alkaline. Additionally, walnut, hickory or pecan wood ashes may contain toxic residues that could harm landscape plants. Since the amount of potassium absorbed by plants is exceeded only by nitrogen, potassium fertilizers have been developed to supply the plant needs and not lock up with soil minerals. See Table 9-2 for sources and concentration.

Calcium (Ca). Calcium is present in most soils and is used in the creation of plant cell walls. This important plant food is essential for the creation of strong plants. A lack of calcium results in weak-stemmed, spindly plants. Plants might also show a lack of vigor and growth points might die.

In areas of high annual rainfall (those averaging 46 in/117 cm), calcium leaches beyond the root zone. The root zone is the limit to which roots extend. A yearly soil pH test of plant beds and lawn areas will determine the need for calcium. Calcium soil supplements are available as calcite and dolomite lime.

Magnesium (Mg). Normally available in soils, this element is necessary for chlorophyll formation and essential for seed germination. Many sandy soils and especially modified sandy soils or created soils can have a magnesium deficiency. Such plantings in these areas will appear yellow and chlorotic. A magnesium deficiency differs from nitrogen or iron deficiency symptoms in that leaf veins are dark green while the remainder of the leaf is yellowish. Also Mg symptoms can be spotted first in mature leaves, not the oldest or newest leaves. Mature leaves also pucker unnaturally and fall prematurely. Epsom salts and dolomitic limestone can provide magnesium.

Recall that in nitrogen deficiency, chlorosis (yellowing) will occur in the oldest leaves first. In iron deficiency, chlorosis occurs in the youngest leaves; chlorosis occurring in mature leaves indicates a magnesium deficiency.

Sulfur (S). This element is present in most soils except those such as in the Southwest that receive little rainfall and are naturally alkaline. Sulfur is a prime component in the chlorophyll making process. Chlorophyll is the green pigment in plant cells significant to photosynthesis.

Soils with a deficiency in sulfur yield plants with light green, chlorotic-looking leaves that otherwise would indicate a nitrogen deficiency problem. If soils are alkaline (above pH 7), the existing sulfur is probably locked up chemically and unavailable to plants. To remedy this, reduce the pH level by adding elemental sulfur or iron sulphate. These elements will both acidify soil and provide sulfur. Be careful when applying elemental sulfur to keep the powder away from plant leaves. Sulfur powder on plant leaves will draw water from the plant and cause the leaf to dry out. Apply no more than 5 lbs (2.3 kg) of the powder per 1000 ft^2 (92.9 m^2) per application. Water it in and wait two to four weeks before adding additional sulfur if needed. Iron sulphate affects soil pH very slowly. If soils do not need to become more acid but plantings need sulfur, use gypsum (calcium sulphate).

Iron (Fe). Iron is a micronutrient that is available in most soils, yet it might not be available in sandy, naturally alkaline, or overlimed soils. Its most significant function in plants is in assisting in the formation of chlorophyll, the green coloring in plants. When a plant is lacking iron, the top leaves where the newest growth is occurring will be pale white and the lower, older leaves will be a pale green color. This is called chlorosis. Insufficient iron causes both fruit and flowers to fail.

Generally, in high rainfall areas (those averaging 46 in/117 cm per year) soils are acidic and sufficient iron is available. In low rainfall areas, soils are alkaline and iron is less available. Normal rainfall has an acid pH of 5.7. Rainfall leaches the calcium and sodium downward in the soil and promotes an acid condition. Where there is little rainfall, naturally occurring calcium and sodium move to the surface during evaporation. This creates an alkaline situation and often a buildup of harmful salts in the top few inches of soil.

Iron supplementation, if needed, can be in the form of iron sulfate or chelated iron. Chelated iron means the iron is water soluble, and immediately and persistently available to plants. Iron sulfate is also water soluble yet it bonds with other soil elements very quickly and does not remain an available element.

Copper (Cu). Copper is used in the transformation of nitrogen into plant food. In plants deficient in copper, dieback first occurs in terminal leaves and progresses to stems where brown, dead-looking areas develop. It is almost always available in soils. In acid soils below pH 5 and in alkaline soils above pH 8, copper binds with other minerals and is less available. Composted humus contains copper in sufficient quantities for plant use.

Manganese (Mn). Manganese is important in the transformation of soil nutrients for plant use. This element is abundant in soils, and is available to plants at between pH 5 and pH 6.5. Controlling soil pH is the best way of ensuring availability of this element. Accidental overliming will create a manganese deficiency in soil. If this occurs, adjust the soil back to its proper pH.

Zinc (Zn). Zinc is a trace element needed for plant growth and seed formation. It also helps plants in utilizing other needed minerals. Small amounts of zinc are present in nearly all soils. Zinc becomes less available to plants at a pH above 7.0. Control soil pH to make zinc available to plants. Zinc is also available in chelated forms.

Boron (B). A shortage of boron stunts leaf growth and causes a yellowing of plants. Blooming and seed development stops. In nature, boron is always found in combination with other minerals. Soils low in organic matter and those that are alkaline can have a boron deficiency. By adding composted humus to the garden and by controlling soil pH, enough boron is usually provided. Boron becomes less available to plants at pHs above 7.0 and below 5.3.

Small amounts of Borax soap (sodium borate) can also be added for quick relief. Since boron is a micronutrient needed in very small amounts, too much Borax soap can easily create toxic conditions harmful to plants.

Molybdenum (Mo). Plants need only very small amounts of this micronutrient. Molybdenum helps in preventing an accumulation of nitrates which can cause chlorosis in older leaves, stunted plant growth, and, eventually, plant death. The micronutrient is abundantly available in alkaline soils and scarcely available in soils with a pH below 5.5. Sewage sludge fertilizers such as Milorganite can provide sufficient amounts of molybdenum.

Chlorine (Cl). Chlorine is the final of the sixteen essential elements recognized as needed for plant growth. Although abundant in plant tissue, only very small quantities of chlorine are needed for plant health and growth. The element is rarely deficient in soils. Watering with chlorinated water increases the availability of chlorine.

Summary of mineral elements. Plants require the following macronutrients in large quantities—nitrogen, phosphorus, potassium, calcium, sulfur, and magnesium. These nutrients are usually supplemented in the garden through the use of manufactured fertilizers and compost.

The micronutrients are elements plants need only in trace amounts from the soil and are generally provided by maintaining correct soil pH. These are: iron, manganese, zinc, copper, boron, molybdenum, and chlorine. Table 9-3 gives a full list of the sixteen essential macro- and micronutrients essential for plant growth tabulated by soil, air, and water.

Table 9-3.
Nutrients essential for plant growth.

Macronutrients in the soil		Micronutrients in the soil		Nutrients in air and water	
Nitrogen	N	Iron	Fe	Carbon	C
Phosphorus	P	Copper	Cu	Hydrogen	H
Potassium	K	Manganese	Mn	Oxygen	O
Calcium	Ca	Zinc	Zn	Nitrogen	N
Magnesium	Mg	Molybdenum	Mo		
Sulfur	S	Boron	B		
		Chlorine	Cl		

10

Composting

It is possible to create a garden landscape design and management plan that will either work one to death from exhaustion or tedium, or require only regular, reasonable chores to keep the garden looking great.

The most critical element in reducing the amount of labor required is establishing a healthy soil environment for plants. Healthy soil requires less watering and fertilizing, and plants develop fewer stresses. A friable, organic mulch applied over soils reduces the amount of weeds growing in planting beds and retains soil moisture. A properly mulched planting bed is not only healthy for plants and a labor-saving feature, it also can enhance a garden's appearance. The dark color of composted mulch acts as a wonderful backdrop for the color and texture of plants.

Composted material is organic matter, either plant or animal, that has undergone a decaying process. When its elements are unrecognizable it can be used as mulch. Microorganisms are responsible for decaying the organic matter. When the microorganisms in the compost pile decay plant and animal matter they are doing two things: they are consuming the plant and animal matter for their own use, and they are converting the proteins in the organic matter into nitrogen, phosphorus, potash, and other macro- and micronutrients. To have a healthy compost pile, provide the microorganisms with a proper environment to flourish. That environment is one that allows heat to reach as much as 150°F (66°C) and has enough available water for the microorganisms to carry out their reproductive and digestive processes.

To feed the microorganisms properly, provide organic matter in a certain blend of proteins and carbohydrates. This blend will be described in detail. The overview is that proteins are used by microorganisms for their own growth and reproduction. The proteins meanwhile are also being converted into nutrients for plant use. Proteins come from nitrogen sources. Carbohydrates are the energy-rich materials that the microorganisms consume for energy. Carbohydrates are the carbon sources supplied by woody plant matter.

To have a fast-acting and effective compost pile, it is important to blend a mixture of protein (nitrogen) sources and energy (carbon) sources so that microorganisms quickly multiply and convert the organic matter into a humus-like compost. Humus is the organic element of soil, such as found in the dark, earthy, decomposed matter of the forest floor. Scientists tell us that the right blend or ratio of carbon to nitrogen (C:N) for the most expedient composting is 25:1 or 30:1. That is to say, for every twenty-five parts of carbon include one part nitrogen.

Most materials available for composting do not come with this 25:1 or 30:1 ratio, yet grass clippings and clover hay are pretty close. Table 10-1 gives the C:N of commonly available organic materials used in composting. Sawdust has a 500:1 carbon to nitrogen

Table 10-1. Carbon-to-nitrogen ratios of organic materials.

sewage sludge; activated	6:1
poultry manure	7:1
humus	10:1
alfalfa hay	12:1
alfalfa	13:1
pig manure	14:1
food wastes	15:1
green sweetclover	16:1
sewage sludge; digested	16:1
sheep manure	16:1
cow manure	18:1
grass clippings	19:1
horse manure	22:1
mature sweetclover	23:1
legume-grass hay	25:1
fruit wastes	35:1
sugar cane residues	50:1
deciduous leaves	65:1
evergreen leaves	65:1
straw	80:1
oat straw	80:1
paper	170:1
sawdust, all types	500:1
wood	700:1

ratio and because of this high ratio it decomposes very slowly. Such a ratio indicates a severe protein shortage and therefore the microorganisms reproduce very slowly.

When creating a compost pile, make sure to blend organic materials so that the overall ratio of carbon and nitrogen is approximately 25:1. This typically means taking high protein wastes—green vegetation from the garden, kitchen wastes like orange and apple peels, grass clippings, pulverized seeds like coffee grounds, and manure—and mixing them with materials high in carbon, such as leaves, pinestraw, and sawdust. In the country of Sri Lanka professional compost makers collect protein-rich human urine and apply it to designer compost piles created from material gathered at a municipal dump. The compost, called Gems from Garbage, is quickly composted (in two weeks) and sold throughout the island country. The main idea is that the blending of protein with carbon allows the microbes an ideal environment in which to reproduce and transform the organic matter into food for the landscape.

Now, what organic materials not to add to one's compost? While the heat in compost piles may reach 150°F (66°C), enough to kill most plant diseases and destructive insects, it is still best not to add diseased and infected plant parts to the compost pile. This will help ensure that specific disease problems are not passed on from season to season. Compost piles do not heat up uniformly; any cooler pockets could allow diseases and insects to survive. Weed seed heads are also best excluded for the same reason. Meat and fish scraps do not normally belong in the compost pile, as they attract rodents, but can be buried in the garden. Most compost enthusiasts, particularly gardeners growing their own food, also do not compost domestic animal manures. The belief is that cat or dog wastes carry disease organisms which are transferable to humans. Such wastes are buried outside food-growing areas rather than being added to the compost pile.

To create a fast-acting compost pile, alternate 12 in (30 cm) layers of leaves on top of 12 in layers of grass clippings. Continue building to end up with a pile that is about 4 ft (1 m) tall by 10 ft (3 m) in diameter. The pile can be freestanding with sloping sides or in bins if space is limited. While a compost bin is neater, a freestanding pile is easier to turn. Mixing grass clippings and leaves in layers will insure a pile near the ideal 25:1 carbon to nitrogen ratio that microorganisms prefer.

Now, leave the compost pile as layered for about a year. It will slowly decompose as long as the pile is slightly damp. The volume of the pile will have reduced by about one-half when the compost is ready. Compost provides an outstanding organic mulch for incorporating into garden soil and for use as a surface mulch to hold moisture and reduce weed growth.

The alternative is to rapidly compost the organic matter for quicker use in the landscape. This is done by turning the compost every three days with a pitch fork or specialized compost-turning tool to aerate the pile. This method produces finished compost in two to three weeks. Some experienced gardeners have found it helpful to chop through the layers of grass and leaves with a tool such as a mattock. Chopping mixes the layers and creates cuts and scratches so microorganisms can get into plant matter more easily. By covering the compost pile with a waterproof covering after turning, excess water will be prevented from cooling the ideal, warm temperature microorganisms prefer. Excess water also leaches out valuable nutrients.

Compost piles with a 25:1 carbon to nitrogen ratio will usually produce enough moisture as part of the decomposition process. If water has to be added, be careful not to saturate the pile. Excess water will smother the fast-acting aerobic bacteria and they will be replaced with slower acting and smellier anaerobic bacteria. Ideally, the moisture level of a healthy compost pile has the water content similar to that of a thoroughly wrung-out dishcloth.

A strong ammonia smell from the compost pile means that too much nitrogen (protein) source, such as fresh grass clippings, is in the compost pile. To remedy this situation add additional matter that is high in carbon, like leaves, shredded paper, sawdust, or straw. A sour smell indicates a lack of aeration, usually stemming from too-infrequent turning of the pile. A compost pile, actively working, will not produce disagreeable odor.

By selecting materials with the correct C:N ratio and by turning the covered pile every three days, composted material will be ready to place in the garden after two to three weeks. How to tell when is it ready? Look for humus, the dark brown, friable material, or measure the temperature of the compost pile. Use a bimetal thermometer with a 2–3 ft (0.5–1m) shaft to take the pile's temperature. Such thermometers are available from many garden centers or nurseries. The compost pile will heat up to 110°F (43°C) the day after it is made. By the second or third turning the temperature will rise up to 150–160°F (66–71°C). If the compost pile does not achieve this temperature, more nitrogen or more moisture is needed.

When compost is finished after two or three weeks of turning, or letting it sit for a year, its temperature will be about 110°F (43°C). The resulting carbon to nitrogen ratio has been reduced to 10:1, which is the same as humus from the forest floor. The pH of the compost should be neutral, or about pH 7.

Another very effective method of composting on a much smaller scale is to recycle household organic garbage into the garden on an every-other-day basis. Do this by digging a shallow hole in the garden and putting in all kitchen scraps. Cover the kitchen scraps with a 4–6 in (10–15 cm) layer of soil. In about three months the scraps will be totally gone and the soil should be full of earthworms and microorganisms. Recycling household garbage into the garden will improve the structure in heavy soils and take the household garbage out of the waste stream of the community.

Composted leaves and grass clippings provide the best soil amendment available. Additionally, homemade compost applied regularly to soils will reduce or eventually eliminate the need to fertilize garden areas. The first-class garden possible begins with composting today for a richer soil and healthier garden tomorrow.

11

Mulching

A mulch is an organic or inorganic material placed on top of the soil for both functional and aesthetic purposes. When effectively used, mulches help maintain healthy plants, reduce garden maintenance, and improve the appearance of planting areas.

There are two principal types of mulch, organic and inorganic. An organic mulch is a natural material that readily breaks down over a period of time. Microorganisms act in breaking down the organic matter by consuming it. In this manner valuable plant nutrients are released for plant use. Typical organic mulches include leaves, evergreen needles, bark, wood chips, and various hulls, such as peanut, cottonseed, pecan, and rice hulls. Organic materials local to one's area usually cost less.

When using organic mulches, care should be taken not to use those that are very fine-textured. Such materials tend to mesh together too tightly, forming a seal and retarding the flow of water and air to the soil and plant roots. Fine-textured peat moss and sawdust fall in this category.

Some materials, such as sawdust, crushed corn cobs, and wood chips use much nitrogen from the soil in decomposing. Use caution in using such materials as some of these mulches actually rob the soil of valuable nutrients. Slow-growing plants with yellowish leaves may indicate a nitrogen deficiency induced by the mulching material. Nitrogen levels can be corrected by using 4 oz (115 g) of ammonium nitrate or ammonium sulfate per bushel (35.24 l) of mulch, or 2 lbs (0.9 kg) per 100 ft^2 (9 m^2) of a complete fertilizer, such as 13-13-13 or 5-10-5. Slow-release nitrogen can also be used with less danger of burning plants. Apply this to the soil before adding mulch or apply on top of old mulch before replenishing it.

Bark nuggets, when used as a mulch, tend to float. This type of mulch is unsuitable for slopes because it clogs catch basins or other drainage systems. Shredded hardwood bark and pine straw are appropriate for slopes because they will not float away. They hold together due to their structural composition. Well-rotted manures and some dried, native field straw materials may be used as mulch, yet they invariably introduce weeds. Exercise restraint when using dried natural materials as a mulch around seating and cooking areas because of the danger of fire.

For established woody plants, organic mulches are applied at a settled depth of 2–4 in (5–10 cm) in the fall and again in early spring, if needed. For heavy clay soils, use 2 in (5 cm) of mulch. For light, sandy soils, 4 in (10 cm) of mulch is best. Pine straw may be applied at depth of 6 in (15 cm) to allow for settling.

Be careful about overmulching. After the mulch has settled, it should be no more than 4 in (10 cm) deep. Overmulching restricts air and water intake. Plant roots will grow into a surface mulch and be susceptible to drought and winter freezes. If plant roots grow in the mulch, it is an indication that the mulch is too heavy and part should be removed. Also, keep the mulch 1–2 in (3–5 cm) from the plant bark, stem, or trunk to prevent fungus, disease, or other injuries and to prevent root sprouts. As termites often develop in shredded bark and wood chips these materials should not be used near foundations of wood construction.

Depending on the region and specific environment, adding new mulch may be limited to every one to three years to avoid overmulching. To obtain the desirable appearance of fresh mulch, when additional mulching is not needed, either rake over the existing one or use one of the mulch colorant sprays.

For new installations of woody plants, mulch may be applied after the soil has adequately settled around the plant root system. For herbaceous plants, the mulch should be applied at planting. For heat and cold protection, it is desirable to mulch bulb plantings, too.

Inorganic mulches include such materials as gravel, chipped stone, river stone, black plastic, and perforated landscape fabric. One advantage of inorganic mulches is that they are less of a fire hazard than many organic mulches. Also, they do not decompose readily though they do have to be restored periodically.

If plastic is used as a mulch it should be black. Clear or translucent plastic is sometimes used in solar sterilization of the soil, yet as an all-round mulch the black plastic effectively blocks light and reduces the incidence of weed seeds sprouting. Punch a limited number of holes in the plastic for necessary water and air flow to the soil. Any plastic reduces the penetration of air and water to the soil, a negative feature, but perforated landscape fabric is especially made for mulching purposes. It is perforated and permits an adequate flow of air and water to the soil, which is essential for good plant growth. To stabilize both plastic and landscape fabric, and to shade and protect it from deterioration, it is best to cover it with a mulch, such as gravel, pine straw, or shredded bark. The perforation in the landscape fabric will help prevent slippage of light mulches placed over it.

The depth of inorganic mulches depends on the type materials used. If mulching with pea gravel or crushed stone, 1–2 in (3–5 cm) of either material will suffice. If using black plastic one layer will do. Overlap the plastic by about 4 in (10 cm) and cut several small slits in it for the penetration of air and water. Plastic must be weighted down to hold it in place, and this may be accomplished by adding a light covering of an organic mulch.

Advantages of using mulch:

1. Conserves moisture by reducing evaporation.

2. Retains water so it will gradually soak into the soil.

3. Moderates soil temperature changes, daily and seasonally.

4. Breaks impact of rain and irrigation spray on soil.

5. Reduces erosion due to slowing surface water movement.

6. Reduces weed growth that would otherwise restrict water, food, and light to desired plantings.

7. Reduces soil baking, crusting, and cracking due to summer and winter sun.

8. Reduces winter kill due to plant desiccation.

9. Adds to the aesthetic value by being attractive and unifying a planting design composition.

10. Increases soil fertility over time by increasing microorganism activity, which increases the availability of nutrients.

11. Adds organic matter to soil, thus improving soil structure.

12. Allows the flow of oxygen into the soil and carbon dioxide out of it.

With the exception of the last three, the above advantages relate to organic or inorganic mulches. In addition, inorganic mulches require replinishing less often and have a more uniform color and texture.

12

Lawns

In a residential landscape, the lawn is often the primary open space in the design. Because of this, lawn areas are subject to a lot of visual inspection. Their color and uniformity of texture are particularly likely to receive visual scrutiny. The lawn is often the place where outdoor activities are held, therefore a healthy, thick turf allows for maximum enjoyment.

Selecting a grass for open space largely depends on climate. One can select either warm- or cool-season grasses. Warm-season grasses grow most vigorously during the warm part of the year when temperatures are 80–95°F (26–35°C). Cool-season grasses grow best when it is cool and wet and temperatures are 60–75°F (16–24°C). Figure 12-1 maps the geographic extent of warm- and cool-season grasses.

Warm-season grasses are indigenous to southern Europe, tropical and subtropical areas of Asia, Africa, South America, and the West Indies. They adapt well to hot, humid areas of the United States. In winter they go dormant and turn brown. Warm-season grasses include bermuda (*Cynodon dactylon*), centipede (*Eremochloa ophiuroides*), *Zoysia*, carpet (*Axonopus affinis*), and St. Augustine (*Stenotaphrum secundatam*). These grasses are thick-growing and constantly spread by sending out runners.

Cool-season grasses are indigenous to temperate and arctic regions of the world and are best adapted to grow in cooler, less humid areas. These grasses retain their green color throughout the year. Some common types include various bluegrasses (*Poa*) and fescues (*Festuca*), and perennial (*Lolium perenne*) and annual ryes (*L. multiforum*).

These grasses are not rapid spreaders like the warm-season grasses. Rye grass, however, is quick to establish and is often used to control erosion on freshly cultivated or unstable soil. Perennial rye tolerates hot and cold temperature extremes better than annual rye. It is also lighter in color and requires less mowing than annual rye grass. In

91

Figure 12-1. Geographic extent of warm- and cool-season grasses.

the South, rye grass is used for winter green color. It can be overseeded on top of warm-season grasses in September. Most rye grass is killed off when the weather heats up. The exception is in shady areas where perennial rye will persist from season to season. Thus, rye grass does not compete with warm-season grasses. In the North, perennial ryegrass can tolerate mild summers and persist as a year-round turf.

Beyond choices between warm- and cool-season grasses, sunlight exposure and soil pH are the two most critical factors in grass selection. Although all lawn grasses grow best in full sunlight, of the warm-season grasses, St. Augustine, zoysia, and centipede will grow under high-branching trees that allow filtered sunlight or bright shade. St. Augustine and zoysia are the most shade tolerant of the warm-season grasses and will get by with bright daylight. A partial to total deep shade condition will not grow lawn grass. Switch to a mulch or ground cover in such situations.

Of the cool-season grasses, both bluegrass and fescues tolerate a half day of shade or a full day of filtered sunlight through high-branching trees. When lawn areas do not receive full sun, make sure growth and health factors such as soil pH, nutrient availability, and moisture levels are ideally maintained for the best performance.

In the South, grass is usually planted in monostands. Using only one variety of grass, such as bermuda (*Cynodon dactylon*), is typical. Because of variances in grass color, texture, and height, warm-season grasses are not planted in blends as cool-season grasses are.

In the North, grass is planted in polystands with two or three species planted together or in a blend. Similar textures allow these species to blend more readily. A common blend of cool-season grasses may be Kentucky bluegrass (*Poa pratensis*) and perennial rye (*Lolium perenne*) for use in the sun, and fine fescues for best performance in the shade.

Soil pH levels can be determined with a simple test kit. Soil pH can be adjusted with ground limestone if soil is too acidic, or sulfur if it is too alkaline. Certain grasses have specific pH requirements for the best health and growth. Table 12-1 includes pH ranges for all grasses discussed.

Table 12-1. Lawn grass culture requirements.

Grass type	Exposure			pH range	Irrigation need	Fertilizer requirements
	Full sun	Some sun	Bright shade			
Warm-season						
Common bermuda	Yes	No	No	6.5	Moderate	Moderate
Carpet	Yes	Yes	No	4.5–5.5	Moderate	Low
Centipede	Yes	Yes	No	4.5–5.5	Low	Low
St. Augustine	Yes	Yes	Yes	6.5–7.5	Low	Moderate
Zoysia	Yes	Yes	Yes	6.0–7.0	Low	Moderate
Cool-season						
Kentucky bluegrass	Yes	Yes	No	6.0–6.5	Moderate	Moderate
Creeping red fescue	Yes	Yes	No	6.0	High	Low
Tall fescue	Yes	Yes	No	5.5–6.5	Moderate	Moderate

The lawn's health and appearance depends on how carefully it is monitored and maintained. Monitoring tasks include taking soil pH tests in the fall or spring and performing a soil nutrient analysis every two years. Additionally, note any visual changes in the turf. A poor color could mean the grass is stressed in some manner. Stress results from disease or pests, drought, extreme air temperatures, excessive compaction, a change in soil pH, and a shortage of soil nutrients. If grass does not spring back after being walked on, it is probably time to irrigate. This lack of resiliency in grass can be an early warning signal to indicate a need to water.

Managing a lawn can include fertilizing, maintaining soil pH, mowing, dethatching, and weed control. The last three management tasks directly relate to the first two. By maintaining a healthy lawn, much of the battle is already won.

Many turf scientists (lawn specialists) do not recommend regular fertilization programs. Instead, they suggest fertilizing only when a greener color is desired or rapid growth is needed to fill in damaged turf. We agree with this philosophy and practice it successfully.

Soil pH is critical to the availability of soil nutrients and to ultimate plant health. Maintaining a correct soil pH is not arbitrary in effective lawn management. We recommend getting a soil pH testing kit and including pH testing as a regular gardening practice.

Lawn specialists will tell us to mow often for the best lawn appearance. Research has proved that frequent mowing increases the density of the grass canopy. Since a dense grass canopy slows water evaporation from soil and leaf surfaces, mowing frequently helps to conserve water.

Removal of more than one-third of a grass blade when mowing can be stressful to turf. However, regular mowing allows weeds to become stressed and ultimately allows a more uniform lawn. Leaving cut grass to filter down to the soil level instead of removing clippings enhances soil fertility and can provide 20–40% of a plant's nutrient need. Table 12-2 gives specific mowing heights and mowing frequencies for the grass types being discussed. It is recommended that grass grown in shaded areas be cut 0.5 in (1 cm) higher so more of the plant can gather light for photosynthesis.

Thatch is a layer of dead and living stems and blades between the soil and green grass blades. All lawns develop some thatch. A layer of thatch 0.5 in (1 cm) or less is beneficial in holding moisture and insulating the soil surface from heat, cold, and compaction. When thatch exceeds one inch in thickness, it creates a tight barrier, and problems in watering or nutrient availability occur. A thick thatch layer slows water and nutrients to plant roots and can actually prevent water from reaching the grass's root level.

Dethatching a lawn is done with a special mower which cuts and pulls the thatch up to the surface to rake off for disposal to the compost pile. Vertical mowing machines are often available to rent. Bermuda grass (*Cynodon dactylon*), St. Augustine (*Stenotaphrum secundatum*), *Zoysia*, and bluegrasses (*Poa*) all develop thatch buildup over the years. Late winter is the best time to dethatch a cool-season lawn. Dethatch a warm-season lawn in the early spring just before it greens and starts to grow.

Weed control in lawns is most soundly a manual effort. We cannot recommend the use of herbicide control techniques for weeds in the lawn or the use of lawn fertilizers containing herbicides. While there are many herbicides available to kill specific weeds to give a perfectly uniform lawn, we think the handling dangers of such chemicals to the home gardener and one's pets could be significant. Also, the insidious effects the chemicals may have on wildlife, water quality, and the food chain urge restraint in their use. Maintaining a healthy turf and mowing frequently controls most of the common weeds. Always strive for visual uniformity and dependability in lawn management.

12-2. Lawn grass management characteristics.

type	Mowing frequency[1]	Mowing height in (cm)	Stress recovery[2]	Establishment methods		Color	Wear tolerance	Susceptibility insects/disease
				Seed	Sod			
-season								
mmon ermuda	High	0.5–1.5 (1–4)	Fast	Yes	Yes	Medium green	High	Moderate
rpet	Low	1.0–2.0 (2–5)	Good	Yes	Yes	Yellow-green	Poor	Moderate
ntipede	Low	1.5–2.0 (4–5)	Good	Yes	Yes	Yellow-green	Poor	Moderate
Augustine	Medium	2.5–3.0 (6–8)	Good	No	Yes	Medium green	Low	High
ysia	Medium	1.0–1.5 (2–4)	Slow	No	Yes	Medium green	High	Low
-season								
ntucky bluegrass	Medium	1.5–3.0 (4–8)	Good	Yes	Yes	Blue-green	Moderate	Moderate
eeping red fescue	Low	1.5–2.0 (4–5)	Good	Yes	Yes	Medium green	High	High
l fescue	Low	2.0–3.0 (5–8)	Slow	Yes	Yes	Dark green	High	Moderate

frequency indicates a need to mow about once every ten days; *high* means once every four days.
ty to bounce back from freeze, drought, insect, or traffic damage.

1. The low shrubs, mulch bed, sidewalk, and fence all create lines in the landscape and impart a distinct feeling. The edge of the pine straw mulch bed, along with the sidewalk edge and lawn, impart a flowing, casual feeling, drawing the viewer toward the pool court of this residential community clubhouse. The shrubs provide a transition from the building to the ground level and also emphasize the gate to the pool. Madison, Mississippi.

MANAGEMENT Prune the evergreen harland boxwoods (*Buxus harlandii*) and India hawthorn (*Raphiolepis indica*) shrubs in late winter. Shape them again as needed in early summer. Mulch in the fall. Refurbish the mulch in the spring. Trim grass away from the sidewalk and bed edging every third mowing. Mow the grass approximately twenty times a season.

2. The line of the low clipped boxwoods echoes the line of the stone edging. This unifying rhythm repeats again in the line of crape myrtle trees which define the space against the enclosing hedge line and privacy screen. In this monochromatic foliage scheme, the light-colored bark of the small trees lends variety and contrast to the dark green background while creating a feeling of spaciousness in an otherwise limited space. Nashville, Tennessee.

MANAGEMENT In late winter, prune small crape myrtle (*Lagerstroemia indica*) trees to maintain size and openness; prune broadleaved evergreen shrubs to remove dead wood and control growth. Shear low boxwood (*Buxus*) border in late winter to control size. In early spring, fertilize all plants to maintain foliage color, and mulch. Fertilize lawn in early spring, if needed. Apply 1 in (3 cm) water to lawn during prolonged drought of three weeks. Mow twenty or more times a season, edge every third time.

3. Although this garden is designed to emphasize feeling, smelling, and hearing for those who are visually impaired, visual unity is established for the sighted by the trunk lines of the sugar hackberry and the espaliered English ivy. Also contributing to the unified design are the symmetrically balanced raised planters, ground cover patterns of carpet bugle in the Bermuda grass lawn, and low clipped holly hedges. The raised planters have touchable, fragrant herbs and these are identified in Braille on top of the wall. The fountain in front of the espaliered ivy provides a cooling sound in a warm climate. Dallas, Texas.

MANAGEMENT Maintenance is somewhat intensive due to the need for frequent pruning, edging, and watering of the elevated planting areas, and maintaining the espalier. Mulch and prune holly (*Ilex*) hedges in late winter. Shear every four to five weeks during the growing season. Prune espaliered ivy (*Hedera helix*) every four to five weeks, or as needed, and mulch. Check sugar hackberry (*Celtis laevigata*) for winter damage and prune as needed. In early spring, remove dead wood or debris from herbs in raised planters. Replant if required. Fertilize herbs and ground cover (*Ajuga reptans*) with a balanced plant food. In early spring, fertilize Bermuda grass (*Cynodon*), if needed. Mow twenty or more times a season, edge every third time. Water garden twice weekly or as needed.

4. Since the front door is hidden from the street, a strong directional planting design was required. This is achieved by the line flow of the liriope ground cover (left) and the linear, dwarf burford holly shrub mass (right) toward the door. Three small crape myrtle trees interrupt the horizontal flat ground cover, define space, soften the house facade, and provide balance to the house and landscape. A small evergreen southern wax myrtle tree on the corner near the front door repeats and balances the evergreen color of the hollies. At the garage, on the left of the photo, is a hetz holly shrub. This holly is visually terminated by the lower mass of Chinese hollies, both plantings repeating the holly color found near the door. An Asian jasmine ground cover, extreme right, continues the flow of the planting around the house facade. The fine-textured zoysia lawn provides contrasting texture and color to the design composition. Starkville, Mississippi.

MANAGEMENT Prune the small crape myrtle and southern wax myrtle (*Lagerstroemia indica* and *Myrica cerifera*) trees in late winter to maintain size, expose trunks to define vertical space, and provide color contrast. Prune all holly shrubs (*Ilex cornuta* 'Rotunda', *I. c.* 'Dwarf Burford', *I. crenata* 'Hetzii') in late winter to maintain size and density. Mow liriope (*Liriope muscari*) ground cover prior to spring growth to keep thickly matted. Prune edge of Asian jasmine (*Trachelospermum asiaticum*) three or four times a season to maintain within space. Add organic mulch to plantings to a settled depth of 4 in (10 cm) in the spring. Mow lawn (*Zoysia matrella*) fifteen or more times a season, edge every third time. During extended drought of three weeks, apply 1 in (3 cm) of water. With an established lawn, fertilize only when an off-color indicates the need.

5. The lines and color of the pindo palms in the center of the photo provide dramatic accent while directing the view down and across the pool. The curvilinear lines of the palm and the curvilinear side of the pool unifiy this design composition. Seasonal color is provided by blooming hydrangeas under the palm, and, in the foreground, by daylilies. Both of these are summer-flowering, thus at their best when the pool is in use. Walterboro, South Carolina.

MANAGEMENT In late winter, remove dead growth from the palms (*Butia capitata*). Prune the other evergreen shrubs to maintain size. Fertilize hydrangeas (*Hydrangea macrophylla*) and daylilies (*Hemerocallis*) with a balanced fertilizer in early spring and remove dead foliage. Prune hydrangeas to retain their shape after they bloom. Fertilize established shrubs only if foliage color indicates need. Divide daylilies every fourth year after they flower. Dead-head any flowering annuals and perennials weekly to prevent seed production and to neaten appearance. Fertilize any container plantings with liquid food every three weeks during the growing season and irrigate twice a week. Mow limited lawn area twenty or more times a season, edge every third time.

6. Three classic plant form types are illustrated: the cattails represent a very erect and upright form, the Japanese maple displays a layered, horizontal branching, and the water lily leaves provide a flat, almost two dimensional appearance. The fine-textured trees in the background act as a backdrop to this feature planting, emphasizing the cattails and Japanese maple. The combination of plant forms insures contrast, variety, and interest. St. Louis, Missouri.

MANAGEMENT Prune the shrubs and the Japanese maple (*Acer palmatum* 'Atropurpureum') in late winter to retain size and form. Cut the cattail (*Typha*) back in late winter and divide every two years to keep it robust. Remove dead growth from the water lily before spring growth emerges. As this pool is designed to be a reflecting pool, maintaining clear water is not a priority since muddy or dingy water works better for reflection. Excessive muck buildup in the pool bottom might have to be dredged every four to five years, depending on the water environment. Adjacent deciduous trees and normal leaf-drop contributes to muck buildup.

7. The weeping form of a cotoneaster, to the right of the steps, serves to contrast the geometry of the red brick and visually soften the wall corner. Its fine-textured foliage also parallels the texture of the adjacent English boxwood. The evergreen southern magnolia screens a background structure on an adjoining property. *Hostas* planted under the edge of the magnolia provide seasonal foliage and flower effects. Atlanta, Georgia.

MANAGEMENT Prune *Cotoneaster* after flowering and periodically during the growing season to maintain size. Shear boxwood (*Buxus sempervirens* 'Suffruticosa') in late winter, remove interior dead wood. Shear boxwood again in early summer if needed. Prune all plants (including the southern *Magnolia grandiflora*) to maintain size and access. Mulch all plantings after pruning. Fertilize *Hosta* lilies with a complete fertilizer in early spring, and dead-head in summer. Mow the lawn twenty or more times a season, edge every third time.

8. The weeping clumps of pampas grass repeat the rhythmic, arching line of the bridge and lead one's view down to the water below. The erect iris clump at the end of bridge contrasts the mounds of pampas grass, architecture, and water, and becomes a focal point along with the bridge. The repetitious use of the pampas grass mass in the background provides actual and reflected unity to a large space. Natchez, Mississippi.

MANAGEMENT   Cut back pampas grass (*Cortaderia selloana*) to 12–18 in (30–45 cm) above ground level in late winter. Prune *Iris* stand only if winter damaged, yet divide iris every three years to maintain size. Fertilize if plant color indicates need. Mulch in late winter. Due to slope and subsequent rapid water and nutrient runoff, the Bermuda grass (*Cynodon dactylon*) lawn area requires a complete fertilizer in early spring and midsummer. Mow lawn twenty or more times a season, edge every third time. During prolonged droughts, apply 1 in (3 cm) water weekly by drip irrigation. To prevent native vegetation developing at water's edge, deepen pool to 3 ft (1 m) to eliminate sunlight required for extraneous plant growth.

9. The mounded littleleaf periwinkle ground cover softly defines the flat turf plane, and adds subtle interest to the lawn space. Mowed turfgrass can be the finest of all plant textures and makes an attractive pairing with the ground cover. The curvilinear ground cover edge and brick line attract viewers to the house entry. Vertical interest is found in the evergreen holly tree (left) terminating the front area. The globe-shaped boxwood shrubs define space, emphasize the entry, and provide color and texture contrasts to the ground cover. The boxwood's globular form also contrasts the conical form of the yew on each side of door. Seasonal color is provided by the potted white caladium foliage. Nashville, Tennessee.

MANAGEMENT Prune holly trees (*Ilex* × 'Nellie R. Stevens') in late winter to control height and form. Remove 6–9 in (15–23 cm) of the past year's growth. Also prune out any interior dead wood on boxwoods (*Buxus sempervirens*) and yews (*Taxus*) to help prevent insect and disease problems. Shear boxwoods and yews in late winter and again in early summer to maintain the formal appearance. Trim back the periwinkle (*Vinca minor*) ground cover 6 in (15 cm) from the brick curbing in late winter and early and late summer. Place an organic mulch around the hollies, boxwoods, and ground cover in late winter. Replenish mulch as needed in midsummer. In the spring, if needed, fertilize the lawn. Mow twenty or more times a season, edge every third time. Throughout the summer, irrigate the container caladiums (*Caladium hortulanum*) every two days. Water in late afternoon so the hot sun does not blister leaves. Fertilize all container plants with a balanced liquid plant food every two weeks. Remove developing *Caladium* flowers to prevent seed production and to improve appearance.

10. An inviting entry space to this home begins with the brick posts flanking the steps, leading from the broad walkway and the Japanese maple on the right and the holly tree on the back left. While the brick posts define the entrance into the space, the two trees personalize the space and direct visitors to the porch steps. The porch foundation is softened by evergreen azalea plantings. Sessums, Mississippi.

MANAGEMENT Prune the Japanese maple (*Acer palmatum*) and yaupon holly (*Ilex vomitoria*) in late winter each year to retain their size and keep an open, balanced, informal plant form. Fertilize the azaleas (*Rhododendron*) with cottonseed meal after blooming. Also right after blooming, informally prune robust azaleas back to retain a size in proportion with the porch and railing. Place compost mulch beneath the trees and azaleas in late winter and early summer.

11. The Boston ivy, draping the wall top (left) projects textural interest while forming a three-dimensional mass and void pattern of light and dark tones. The projecting mass of Virginia creeper (right) establishes balance. The vines soften the wall material, and also by repeating the basic green color in the space the area appears larger. The deciduous foliage of the Boston ivy provides brilliant red tones in fall. The warm accent color and form of the spreading Japanese maple tree draw attention to the pool. Nashville, Tennessee.

MANAGEMENT In late winter, early summer and midsummer, prune and thin the ivy (*Parthenocissus tricuspidata*) and Virginia creeper (*P. quinquefolia*) vines to maintain balance within the space. In late winter, prune the maple (*Acer palmatum* 'Dissectum') tree to maintain within the space. Add organic mulch in early spring. During extended drought of three weeks, apply 1 in (3 cm) water by drip irrigation. Clean pool as needed.

12. Petals are used here to provide variety through texture and color. The foreground iris blossoms are solidly textured relative to the cream-colored, feathery astilbe blossoms behind. The red roses are texturally somewhat between the two, providing a medium to the extremes. Green foliage quite naturally enhances the flower colors. Kew, England.

MANAGEMENT Every two to three years divide the *Iris germanica* and *Astilbe japonica* after flowering. Mulch. Add compost in spring and summer. Prune roses (*Rosa*) in late winter before growth begins. Remove and replace the old mulch under the roses, since it may carry disease. Fertilize roses in early spring. Roses may also require weekly fungicide spraying to control outbreaks. Water by drip system, as needed.

13. The coarse-textured, erect lotus foliage against the fine-textured, mounding forms of the pampas grass makes a bold statement about the value of foliage textures in the landscape. This is evident here particularly, with foliage textures contrasting the placid water surface. The texture of the lotus foliage is repeated in the water lilies in the foreground, thus providing a unified composition and a double exposure of beauty in the water. Starkville, Mississippi.

    MANAGEMENT Remove dead foliage from all plants—lotus, water lilies, and pampas grass (*Nelumbo, Nymphaea,* and *Cortaderia selloana*)—in late winter. Fertilize with a balanced fertilizer. Mulch plants in soil areas. Clean pool as needed.

14. Bright, pastel-colored annuals bloom among an evergreen bigleaf periwinkle ground cover, insuring color for all seasons. This special garden is raised to enhance gardening activities by its owner, who has arthritis. The evergreen white pine screen at the back serves to block out the view and soften the sounds of a busy traffic intersection, and provides a backdrop for viewing the flower garden. Ladue, Missouri.

MANAGEMENT Remove weeds in spring, summer, and late summer. Add composted mulch in late winter, early summer, and fall. Remove dead annuals from the raised bed after the first frost and mulch the adjacent hawthorn trees (*Crataegus phaenopyrum*) to conserve moisture and deter erosion. Fertilize the trees with a complete, slow-release fertilizer in early spring to keep them thick and luxuriant. Fertilize the annuals and periwinkle ground cover (*Vinca major* 'Variegata') with a complete, slow-release fertilizer in the spring when preparing the soil for planting.

15. The alternating groups of white and pink caladiums act to attract summer views to this suburban residence and emphasize the house trim color. The caladiums in this landscape are planted 8 in (45 cm) apart in two rows. By planting large bulbs close together, staggered in an 18 in (20 cm) wide bed, the plants grow tall and appear fuller. The dark green liriope ground cover in front of the caladiums acts as a unifying element in the design and enhances the composition even when the caladiums are not present. The azaleas behind the caladiums help give the planting a living earth mound appearance, creating a private space on the house side of the plant mound and also imparting a greater illusion of depth. Seasonal color begins with spring-blooming azaleas and follows with colorful summer caladium foliage and liriope blossoms. Amory, Mississippi.

MANAGEMENT Prune the azaleas (*Rhododendron*) as needed after spring bloom. Plant *Caladiums* after all frost danger has passed and the soil begins to warm. (Caladiums will not start growing until the soil is 70°F/19°C). Add 1 in (3 cm) of compost around the plant in early summer to reduce weeding and to hold moisture.

Remove dead leaves and caladium blooms twice a week for appearance and to keep the plant in an active growth cycle. Water caladiums late in the afternoon once a week with 1 in (3 cm) of water throughout the growing season. Hot sun shining through water droplets on leaves causes brown heat blisters on foliage.

Since caladiums are tropical perennials, dig in fall after the first frost and store at room temperature until spring planting. Wash all soil off bulbs and let dry for two weeks. Store bulbs in plastic trays so they do not touch one another. While caladiums are spectacular, it should be noted that they peak about 8–10 weeks after planting and can look scraggly in late summer.

Cut the *Liriope muscari* ground cover back in late winter to allow for new growth. Mulch the caladium area and the azaleas with composted organic matter in late fall and early spring. Add a minimum of one cup of cottonseed meal around each azalea after blooming to provide nitrogen and to acidify the soil.

16. Rose gardens are often visually chaotic due to the large variety of rose colors. Through grouping roses by color, as seen here, chaos can be eliminated. Additionally, the visually imposing feature of a white-painted fence and archway encourages visual unity. Large rose groupings benefit markedly from pairing with a visually dominant feature. Such an element can provide unity both when there is a storm of beautiful blossoms and when there are just scraggly stems in the off-season. The decorative white wood structure in this garden provides enclosure, and the arched gate acts as the visually dominant feature or focal point. Finally, though not the case or need in this photo, surrounding the edges of rose gardens with dark green plants can act as a backdrop to show off the colorful blooms. St. Louis, Missouri.

MANAGEMENT Water roses (*Rosa*) weekly and carefully during the growing season. Do not get water on leaves or blossoms as this invites the common fungal disease black spot. Cut spent blossoms weekly. Treat rose bushes to combat insects and the fungal disease every nine days in spring and summer. Mulch the beds in late winter, early summer, and fall with composted mulch. Cut rose canes back to within 16 in (40 cm) of the ground in late winter. Do not compost prunings. Conduct a yearly soil test in the spring to see if compost is providing enough nutrients. Supplement compost applications with a complete fertilizer on a monthly basis during the growing season if soils are very porous and plants are not growing or producing blooms prolifically.

17. The repetition of the color of the background house and the flowers begins a unified composition. The yellow of the flowers in the background enlivens this composition of primarily purple coneflowers, as yellow is a complement of purple on the color wheel and complementary colors used together provide a contrast. Foreground sedum provides a transition in height, soft foliage mass, and green and white flowers. New Bern, North Carolina.

MANAGEMENT Mulch perennials with a composted material in late winter, early summer, and fall to provide nutrients and moderate temperature and moisture. By late spring, some coneflowers (*Rudbeckia maxima*) may require staking for support. All flowering plants will need to be dead-headed, daily or weekly, depending on the type. Remove any dead and diseased leaves too. Any week without rain, provide perennial borders 1 in (3 cm) of water, preferably with soaker hose or drip irrigation.

18. Under eaves in a small microclimate environment, this planting enriches the walkway and provides an interesting monochromatic color scheme. Variety is provided by different shades of green foliage, and contrasts are created by fine and coarse textures of foliage and stone. Plantings are ground covers of glossy, dark green bugle weed (foreground) and dull, light, grayish green mondo grass (background, right). To soften the house wall and define the vertical space, a small Japanese maple tree is planted in the mondo grass. Upright, feathery wood fern adds seasonal variety of line pattern and color. An evergreen camellia (left) screens the adjacent property and contributes seasonal flowering. The bold upright foliage plants in background (right) surrounding the bird bowl are cast-iron plants. Beyond is a holly leaf fern. Under the eaves dripline, the gray, broken slate pieces control erosion and serve as a non-living mulch to conserve moisture. Jackson, Mississippi.

MANAGEMENT In late winter, remove any cold-damaged foliage, and prune Japanese maple (*Acer palmatum*) and *Camellia* shrub to maintain size and access. In late spring and midsummer, remove overgrowth of bugle weed (*Ajuga reptans*) and mondo grass (*Ophiopogon japonicus*). Also thin back the wood fern (*Dryopteris marginalis*). Remove to ground level any winter-damaged foliage of the bold, coarse-textured cast-iron plant (*Aspidistra elatior*) and holly fern (*Cyrtomium falcatum*). Fertilize in late spring, if needed. Established plantings will require little or no feeding. If needed, water with a soaker hose or drip system weekly in dry periods in the growing season. For this microclimate area, adequate moisture will be a major management matter for the bugle weed as its northern exposure receives little rainfall. In late fall, remove fallen maple and fern foliage to compost bin.

19. Extended seasonal color is provided by the red of a Japanese maple tree and yellow-green of a potted azalea. The repeated greens of the global boxwoods, the espaliered camellias on the pierced brick wall, the zoysia turfgrass, and the sedum ground cover near the rock outcrop unify the design composition. The native oakleaf hydrangeas near the maple provide cool white summer blossoms. Flowers are succeeded by bronzing and yellowing of the hydrangea leaves in fall and interesting dried flowers and peeling stem bark in winter. This limited planting design composition provides maximum seasonal effects of flowers, varying foliage colors and textures, and branch patterns. Birmingham, Alabama.

MANAGEMENT In late winter, prune and remove interior dead wood and shear boxwoods (*Buxus*) to maintain size and shape. Judiciously prune espaliered shrubs (*Camellia sansanqua*) and Japanese maple (*Acer palmatum*) in late winter. Mulch all trees and shrubs, including azalea (*Rhododendron periclymenoides*). If needed to retain within space, edge and thin *Sedum* ground cover. Prune potted azalea and oakleaf hydrangeas (*Hydrangea quercifolia*) after flowering. Water potted azalea twice weekly and fertilize with a complete fertilizer in late spring and midsummer. Trim turfgrass (*Zoysia matrella*) fifteen or more times a season. For any week without rainfall, apply 1 in (3 cm) of water by drip irrigation.

20. A wide expanse of wall is unified and defined by the repetition of white begonia flowers contrasting the darker background. The use of a continuous flower color, here, pink impatiens, on ground level unifies the horizontal planting composition and provides variety. The green background for the pink flowers enhances their color quality. New Orleans, Louisiana.

MANAGEMENT During the growing season, fertilize the wall container *Begonia* plants with a balanced liquid plant food every two weeks. Water containers every two days. Replant in fall with possible winter hardy annuals, such as pansies (*Viola wittrockiana*). Fertilize *Impatiens* when planted and several times a season. For any week without rainfall, apply 1 in (3 cm) of water by drip irrigation. Remove faded blossoms.

21. An orderly asymmetrically balanced mass and void composition of water and plants is unified by the repetition of color, texture, and line. The overall green color unifies the plants, yet variety is provided by the contrast of the repeated yellow azaleas (*Rhododendron*) in the background and the vertical lily foliage masses. The hostas in the foreground are accent plants, their variegated foliage being subtly echoed by the iris at water's edge. Inverewe, Scotland.

MANAGEMENT The foreground planting consists basically of perennials. The variegated *Hosta* need regular watering. For ground plantings, fertilize in late spring and midsummer, mulch, and remove flowers to eliminate seed production and to improve appearance. Every two to three years, as needed, divide perennials. In early spring, drain, clean, and replenish the pool with water. In late winter, prune and judiciously thin the mass of woody ornamental plants in the background to remove dead wood and to control size.

22. What is virtually a monochromatic plant color scheme is enhanced by the patterns of azalea shrub forms defining the flat mondo grass ground cover, curvilinear sago palm foliage, and the dark live oak sculptural limb canopy. Contrast is through the coarse-textured foliage of dark green palms, cast-iron plants, and seasonal amaryllis bulbs, with the fine-textured, light green mondo grass. The repetition of these plants unifies a large area under the canopy of live oak trees. New Orleans, Louisiana.

MANAGEMENT If cold-damaged, prune mondo grass (*Ophiopogon japonicus*) prior to spring growth to 2 in (5 cm). Mulch. In late winter, remove dead foliage of sago palm (*Cycas revoluta*) and cast-iron plants (*Aspidistra elatior*). Prune background shrubs to control size and density. Every five to eight years, in winter, prune live oak (*Quercus virginiana*) to remove dead wood, to open interior for better air circulation to help prevent diseases, and to enhance the branch pattern. Prune azaleas (*Rhododendron*) after flowering in the spring. In early spring, apply a complete fertilizer to maintain good color and health. Plant *Amaryllis* bulbs in fall for the next spring's bloom, fertilize every four weeks during the growing season, and mulch.

23. This superb country garden radiates an abundance of both annual and perennial flowers, herbs, and shrubs. Trees are used for structure and backdrop. Note the evergreen tree serving as a focal point and visual terminus at the end of the garden path. Also, note the garden is surrounded by a simple palette of green trees to enclose and serve as a backdrop. Within the garden, purples, yellows, and oranges are repeated throughout to give visual unity to the spring and summer garden. Nashville, Tennessee.

MANAGEMENT Place compost around all plants in late winter, early summer, and in the fall to provide nutrients and conserve water. Prune shrubs in late winter to retain their form. Most perennials will require dividing and replanting every three years. Weed the garden in the spring, early summer, summer, and fall. Dead-head all flowering plants every week. Compost all spent blossoms and weeds. A 1600 ft^2 (150 m^2) garden will produce an abundance of material for composting. Provide a minimum of 100 ft^2 (9 m^2) for adequate composting space.

24. The active lines of the summer-flowering liriope ground cover and the low holly hedges on each side of the walk focus attention to the door. Additional emphasis to the door is gained by tree-form, evergreen ligustrum shrubs providing strong vertical spatial definition and contrast to the horizontal ground cover and shrub masses. The tree-form shrubs are repeated behind and at the ends of the hedges for enframement of entry area. Against the house is Asian jasmine ground cover. Live oak trees provide canopy and shade and soften the roof line. Jackson, Mississippi.

MANAGEMENT In late winter, prune the wax leaf ligustrum (*Ligustrum japonica*) to maintain openness and size. Remove winter-damaged foliage from all plants and mulch. Prune holly hedges (*Ilex cornuta* 'Burfordii Nana') to maintain size. In early spring, cut back old leaves on the summer-flowering ground cover (*Liriope muscari*) before new leaves appear. Also cut back upright shoots of the Asian jasmine (*Trachelospermum asiaticum*) to maintain ground cover habit. If needed, fertilize St. Augustine grass (*Stenotaphrum secundatum*) lawn in early spring and midsummer. Apply 1 in (3 cm) water during extended drought of three weeks. Mow twenty or more times a season, edge every third mowing. Prune oaks (*Quercus virginiana*) every five to eight years in winter to remove dead wood, to permit circulation of air to reduce disease, and to enhance the sculptural quality of the branches.

25. Repetition of the planting design on each side of the center walk dividing the front lawn creates symmetrical balance. A feeling of spaciousness is created by the use of fine-textured nandina shrubs against the porch, globed holly shrubs on each side of steps, and boxwood shrubs at porch corners. Semi-privacy is provided on the porch by the dogwood trees fronting the house. The trees also serve as a visual transition from roof line to lawn plane. The creeping juniper ground cover defines and encloses the lawn space, discourages pedestrian circulation on the lawn, and is easier to maintain on a slope. Seasonal annual color of begonias is intensified by the effective green foliage backdrop of shrubs. Franklin, North Carolina.

MANAGEMENT In late winter, remove to ground level two or three vertical stems of each nandina shrub (*Nandina domestica*) adjacent to the porch. Prune a majority of the remaining nandina stems at different heights, just above a joint, to maintain desirable foliage density. Remove interior dead wood from smaller, globe-shaped hollies (*Ilex crenata*) and boxwoods (*Buxus sempervirens*) in late winter. To maintain global shape, shear smaller shrubs in late summer and again in midsummer. Prune edges of *Juniperus* ground cover in late winter and again in midsummer. After dogwood (*Cornus florida*) trees flower in spring, prune to maintain size and spacing from structure. After pruning, sift a light organic mulch over all planting areas. In late spring, fertilize lawn if needed. Mow twenty or more times a season, edge every third time. In early spring, plant, fertilize, and mulch *Begonia* plants. Fertilize annuals with a complete liquid fertilizer every two to three weeks. Water annuals weekly as needed. Remove annuals in late fall, cultivate soil, replant if possible with winter-hardy annuals, such as pansies (*Viola*). Mulch.

26. This asymmetrically balanced country home is sited in such a way that an earth mound and ever-green trees were needed on the left side of the house to give it a feeling of balance. In the before picture (top photo), the land falls to the left, causing the house to appear out of balance. In the completed six-year-old landscape, the earth mound and clump of red maple trees establishes a balance as one approaches the residence. The shrubs on the mound have a naturally mounding form and help to give height to the 5 ft (2 m) tall mound. Guest parking is tucked out of priority view behind the mound. Small-scale trees lining the drive to the garage visually subordinate the garage area and accentuate views to the house. Sessums, Mississippi.

MANAGEMENT Cut the showy jasmine (*Jasminum floridum*) shrubs on the berm back to their trunks every 5 years or when the plant gets scraggly looking. New growth will emerge and fill in the space by midsummer. Mulch beneath the shrubs when they are cut back and mulch all areas not covered by shrubs in the fall and again in spring.

Prune the crape myrtle (*Lagerstroemia indica*) trees lining the drive in late winter each year to create a tree-form plant. Remove suckers at the base of the trees in early summer and fall. Fertilize trees with a high phosphorus, high potassium, low nitrogen fertilizer in the fall to prepare the cold sensitive tree for winter. Mow the slow-growing centipede lawn grass 15–20 times a year. Take yearly soil pH tests in the spring to maintain acidic soil conditions, a must for centipede grass. Correct soil pH if needed in the spring. Fertilize only when needed to fill in diseased or winter-damaged grass.

27. This symmetrically balanced house front is linked asymmetrically to the street by the brick walk coming up one side of the property and angling over to the front door. An informal balance is created. Along with the shrubs and ground cover along the walk and the coarse-textured ivy vine on the building, all elements act to provide an informal and friendly entry approach. Clayton, Missouri.

MANAGEMENT Remove turfgrass from the edges of the wintercreeper (*Euonymus fortunei*) ground cover beds in the spring, summer, and fall. Prune shrubs in late winter and shape again as needed in early summer. Cut the ivy (*Hedera*) back on the house in late winter of each year to discourage it from growing into its shaggy mature stage. Prune ivy 6–12 in (15–30 cm) back from wood construction materials. Control the extent of ivy growth in the spring and summer with frequent pruning and little or no fertilizer or irrigation.

28. This landscape illustrates all four rules that create unity. (1) It has both dominant and subordinate components; (2) features such as color, texture, line, shape, or form are repeated; (3) the number of objects, forms, colors, textures, and lines is limited; and (4) the area is surrounded by an enclosure. The brick work, lamp post, and iron fence are visually dominant while the plantings are subordinate. The ground cover and fence are repeated throughout the design, creating repetition of color, texture, line, and form. The number of objects, forms, colors, textures, and lines used are limited, and the space inside the gate is enclosed with a screen planting. Note how the potted fern near the lamp post adds variety in color, texture, and form, and helps accent the entry. Kosciusko, Mississippi.

MANAGEMENT Mulch the azalea (*Rhododendron*) bed at the rear of the garden in the fall and again in the early spring. Prune the azalea and *Forsythia* screen planting above the ivy bank to keep it from intruding into the small space. Prune the ivy ground cover and vines (*Hedera*) back in late fall. Cut the ivy flat against the post in early spring and again in summer to restrain it from becoming too leggy. Trim the edges of the lawn area every third mowing. Water the potted fern (*Nephrolepis*) every week during the growing season and fertilize with a complete fertilizer each month. Move the fern indoors in late fall before frost.

29. The repetition of white-flowering foreground daisies, tall summer phlox against the background wall, and short white blossoms from impatiens above the wall on the right provides compositional unity and a seasonal cool feeling in a warm climate. The gray foliage of lamb's ears in the foreground and the light tones of the center pavement and stone wall contribute to unity. The green lawn, boxwood foliage, and Boston ivy on the wall provide a contrast and color unity, too. Note the asymmetrical balance of the shrub-enclosed open lawn space above the vine-covered wall. Background planting provides privacy in the entertainment area below. Nashville, Tennessee.

MANAGEMENT Prune boxwood (*Buxus*) shrubs in late winter to maintain size and to remove interior dead wood. Mulch. Add organic mulch to annuals and perennials (*Chrysanthemum, Phlox, Impatiens, Stachys byzantina*) in late winter, spring, and summer. Provide an additional complete fertilizer for shrubs in early spring if foliage color is not a healthy dark green. Fertilize lawn (*Festuca*) in late spring, if needed. Mow twenty or more times a season, edge lawn every third time. In late winter and midsummer, judiciously thin the Boston ivy (*Parthenocissus tricuspidata*) to expose stones for contrast. Each week in summer without rain, provide 1 in (3 cm) of water to flowers by drip irrigation.

30. The repetition of the live oaks, juniper hedge, and curvilinear walk creates unity. Emphasis is provided by the pink geraniums and the bold-textured shrub background. The trees enclose the space, provide privacy, and serve as a windbreak. This composition displays all the essentials for unity: (1) house and accent planting of geraniums are visually dominant while lawn space and walk are subordinate; (2) repetition of color, form, and texture, and the line rhythm of walk and hedge; (3) limited number of objects; and (4) space enclosed by hedge, trees, and house. Sonoma, California.

MANAGEMENT Every five to eight years in winter, prune to remove dead or diseased wood from oak (*Quercus agrifolia*) trees, judiciously remove interior growth to provide air circulation to help reduce diseases and enhance the branch pattern. Fertilize trees if needed for healthy color. Prune the evergreen hedge in late winter and midsummer to maintain form and shape. Mulch hedge in early spring. Fertilize lawn in late spring, if needed. Mow twenty or more times per growing season, edge every third time. Depending on the region, the *Geranium* may require replacement in late fall with a winter-hardy annual. Prune geranium background shrub in late winter to maintain size. Mulch.

31. This classical garden has all of the elements that provide unity. The gazebo is a focal point and the mostly curvilinear forms are repeated throughout the composition. The open space is defined by lush, tropical plantings, and there is repetition of yellow, red, and orange flowers. The rich composition has variety due to the controlled use of a diversity of materials, forms, spaces, colors, lines, and textures. Winterhaven, Florida.

MANAGEMENT As this garden is designed to be seen from a distance, management emphasis is on getting the most color and contrast in forms and texture. Tropical plants on the right side of the composition that add to the coarse texture and weeping forms include the sago palm (*Cycas revoluta*), pindo palm (*Butia capitata*), and banana trees (*Musa*). Pine (*Pinus*) trees are used as backdrop to this composition and their form is sculptural. Details like getting neat edges along a walk or bed line are less important. Intense management of flowering plants, including dead-heading, is important. A frequent mowing and lawn fertilization program will keep the ground plane crisp in texture and color.

32. The flat, smooth expanses of water and lawn contrast with the variety of plant forms and colors. This is a setting in which only the boldest of sculptures could compete and contribute to the exquisite variety the scene imparts. Note how evergreen trees branching to the ground create a backdrop, emphasizing both the sculpture and the sculptural forms of the deciduous trees like the white birch and weeping willow. Madison, Wisconsin.

MANAGEMENT Mow the grass twenty times a season. Remove grass 12 in (30 cm) from tree trunks, sculptures and shrub masses to allow for easier mowing. Mulching the tree and shrub masses in the fall and early spring will also facilitate mowing and conserve moisture. Rake leaves from deciduous birch (*Betula pendula*) and willow (*Salix babylonica*) off lawn areas if needed.

33. This wildflower garden is an example of the pleasing variety that can occur in a meadow-type planting. Unity is achieved in this rich mix of colors due to the repetition of similar heights, textures, green foliage, and yellow and white flowers. St. Louis, Missouri.

MANAGEMENT Poppies (*Papaver rhoeas*), baby's breath (*Gypsophila elegans*), larkspur (*Consolida ambigua*), wallflower (*Erysimum allionii*), and bachelor's button (*Centaurea cyanus*) are included in this planting. All meadow plantings need special management. After weeds are removed from the area, flower seeds are scattered over tilled soil and then mulched with straw. Intruding plants like vines and trees need to be removed by hand in early spring, early summer, and late summer. Meadow plantings are usually burned once every two years. Alternate burning in the summer and fall to ensure the broadest diversity of plants. If meadows are burned in the summer, a mixture of grasses and non-grasses will emerge and woody plants will be eradicated. Burned in the fall, broad-leaved plants such as primrose (*Oenothera*) and black-eyed susans (*Rudbeckia*) tend to emerge. This wildflower planting is featured at the Missouri Botanical Garden and they call it their "Nature Scape Wildflower Mixture." Regional collections are available from many sources.

34. This rich, diverse composition emphasizes a variety of forms. Although attention initially focuses on the small, dark sculpture, the eye travels easily to the flat leaves of the lotus plant and fine-textured ferns at the base of the sculpture while investigating the swordlike leaves of the iris plants. The entire composition is successful because of the dark background shrubs defining the garden space and providing a backdrop for the varied forms and colors of the plants. The large tree creates an overhead canopy, defines the space, and provides a comfortable human scale. Atlanta, Georgia.

MANAGEMENT Cut the *Iris* plants to within 3 in (8 cm) of the ground after several hard winter frosts. Dig and divide the iris clumps every three years in late fall. Side-dress iris with super phosphate or wood ashes in late winter to improve growth and bloom. Remove grass and weeds from the gravel mulch in the spring, summer, and fall. Remove algae from pool if it becomes excessive. Try to establish both underwater and emergent aquatic plants that will create shade and reduce algae growth. By creating a balanced pool with fish, snails, and plants, little or no maintenance of the pool will be necessary. Leave the dead leaves of the American lotus plant (*Nelumbo lutea*) for their wintertime beauty. Remove them after the first of the year so they do not add to the sediment in the pool.

35. The window box and plantings have a perfect size and color relationship with the white window. The space covered by the Boston ivy vine is in proportion with the window and the box planter and the bare brick wall area. The colorful mix of petunias acts as a focal point. Clayton, Missouri.

MANAGEMENT Contain the Boston ivy vine (*Parthenocissus tricuspidata*) to a general area by restricting its growth. Prune the vine in spring and summer. Replant *Petunia* in the spring. Prune petunias back to a height of 6–8 in (15–20 cm) in early summer and again in late summer to maintain plant vigor and stimulate blooming. Fertilize petunias monthly with a liquid plant food and water them three times a week in the hottest and driest part of the summer.

36. The amount of plantings relative to the massive house facade is well proportioned. The planting design composition on the right is simplified by the use of only Asian jasmine ground cover, evergreen camellias, and a deciduous crape myrtle. This planting is repeated on the left side of the house for design unity, adding live oaks for enframement. Natchez, Mississippi.

MANAGEMENT Shear Asian jasmine (*Trachelospermum asiaticum*) ground cover to 6–8 in (15–20 cm) in late winter, fertilize, and mulch. Fertilize lawn in early spring, if needed. Mow twenty or more times a season, edge every third time. Check camellia (*Camellia japonica*) shrubs for scale. Spray as needed in growing season. With established plants, limit fertilizer to requirements for foliage color and health. Fallen crape myrtle (*Lagerstroemia indica*) foliage within planting area may remain as a mulch. Apply 1 in (3 cm) of water by drip irrigation during extended drought of three weeks. In winter, prune oaks (*Quercus virginiana*) to remove dead wood, provide better air circulation to reduce diseases, and enrich sculptural design quality of limb structure.

37. The large amount of fine- to medium-textured plants is in proportion to the smaller amount of coarse foliage of the cast-iron plants under the window. The limited amount of warm-colored red begonias is proportionate to the larger amount of green foliage due to the intensity of the warm color. The border of liriope foliage encloses the colorful annuals and repeats the tone of the cast-iron plants and burford holly hedge. New Orleans, Louisiana.

MANAGEMENT   Replant, fertilize, and mulch *Begonia* annuals in early spring and fall. For fall at this site, pansies (*Viola*) would be suitable to replace the begonias. Fertilize annuals several times during the growing season. After establishment, if no rain falls, water weekly. In late winter, remove cold-damaged foliage from *Liriope* border and cast-iron plants (*Aspidistra elatior*). In late winter, remove dead wood from holly (*Ilex cornuta* 'Burfordii'), prune for space, and remove fallen leaves. Mulch. Prune three times during growing season to maintain holly in space. Inspect hedge for scale in summer. Spray if needed. In late fall, compost the fallen foliage from oriental magnolia (*Magnolia soulangiana*) tree on the right.

38. The lawn and stones contrast in color and texture and provide a strong curvilinear line emphasizing the pool. The round shrub on the left gives a vertical curve to echo the horizontal curve of walk and lawn. The whole shrub composition on the left heightens the view of the pool from the walk and balances the vertical forms of the background trees. Tall vertical background trees provide enframement and backdrop, defining the horizon. Near the base of the white birch tree on the right, note how unmowed meadow grass adds spatial definition, line, and a contrast of form with the mowed lawn in the foreground. Arundel, England.

MANAGEMENT In late winter, prune the birch (*Betula*) tree above pedestrian height. Remove dead foliage from water plants. Check nutrient level and soil pH of lawn area during late fall. Add fertilizer as needed in spring for color and to improve health. Mow lawn twenty or more times a growing season to keep it thick and healthy. Edge every third time. Mow to maintain meadow effect: twice during the growing season or as needed, and in the winter after seeds have fallen. Apply 1 in (3 cm) water to lawn during prolonged droughts of three weeks.

39. The three Italian cypresses in the background contrast in form and texture to the stark roof line and foreground palm trees, thereby providing emphasis. They also contrast the hedgerow of trees. Monterrey, Mexico.

    MANAGEMENT Fertilize lawn in early spring, if needed. Mow twenty or more times a season, edge every third time. For extended drought of three weeks, apply 1 in (3 cm) of water to lawn. Remove dead foliage from the Canary Island date palms (*Phoenix canariensis*) and *Yucca* at bathhouse in late winter. If needed, prune to shape the Italian cypresses (*Cupressus sempervirens*).

40. The sculpture, a sundial in a thyme garden, is visually dominant because its smooth, light-colored form contrasts both in color and texture with the surrounding ground covers. The ground covers are all types of thyme, all of which are drought tolerant and prefer well-drained soils. Note how variety enriches the composition through using different colors of thyme in a geometric pattern. The basket-weave pattern of brick is a coarse texture and emphasizes the fine texture of the ground cover. St. Louis, Missouri.

MANAGEMENT Prune to keep the geometric pattern of the *Thymus* ground cover bed. Weed in the spring, summer, and early fall. Fertilize with sifted compost in late winter, early summer, and early fall.

41. This simple, low maintenance planting is nonetheless able to provide viewer interest. By placing small groupings of coarse-textured hostas in a large bed of fine-textured liriope, contrast is established. The hostas are visually dominant and emphasized except when the liriope is blooming. St. Louis, Missouri.

MANAGEMENT Cut the liriope (*Liriope muscari*) back in late winter to allow for new spring growth. Fertilize the shade-tolerant *Hosta* with compost in late winter, early summer, and fall. Remove spent bloom spikes of hostas every two weeks during the flowering season. Divide and replant the hostas every three to four years. While the liriope is drought tolerant, the hostas are not. Water hostas every week there is less than 1 in (3 cm) of rainfall.

42. The progression of plant materials—the vines against the wall, the tree roses, and the mass of Summer Snow roses leading to the brick path and the hybrid Bermuda grass lawn—is well-balanced and proportioned. This planting design provides effective transition from house to lawn. The large live oak in the background provides enclosure for the space. The use of only two flower colors of roses along the walk allows bright color unity. The vine at the far end is a wisteria, the wall vine in foreground and the one adjacent to the wisteria are evergreen jessamine vines. The vining plant between the jessamines is Lady Banksia rose. New Orleans, Louisiana.

MANAGEMENT Prune and judiciously thin vines (*Wisteria sinensis, Gelsemium sempervirens,* and *Rosa Banksia*) after flowering to maintain space. Tie loose vines to wall. Mulch vines. In late winter, prune roses (*Rosa floribunda* and hybrids). Fertilize roses in early spring, remove old mulch and add new mulch. Remove dead blossoms to prevent seed production and to improve appearance. Drip irrigate roses weekly or as needed. In midsummer, lightly prune and fertilize roses for fall blossoms. Spray roses weekly to control diseases. In late winter, remove dead wood from oaks (*Quercus virginiana*). Prune limbs to provide interior air circulation and sculptural design quality. In the spring, remove oak leaves from lawn and compost.

43. A beautiful transition is made here with plants and materials—from the foreground lawn and white-flowering annuals to the evergreen azalea shrubs at the brick pillars, the summer-flowering clematis on the iron fence up to the large pear tree and mature shade trees behind the fence. Without the plant materials, the brick and wrought iron gates would be out of proportion with the space. Nashville, Tennessee.

MANAGEMENT After spring flowering, prune pear (*Pyrus*) trees to provide better air circulation within, to remove dead wood and rubbing branches, and to control size. Prune azaleas (*Rhododendron*) after spring flowering to control size. Mulch. Apply 1 in (3 cm) of water to azaleas during extended drought of three weeks. Thin *Clematis* to control size. In early spring, to establish a wider color range for summer, fertilize bedding area with complete food, cultivate soil, plant *Impatiens* or other annuals, water, and mulch. Water annuals weekly. Feed annuals with a complete fertilizer three or four times during the growing season. In the fall, fertilize and cultivate soil and replant winter hardy annuals. Mow lawn (*Festuca*) twenty or more times a season, edge every third time.

44. The Japanese irises create a gentle, elegant, transition from the water's edge and deck to the shore. Without the irises, the transition from shoreline to deck to lake would not be as comfortable or pleasing. St. Louis, Missouri.

MANAGEMENT Since the Japanese iris (*Iris ensata*) prefer to be 3–4 (8–10 cm) above water, it is best to not fertilize them and chance damaging water quality or creating algae blooms. Mulch to a total depth of 3–4 in (8–10 cm) in the fall. Divide and thin clumps of iris in the fall every three years. Peak blooms will result two years after thinning.

45. The large bed of common periwinkle ground cover provides a strong base for the attractive clump of trees. In addition to creating a transition from the trees to the lawn, the circular base makes the vertical trunks visually prominent. Kosciusko, Mississippi.

MANAGEMENT Mulch the periwinkle (*Vinca minor*) with compost or a shredded bark mulch in the fall and again in the early spring. To make the ground cover bed stand out, trim back the ground cover 8–10 in (20–25 cm) from the lawn edge to expose the dark brown mulch. Use either plastic or steel edging at ground level, or a ground level brick or concrete mowing strip, to separate the lawn from the ground cover. If shredded bark mulch is used, apply a slow-release, complete fertilizer in late winter to feed the ground cover.

46. A single, small-scale, multi-trunk crape myrtle tree canopies the house entry, reducing vastness by defining the vertical space. Container-grown evergreen shrubs echo the green foliage of the tree and the small boxwood shrub border beneath it. Also, the boxwood border softens the hardness inherent to brick construction. Seasonal flower color is provided by the begonias in the basket by the door. New Orleans, Louisiana.

MANAGEMENT To maintain size and openness of the crape myrtle (*Lagerstroemia indica*) tree, prune in late winter. For extended summer flowering, tip prune branches after flowering to produce new growth on which flower buds grow. Several times each season, as needed, shear the low boxwood (*Buxus*) border and evergreen container shrubs (*Podocarpus*) to maintain compactness and size. Mulch all plantings. Fertilize the container shrubs in early spring and midsummer; water twice a week. Every other day water the annuals in the basket. Fertilize the annuals three or four times a growing season. In late fall, cultivate the soil in the basket and replace the annuals with winter hardy annuals, such as pansy (*Viola*) plants.

47. By introducing the turf-covered mounds and the tree and shrub plantings, the open space of a drive and parking area for this high density housing site is pleasingly defined. Chicago, Illinois.

MANAGEMENT Fertilize the lawn in early spring, late spring, and midsummer; the slopes cause a rapid water runoff and leaching of soil nutrients. During extended drought of three weeks, apply 1 in (3 cm) of water to the lawn. Mow lawn twenty or more times a season, edge every third time. Prune trees as needed for removal of dead wood, to permit better interior air circulation to help reduce diseases, and to enhance branch pattern beauty.

48. This early spring picture (above) shows how the existing landscape lacked definition of spaces and edges. Poor turf quality and the row of irises floating in the open lawn area contributed to a lack of uniformity and order.

The landscape rejuvenation began (above opposite) by moving the irises to a newly created flower bed at the edge of the driveway beside the carport. This bed provides an attractive accent for guests arriving at the parking court. The slight hillside beyond the house was converted from turfgrass to a coarse-textured ground cover and an ornamental shrub bed.

In the close-up photo (below opposite) of the hillside planting, treated timbers separate the lawn space from the shrub border screen and create an edge which helps to define space and provide order. At the base of the old oaks, azaleas are planted to create an enclosure and provide seasonal color. Thrift ground cover was planted at the top of the curvilinear brick wall and now cascades down, providing a fiery purple splash for three weeks in the spring. Turf quality was improved by switching to a more shade tolerant grass and through the addition of an irrigation system. Kosciusko, Mississippi.

MANAGEMENT Cut the coarse-textured, bigleaf periwinkle (*Vinca major*) ground cover on the hill back to the ground every two years to encourage new growth and remove woody stems. When the thrift (*Phlox subulata*) ground cover grows down the wall to the grass level, begin cutting it back 6–8 in (15–20 cm) above the ground in late spring each year. Take yearly pH tests in the centipede lawn area and azalea (*Rhododendron*) beds to be sure acidic soil conditions are being maintained. Fertilize azaleas after they bloom with cottonseed meal. Remove turfgrass from all beds and along wall edges in the spring, summer, and fall to allow for easier mowing.

49. Before a landscape architect was called in to work with this residence, all of the ground cover and shrubs were lined up against the house. There was no creation of outdoor spaces. The new landscape design shows definition of an entry space. Ground cover was extended out and around the large tree to provide unity in the design and to create a soft, inviting, human-scale entry. Ground cover plants also cover bare soil under the tree where grass would not grow. A mass of nandina shrubs separate the entry space from the arrival space.

The view into the entry space approaching the front door shows a multi-trunk possumhaw holly tree planted as a visual terminus for the entry walk (lower photo). Between the porch and walk, ivy serves as an all-season backdrop for pansies in the winter and spring and impatiens or begonias in the summertime. Starkville, Mississippi.

MANAGEMENT Mow the liriope (*Liriope muscari*) ground cover to the ground in late winter. Compost the clippings. Remove one-third of the oldest nandina (*Nandina domestica*) shrub canes in late winter. Shape the possumhaw holly (*Ilex decidua*) in late winter and again in early summer to keep the ideal plant form and size. Plant winter annuals in the fall and summer annuals in the spring. Each season when planting annuals, work compost into the soil for plant health and growth.

50. The support posts of an arbor define the wall space as the arbor plants cast a beautiful mosaic shadow pattern on the plain wall. To screen the view from a house at a higher elevation across the street, the arbor lends privacy to this walled patio. Privacy, shade, and interesting patterns for limited spaces result from this use of plants on arbors. San Francisco, California.

MANAGEMENT In winter and midsummer, prune arbor tree (*Platanus*) to control size, remove dead wood, and permit air circulation to help prevent diseases. Tie loose stems to arbor frame. Replenish mulch of arbor plant, and fertilize as foliage indicates need. During extended drought of three weeks, apply 1 in (3 cm) of water by drip irrigation to trees. Remove leaves to compost area in the fall.

51. The tree-form evergreen yaupon holly (left) creates a pattern against the white wall and defines space, thereby creating depth. Repetition of its fine-textured foliage in the lower boxwood shrubs provides unity and a feeling of spaciousness. The spring-flowering, evergreen Carolina jessamine vines on the right soften the structural corner and provide line patterns for the wall. Starkville, Mississippi.

MANAGEMENT In late winter, prune and thin tree-form holly (*Ilex vomitoria*) to maintain size and openness in the limited space. Remove dead wood within and shear the lower boxwood (*Buxus semper-virens*) shrubs in late winter to maintain shapes and sizes. Shear again in midsummer. Judiciously prune to thin jessamine (*Gelsemium sempervirens*) vine at top after flowers drop in the spring. Add organic mulch to the planting areas. During extended drought of three weeks, apply 1 in (3 cm) of water by drip irrigation.

52. Notice the vastness and inhuman scale along this street of newly completed houses (top photo). Compare that with the established neighborhood across the street where eight-year old trees separate the pedestrian and family living spaces from the public street space (lower photo). Trees planted between the sidewalk and curb act as a baffle to cut off the street and parked cars. Street trees enclose the pedestrian space and encourage people to walk. Florissant, Missouri.

MANAGEMENT Prune the maple trees (*Acer saccharinum*) to keep branches out of the pedestrian path and above cars and trucks. Plant large-scale trees, such as oaks (*Quercus*) and cypress (*Taxodium distichum*), 40 ft (12.2 m) apart. Small-scale trees, such as red maples (*Acer rubrum*) and hawthorns (*Crataegus*), can be planted 30 ft (9 m) apart to encourage branches to grow upward rather than outward and downward. Remove turfgrass a minimum of 12 in (30 cm) from around tree trunks to allow for easier mowing. Trim along curbs and walks every third mowing to keep lawn edges neat.

53. The trailing juniper ground cover and daylily bed define the central St. Augustine grass lawn space by enclosure. An additional feeling of enclosure is provided by two large tree canopies in the background. A pecan tree is growing on the left and a pine on the right, both in harmony with the landscape. The two smaller crape myrtle trees in the foreground complete the sense of enclosure and definition. Note the attractive monochromatic color contrasts of ground covers and lawn floor. Hilton Head Island, South Carolina.

MANAGEMENT In late winter, prune to judiciously thin and edge the juniper (*Juniperus conferta*) ground cover to maintain within the space. Sift lightweight mulch down into it. Since the lawn is competing with trees and their feeder roots, feed lawn grass (*Stenotaphrum secundatum*) with a complete fertilizer in early spring and again in midsummer. Mow lawn twenty or more times a season, edge every third time. During prolonged drought of three weeks, apply 1 in (3 cm) of water to lawn. Fertilize daylilies (*Hemerocallis*) in early spring, remove dead foliage, and mulch. During the summer, remove faded flowers and dry stalks to prevent seed production and to neaten appearance. Rake and remove fallen pecan (*Carya illinoensis*) and crape myrtle (*Lagerstroemia indica*) leaves, as well as any pine (*Pinus*) needles in the fall. In late winter, prune crape myrtle trees to maintain size and space. Remove dead limbs from pine trees anytime they are noticed. Prune background shrubs in late winter to maintain size.

54. The natural, tall, slender form of the sweet bay magnolia tree (right) encloses the entry space and screens the neighbor's house in the background. The coarse texture and form of the magnolia tree accents through contrast the low, fine-textured, rounded mass of Japanese holly shrubs. To provide compositional unity with a vertical, left of the door is a medium- to coarse-textured upright camellia shrub which relates to the magnolia tree. To define space and provide seasonal effects, on the entry landing is a potted dwarf crape myrtle tree. Jackson, Mississippi.

MANAGEMENT In winter, prune *Magnolia virginiana* tree and holly (*Ilex crenata* 'Helleri') shrubs to maintain size and to remove dead wood. Mulch with organic material. Fertilize trees and shrubs if foliage color indicates the need. Mulch potted dwarf tree (*Lagerstroemia indica* 'Nana'). Fertilize early spring, early summer, and midsummer. Water every two to three days during the growing season. After flowering in the spring, prune the *Camellia japonica* to maintain slender form and size. Remove faded blossoms. Mulch.

55. The live oaks and low, clipped juniper hedge beyond enclose the pool area and separate it from the background open space. Overlooking the bay, this garden was designed by Thomas Church and completed in 1949, and it illustrates the fact that effective design is enhanced by age and time.

The vertical tree trunks against the horizon provide a depth of view and reduce the sense of overwhelming vastness. The lawn areas to the right and in the background contribute unity to the composition. Donnell Garden, Sonoma, California.

MANAGEMENT Every five to eight years, prune oak (*Quercus agrifolia*) trees to remove dead and diseased wood, to provide better air circulation to help prevent diseases, and to enhance silhouette. In late winter, remove dead wood from *Juniperus* hedge and shear. Shear lightly two or three times during the growing season to maintain size, foliage density, and the view. Fertilize the lawn early in spring, if needed. Mow twenty or more times a season, edge every third time.

56. The floor material couples stone with pine straw, pine straw with pea gravel. It also changes with the season. To reduce maintenance during the growing season, when the large background water oak tree (right) absorbs much moisture from the soil, the ground is covered with pine straw rather than lawn. The straw permits the flow of water and conserves soil moisture, adds organic material to the soil, and provides a clean, easy surface for access. In the winter, annual Italian ryegrass replaces the pine straw, adding winter color and variety to the space. In the background area, there is a year-round surface of loose pea gravel mulch. The two materials are separated by a brick border level with the surfaces. The garden is enclosed with additional tree canopies on adjoining properties, a planting of evergreen camellia shrubs, and English ivy ground cover in planters. The ground cover is repeated on the right to add to compositional unity. The ivy also balances the focal point of the iron kettle pool and vertical timber sculptures. Walterboro, South Carolina.

MANAGEMENT Every five to eight years, prune oak (*Quercus nigra*) tree in winter to remove dead and diseased wood, provide better interior air circulation to help prevent diseases, and to enhance the branch pattern. In late fall, apply a balanced fertilizer, cultivate straw into soil, and sow annual rye grass (*Lolium multiflorum*) seeds. Keep soil moist until seeds sprout. Water lawn in drought of more than three weeks. Mow as needed. After spring flowering, prune shrubs (*Camellia japonica*) to maintain within space. In late winter and as needed, trim ivy (*Hedera helix*) ground cover to maintain within planting areas. In late spring, as the seasonal winter lawn begins to wilt, mow it closely. Cover it with several inches of pine straw or other fine-textured, porous, organic material to conserve soil moisture. This people space requires minimum maintenance in the growing season.

57. The line of flowering pear trees with liriope ground cover beneath separates vehicular circulation from pedestrian circulation. Stepping stones give pedestrian access to parked vehicles in the street. The trees will eventually provide canopy and shade over the walk and a greater feeling of enclosure and protection. The ground cover is repeated at the wall for compositional unity. The wall is softened by a fine-textured, evergreen creeping fig vine. New Orleans, Louisiana.

MANAGEMENT After pear (*Pyrus Calleryana* 'Aristocrat') trees flower in the spring, prune to keep branches above pedestrian height. At the same time, prune to permit interior air circulation to help prevent diseases and remove any cross branching. Both the pear tree and *Liriope muscari* ground cover are well suited to restricted space and soil conditions. Mulch all areas to conserve moisture. During prolonged droughts, drip irrigate to soak plants deeply. Every two to three years, judiciously thin creeping fig vine (*Ficus pumila*) to maintain within space.

58. The vastness of a residential open lawn is partially reduced by the plantings (right) of live oak and southern magnolia trees. The Boston fern ground cover and mulched area (left) with a large common bald cypress personalize the space. This photo expresses the value of mulch with limited plant materials to define space and, here, to provide a semi-private lawn area adjacent to the house and garden. The ground cover under the oaks defines the lawn space, absorbs their fallen leaves, and eliminates lawn maintenance under the tree canopies. New Orleans, Louisiana.

MANAGEMENT In the spring, fertilize the hybrid Bermuda grass (*Cynodon*) lawn, if needed, and replenish the organic mulch. For the fern (*Nephrolepis exaltata* 'Bostoniensis') ground cover, add light weight mulch to sift down among the plants. Mow the lawn twenty or more times a season, and edge it every third time. Rake and remove evergreen *Magnolia grandiflora* leaves throughout the year. Also remove fallen foliage from the bald cypress (*Taxodium distichum*). Every five to eight years, remove interior branches of oaks (*Quercus virginiana*) to improve air circulation for disease prevention and to enhance branch patterns. Maintain oak and cypress limbs above pedestrian access.

59. The white-flowering oakleaf hydrangeas and yellow daylilies break up the open space of a rock out-cropping and delicately relate the composition to the natural plantings in the background. The large shade trees enclose the deck space and make the distant view more interesting by defining the open space. The vertical tree trunks establish a greater feeling of depth and enhance the view. Birmingham, Alabama.

MANAGEMENT In early spring, remove dead foliage from daylilies (*Hemerocallis*) and hydrangeas (*Hydrangea quercifolia*). Fertilize, and mulch. Due to limited soil in the rock area, drip irrigate plants twice weekly, or as needed, during the growing season. Remove faded flowers from daylilies to prevent seed production. Remove dried flower stalks for tidy appearance. Fertilize lawn in early spring, if needed. Mow twenty or more times, edge every third time. Prune trees periodically to maintain open view of background and to remove dead wood. Fertilize trees as needed. Leave fallen foliage as mulch under trees on natural soil slope.

60. The drive curves at the end, providing concealment and a feeling of greater depth. The open live oak tree canopy provides interesting contrasts of light and shadows. Mature azaleas and gardenias enclose the drive and provide seasonal flower color in the spring and summer. St. Francisville, Louisiana.

MANAGEMENT Prune oak (*Quercus virginiana*) trees in the winter, every five to eight years. Remove dead wood, to provide better interior air circulation to help prevent diseases, and prune to enhance the branch pattern and the light and shadow feature. Prune azalea (*Rhododendron indicum*) and gardenia (*Gardenia jasminoides*) shrubs after flowering to maintain size. Also, eliminate dead and diseased wood or rubbing branches. Mulch shrubs with fallen tree leaves and add organic material. Fertilize only to maintain foliage color, perhaps annually or every two to three years. Mow native grasses and annuals along drive every three weeks or as needed.

61. The trunks of the tree-form yaupon holly and the raised planting area partially conceal the view, enticing one to look further. The repetition of the red begonias and border liriope plant in the foreground and background contribute compositional unity. A cool white summer color is provided in the background by caladium foliage and shrub althaea blossoms. The coarse texture and patterned foliage of the Chinese fan palm in the container create accent. New Orleans, Louisiana.

MANAGEMENT Prune the yaupon holly (*Ilex vomitoria*) to maintain tree-form effect. Maintain side branching above pedestrians. Mulch and fertilize *Begonia* and *Caladium* every three weeks during the growing season. Water during any week without rainfall. Replace annual plantings in the fall with winter-hardy plants and mulch. Each season before replanting annuals, add fertilizer and cultivate. Fertilize container palm (*Livistona chinensis*) plants in early spring and several times during the growing season. Mulch. Water container plants two or three times weekly. Prune shrub althaea (*Hibiscus syriacus*) to maintain within space. Fertilize as needed.

62. The container plants and vine on the fence and the small trees outside of the fence partially conceal what is beyond, leaving something to the viewer's imagination. The potted plants define the court space, soften the hard construction materials, and provide contrasts of texture and color. Baton Rouge, Louisiana.

MANAGEMENT Prune vine on fence to maintain partial fence exposure. In winter, prune tree outside of fence (right) to control size and to open up the interior. Mulch potted plants, fertilize every two weeks with a liquid plant food. Water containers every two days or as needed during the growing season. Remove dead blossoms to prevent seed production and to neaten appearance. Container plants require high maintenance, yet provide colorful plant and pot color.

63. In a limited space, tall, narrow evergreen Foster's hybrid holly trees provide a privacy screen for this outdoor living area. The trees, being a darker color than the walls and pavement, allow a much needed feeling of depth. They also soften the effect of the hard construction materials and help create a feeling of spaciousness against the high masonry wall. The pool is painted a dark color which allows the water to be more reflective. This composition provides a pleasing transition of water, stone, and plants. Foliage shadows add drama to the smooth building materials of the floor. New Orleans, Louisiana.

MANAGEMENT Prune evergreen holly (*Ilex × attenuata* 'Fosteri') tree hedge in late winter to remove dead wood and maintain height and density. Apply a complete fertilizer in early spring. Mulch. Each week without rain apply 1 in (3cm) of water by drip irrigation.

64. The evergreen holly shrub hedge provides a desired privacy enclosure for the pool and outdoor seating area. The coarse-textured, patterned foliage of the sago palms contrasts and accentuates the finer textured hedge backdrop. Weeping plant forms at the pool edge direct the view to the water and help unify
the upper and lower levels. Background live oak trees enhance the composition by adding height to the
backdrop and screening any distracting structures beyond. The use of primarily fine-textured plants
creates a feeling of spaciousness in this limited area. New Orleans, Louisiana.

MANAGEMENT Prune background holly (*Ilex* × 'Nellie R. Stevens') hedge in late winter and as needed
during the growing season. Prune oak (*Quercus virginiana*) trees to eliminate dead or diseased wood and
maintain within the available space. Remove dead foliage from the palms (*Cycas revoluta*). Replant annuals
in the raised stone bed in spring and fall after cultivating the soil. Fertilize. Mulch all planted areas with
organic material. Prune weeping perennial (*Lantana montevidensis*) during growing season to keep vines
out of the pool.

65. The tall yew hedge on the left of the drive creates a solid, evergreen screen between these two-story residences. The screen is tallest where privacy in the house and outdoor living spaces is desired. Nearer the street, the tall part of the screen changes to a more informal, mounding hedge—still separating the two residential properties but also allowing views to the homes from the street. The fine texture of the yew hedge insures it will be visually subordinate and provide its function quietly. Ivy ground cover is planted beneath the hedge to provide a transition from the hedge to the drive. Clayton, Missouri.

MANAGEMENT Prune the yew (*Taxus*) hedge in late winter and early summer to keep its geometric form. Mulch beneath the hedge in the fall and spring. Trim the ivy (*Hedera*) ground cover back from the edge of the drive in spring, summer, and fall. Create a 12 in (30 cm) mulched bed beyond the trunk of the littleleaf linden tree (*Tilia cordata*) on the right to facilitate mowing.

66. Primarily, trees can be seen here as moderating the hard construction materials of house, garage, garden pavements, pool, and fence. Secondarily, for this two-story house on a narrow lot, the single, specimen sugar maple, pink-flowering crape myrtles, and the evergreen lusterleaf holly trees behind the fence are used in an aesthetical and functional manner for enframement, backdrop, seasonal color, and privacy screen. Adjacent to the house, an arbor draped with English ivy relates the two-story house and open space to the scale of people. The dwarf yaupon holly mass on the left and single cleyera on the right provide a feeling of enclosure for the pool area. Atlanta, Georgia.

    MANAGEMENT Prune the trees in late winter every five years. Prune to remove dead wood, to permit better interior air circulation to help prevent diseases, to increase the density for screening, and to enhance the branch pattern effect. Also remove any sugar maple (*Acer saccharum*) limbs interfering with the roof. Prune crape myrtle (*Lagerstroemia indica*) and holly (*Ilex latifolia*) annually to maintain within space. Prune dwarf yaupon holly (*Ilex vomitoria* 'Nana') and cleyera (*Ternstroemia gymnanthera*) shrubs in late winter to maintain size and remove dead wood. Thin English ivy (*Hedera helix*) on the arbor for better air circulation and tip prune to maintain pedestrian clearance as needed. Mulch all planting areas. During extended drought of three weeks, apply 1 in (3 cm) of water to all planted areas. In late fall, rake and remove fallen foliage of deciduous trees.

67. A landscape baffle is a planted screen with openings allowing for limited views or pedestrian circulation while subordinating views beyond the baffle. These mature crape myrtle trees create a baffle between the sidewalk and parked cars. The trees visually minimize the impact of the cars and separate the parking space from the sidewalk space. Baton Rouge, Louisiana.

MANAGEMENT Until crape myrtles (*Lagerstroemia indica*) are 8–10 ft (2–3 m) tall they need consistent pruning to develop an attractive shape and to keep from becoming so top heavy with blooms that falling over becomes likely. Prune in early spring and summer of each year. These mature crape myrtles will rarely need pruning. Fertilize with a low nitrogen, high phosphorus, high potassium fertilizer in late fall. Remove a 6 in (15 cm) band of turf around tree trunks in the spring, early summer, and in the fall.

68. The planting compositions enclosing the St. Augustine grass lawn provide ground forms to define and enrich the space while balancing the coarse or hard texture of the stone building. The similar textures and shrub forms establish unity and spaciousness in a limited area. The varying plant heights and colors add interest to the mass. The use of the continuous mondo grass ground cover also offers a unifying element. This planting shows the effectiveness of a monochromatic scheme using varying tones of green. In the outcurve of the shrub mass, the three flowering dogwood trees serve as a transition from house to the shrub planting, asymmetrically balancing the planting mass, providing partial concealment and enticement to the background, and adding seasonal color highlights. The fine texture and light color of the lawn create contrast and a feeling of spaciousness in relationship to the darker, textured plant mass. New Orleans, Louisiana.

MANAGEMENT Judiciously prune shrubs and small trees in late winter to maintain size. Every third year the mondo grass (*Ophiopogon japonicus*) ground cover will need mowing to maintain even density. Set mower at lowest height when pruning mondo grass. Mulch all plants with organic material. Mow St. Augustine grass (*Stenotaphrum secundatum*) lawn twenty or more times during growing season, edge every third time. With established plantings, such as those pictured, fertilize only when foliage indicates a need. During extended drought of three weeks, apply 1 in (3 cm) of water.

69. These large ivy beds act as ground forms helping to create a void or space in the lawn area by their mounding habit and because the ivy is taller, darker, and of a coarser texture than the lawn. The form and texture of the ivy planting creates a big enough visual difference to define the lawn space. Pasadena, California.

MANAGEMENT Cut the Algerian ivy (*Hedera canariensis*) back to the ground with a mower once every two years in late winter to remove woody stems and maintain vigorous growth. Prune the ivy back from its bed edges in spring, early summer, and in the fall. Mow the grass twenty times a season. Trim along the walk and bed edges every third mowing.

70. The single hawthorn tree underplanted with a ground cover creates depth against the solid plant mass background, defines the lawn space, and provides color contrast. This multi-trunk, small-scale, sculptured tree form is suitable accent for this space. The ground cover below adds to the focusing effect and provides weighted balance for the delicate trunks and substantial tree crown. In winter, the line pattern of the light gray tree trunk and limbs against the dark background screen provides a seasonal color contrast and pattern interest. Chicago, Illinois.

MANAGEMENT After the hawthorn (*Crataegus*) tree flowers in spring, prune to remove dead wood, to lessen disease by opening the interior for air circulation, and to enhance the next winter's branch pattern. In early spring, fertilize and mulch the *Euonymus* ground cover at base. Fertilize the lawn area in early spring, mow twenty or more times, and edge every third time. Thin the *Juniperus* ground cover in late winter, and prune occasionally to maintain it in the space. Mulch with lightweight organic material by sifting down through the branches.

71. The vertical, light-colored crape myrtle tree trunks define the space in front of the dark evergreen holly screen and impart a greater feeling of depth to the area. In this symmetrically balanced design the rectilinear boxwood-enclosed planting areas also create depth. Seasonal summer color is provided by the pink blossoms of the crape myrtle trees, the pink caladium foliage and begonia blossoms, and the use of bench cushions. Repetition of the pink color provides compositional unity. The high background hedge screens the adjacent house. New Orleans, Louisiana.

MANAGEMENT In late winter, prune holly (*Ilex cornuta* 'Burfordii') hedge to maintain desired size and density. Prune interior of crape myrtle (*Lagerstroemia indica*) trees for better air circulation to help prevent diseases and to enhance branch pattern. In early spring and late fall, fertilize and cultivate annual planting areas. Replant with seasonal flowers, if appropriate, water and mulch. Any week without rain, apply 1 in (3 cm) of water by drip irrigation. Shear boxwood (*Buxus*) borders in late winter and during the growing season as needed to maintain effect. Mulch potted *Begonia* and *Caladium* plants. Fertilize every two weeks with liquid plant food, and irrigate every two to three days.

72. This house sits on a narrow lot close to the street. The verticle trunks of the old cedar trees create depth and give the perception that the house is farther back from the street than is actually the case. The trees act as a baffle and enclose the lawn space. The liriope ground cover beds reduce mowing and trimming effort around the cedars and act as a ground form helping to define the open lawn space in front of the house. Starkville, Mississippi.

MANAGEMENT Mow the liriope (*Liriope muscari*) ground cover back in late winter to allow fresh, spring growth to evolve. Mow the lawn twenty times a season. Trim along walk and bed edges every third mowing. Fertilize the lawn in early spring if needed to fill in winter-damaged turf.

73a. Three crape myrtle trees were planted on the north side of a paved terrace to provide summer comfort and enclosure. At the opposite end of the terrace is a winged elm for balance. Since the neighbor's property on the north had a direct view to the garden, a shrub and tree composition was planted for privacy. This photograph was taken in August, 1974, nine months after planting. Starkville, Mississippi.

MANAGEMENT A balanced fertilizer was applied to the crape myrtle (*Lagerstroemia fauriei*) and winged elm (*Ulmus alata*) trees in March, 1975, and every spring for five years, then no more. The Bermuda grass (*Cynodon dactylon*) lawn was fed a balanced fertilizer annually for the first three years after planting, then only as its color indicated a need for fertilizer. The lawn was mowed twenty or more times per growing season and edged every third time.

73b. In August, 1976, nearly three years after planting, the three crape myrtles trees provide summer shade, and the adjacent background property is sufficiently screened for privacy. The winged elm is defining the space and visually balances the other trees. The variegated liriope ground cover at the edge of the pavement is providing colorful foliage year-round, and cool, lilac, spiked flowers in August. A Chinese tallow tree was added (right) to define the Bermuda grass lawn space and to serve as a child's climbing tree. The tallow tree also provides bright purple to pink fall foliage, and its white winter seeds show a delightful resemblance to popcorn. Starkville, Mississippi.

MANAGEMENT All trees—crape myrtles (*Lagerstroemia fauriei*), elm (*Ulmus alata*), and tallow (*Sapium sebiferum*)—were fertilized every March for five years beginning the second year after planting. No further fertilizer was applied. The areas under the crape myrtle trees and the shrub border were mulched each spring. Late each winter, the trees were pruned to open up the interior for better circulation of air to help prevent diseases, to remove cross branches, and to enhance the branch pattern. The ground cover (*Liriope muscari* 'Variegata'), planted in late spring, 1974, was given a complete fertilizer that midsummer. Thereafter, only when the foliage indicated a need. The Bermuda grass (*Cynodon dactylon*) lawn was given a complete fertilizer when seeded in summer, 1970, and each spring for three years. Now (twenty years later) the lawn is fed in early spring only when the need is evident. Mow lawn twenty or more times a growing season, edge every third time.

74. To provide spatial definition to the St. Augustine grass lawn area, and to reduce lawn maintenance, part of the site is simply mulched with pine straw and hardwood foliage. This use of mulching is a practical, attractive way to reduce garden maintenance, define space, and provide seasonal color. Three American holly trees on the lower right side asymmetrically balance the visually lightweight deciduous plants in the mulched area to the left. The hollies also enclose and focalize the front entry area and screen a neighbor's drive and garage across the street. The repeated use of the straw under the hollies on right unifies both compositions. Starkville, Mississippi.

MANAGEMENT The area under the trees to the left is basically maintenance-free. It will accommodate pine straw raked from other parts of the lot. For additional seasonal color it may be underplanted with naturalized bulbs, such as *Narcissus* planted in drifts. Fertilize lawn grass (*Stenotaphrum secundatum*) in early spring, if needed. During extended drought of three weeks, apply 1 (3 cm) of water to lawn. Mow twenty or more times in growing season, edge every third time. Prune holly (*Ilex opaca*) trees lightly in late winter to maintain density for screen and enclosure.

75. Mulch is used in this composition to eliminate mowing in shrub beds and around trees, and to provide interesting lines in the landscape. Mulch also defines space in the lawn area. The rich colors of this late winter landscape derive from the use of different browns and the silver bark of red maples. The light brown of St. Augustine grass contrasts with the dark brown of pine straw mulch. Starkville, Mississippi.

MANAGEMENT Mulch around the maple (*Acer rubrum*) tree clump and the shrub bed in the fall and again in early spring to reduce weed growth and soil moisture evaporation. Prune the azaleas (*Rhododendron*) after they bloom to retain plant size if needed. Cottonseed meal can be applied around the azaleas each year after blooming to provide a slowly released organic nitrogen source.

76. This novel planting of ivy on a 6 ft (2 m) tall chain link fence creates an attractive and effective headlight glare screen from the adjacent roadway. The English ivy seems to be thriving, even though it faces west toward the hot afternoon sun. Columbus, Mississippi.

MANAGEMENT Fertilize the English ivy (*Hedera helix*) in late winter with a slow-release, complete fertilizer. Repeat fertilization again in early summer for maximum growth. Stop the fertilization program once the desired screening effect is achieved. Ivy matures into a coarse-textured stage once it reaches the top of a structure. To keep the ivy from evolving into its mature stage shear it back to the fence in late winter of each year.

77. This diverse planting reduces vehicular headlight glare, encloses a walk space, and screens a street intersection. The juniper ground cover repeats the needlelike foliage of the background eastern white pines, lending compositional unity. The flowering oakleaf hydrangeas provide varied seasonal effects with summer white blossoms, contrasting coarse-textured foliage, colorful fall foliage and attractive dried flowers, and textured peeling bark in winter. Athens, Georgia.

MANAGEMENT Mulch all planted areas in late winter with an organic material. To maintain density of foliage and limit the height of pines (*Pinus strobus*), remove some of the growth sprouts (candles) at branch tips in the spring. Prune to judiciously thin the juniper (*Juniperus*) ground cover in late winter. If needed to maintain oakleaf hydrangeas (*Hydrangea quercifolia*) within the available space, prune shrubs after flowering in summer.

78. A streetlight pole in the background on the right is partially screened by flowering dogwood trees and shrubs. This reduces undesired night light in the garden, as well as minimizing the unattractiveness of a bare pole and electrical wires. The planting design also partially screens sights and noises from the street. This planting creates a feeling of concealment and revealment, thus making the space appear larger. Potted annuals provide seasonal color, define space on the brick pavement, and invite viewers toward the benches. Monroe, Louisiana.

MANAGEMENT Prune lower shrubs to maintain privacy screen in late winter. After spring flowering, prune background dogwoods (*Cornus florida*) to maintain density for screening streetlight glare. Mulch all planting areas in early spring. Fertilize potted annuals every two weeks with a liquid plant food. Irrigate pots every day or as needed during the growing season. Cultivate soil and replant pots with winter hardy annuals, if appropriate, and mulch in late fall.

79. The low juniper planting encloses the parking area and directs pedestrian circulation. A 2 ft (0.5 m) wide mulched space inside the brick edging accommodates the overhang of vehicle bumpers and avoids serious damage to plants. The trees add shade, shadow patterns, vertical balance, and spatial definition to the low, horizontal plane of the planting composition. Chicago, Illinois.

MANAGEMENT In late winter, prune junipers (*Juniperus*) in a naturalistic manner to retain a compact form. Mulch. Remove intrusive weeds and grasses from the shrub border in the spring and again in early summer. Every five to eight years, in winter, prune trees to remove dead wood, to open interior for better air circulation to help prevent diseases, and to enhance the branch pattern.

80. Flowering bradford pear trees in a narrow soil strip separate a drive on the right from parking on the left. The trees serve as a directional guide for traffic and to separate use areas. Columbus, Mississippi.

MANAGEMENT In late winter, prune bradford pear (*Pyrus calleryana* 'Bradford') trees to remove dead wood and to permit better air circulation to help prevent diseases. Bradford pear trees also tend to develop many cross branches. If these are not also removed there is a likelihood of significant limb breakage. Due to the deep shade and root competition under the tree this area would be easier to maintain if planted with a ground cover, such as wintercreeper (*Euonymus fortunei*) or ivy (*Hedera*).

81. Rock has been placed on the nearly 2:1 slope of this embankment to hold the soil, stabilize the dogwood tree behind the slope, and protect from erosion. Such coverings, whether of rock, concrete, or another stable material, are known as revetments. Flat limestone rock is laid here on the angle of repose, the angle at which the soil would stabilize naturally. A soil cut graded to its natural angle of repose, that is, the natural slope to which it will weather without sloughing off further, allows hard materials like slabs of rock or wood timbers to be placed on the slope without fear of collapse. Atlanta, Georgia.

MANAGEMENT Rake leaf buildup from rock face in the fall to maintain an attractive appearance. Remove weeds in spring, early summer, and late summer.

82. The use of ground covers on this steep, uneven topography controls erosion and reduces maintenance. The use of different ground cover varieties, such as fine-textured mondo grass in the foreground and a coarse-textured English ivy in the background, creates contrast and varied spaces. This informal planting is in deep shade adjacent to an approach drive. The view here is from the house entry. Seasonal effects are provided by the summer-flowering hydrangeas, spring-flowering dogwoods and azaleas, and winter- and spring-flowering camellias. In addition, dramatic winter color is provided by the red berries of the dogwoods and the branch colors against the green ground cover background. This planting design provides a great deal of seasonal effect with little maintenance. Birmingham, Alabama.

MANAGEMENT Every five to eight years, prune the dogwood (*Cornus florida*) trees after flowering to remove dead wood, to permit more light for the ground area, and to improve air circulation within the crown interior to help prevent diseases. Every two to three, years prune hydrangeas (*Hydrangea macrophylla*) after flowering to maintain compactness. If winter-damaged, mondo grass (*Ophiopogon japonicus*) may be mowed back to 1 in (3 cm) in late winter before growth begins. Hand prune English ivy (*Hedera helix*) to control growth or if winter damaged. Prune to shape azaleas (*Rhododendron*) if required to maintain form. In prolonged drought of over three weeks, apply 1 in (3 cm) of water.

83. This liriope ground cover controls soil erosion and provides cool, lilac-colored, summer blossoms followed by black berries in the fall. The soil grade is depressed between the liriope and the centipede grass lawn area to help direct rainwater flow away from the pool. The turfgrass strip relates this area to the lawn in the background and provides a feeling of a more spacious walk. Starkville, Mississippi.

MANAGEMENT If damaged by cold weather, the liriope (*Liriope muscari*) ground cover may be pruned or mowed back to 2 in (5 cm) above ground level in late winter. Prune before growth begins or foliage tips will remain brown throughout the summer. Mulch. Remove weeds from the ground cover in late spring and again in midsummer. Apply a complete fertilizer to the liriope in the spring and midsummer. During drought of three weeks, apply 1 in (3 cm) of water by drip irrigation. Fertilize the centipede grass (*Eremochloa ophiuroides*) lawn as needed for color and health. Mow twenty or more times a season, edge every third time.

84. A limited area of St. Augustine grass is used on the slope around the water to control erosion. When constructed, the lake bank was graded to a desirable slope of 3:1—3 ft (0.9 m) horizontal to 1 ft (0.3 m) vertical. Such a grade can support a lawn and provide easy access to the water for recreation and fishing. Fallen tree foliage is left in place to reduce maintenance and serve as a mulch. This natural area retains existing native trees, including cabbage palm, American sweet gum, and the evergreen shrub palmetto. Hilton Head Island, South Carolina.

MANAGEMENT Apply a complete fertilizer to the St. Augustine grass (*Stenotaphrum secundatum*) lawn in early spring and every five weeks during the growing season to maintain growth on slope. Mow twenty or more times during the season. Water during prolonged drought of two weeks. Maintain natural foliage mulch under trees to conserve moisture, reduce weed growth on edges, and enhance appearance. Every two or three years in winter, remove dead branches of cabbage palm (*Sabal palmetto*) and shrub palmetto (*S. minor*). Every five to eight years, in winter, prune sweet gum (*Liquidambar styraciflua*) and other trees in the natural area to remove dead wood and provide air circulation to help reduce diseases. Weed growth at the edge of the water is eliminated by the water depth being 3 ft (1 m), too deep for light to penetrate sufficiently for plant growth.

85. The most popular spaces in any summer parking area are those in the shade. In this situation mesquite trees are use to reduce heat gain in the cars, provide human scale and create a more comfortable space for people. Dallas, Texas.

MANAGEMENT Mulch the mesquite (*Prosopis glandulosa*) trees in the fall and spring to conserve moisture and reduce weed growth. Prune *Ligustrum* shrubs in a naturalistic manner that creates uniformity yet is low enough to minimize places for concealment. Prune in late winter and early summer.

86. The line of small trees creates shade for the house porch, provides enclosure and canopy for the walk, and softens the roof line. The crape myrtle trees provide seasonal flower, foliage color, and year-round bark effect. By repeating trees on the right, balance and repetition is established for a unified composition. Baton Rouge, Louisiana.

MANAGEMENT Prune crape myrtle (*Lagerstroemia indica*) trees in late winter to prevent possible branch damage to the house structure, to provide air circulation to help prevent diseases, and to enhance the branch pattern effect. Mulch the planting area in late winter. Mow the lawn twenty or more times each growing season, edge every third time.

87. The use of a wisteria-covered arbor provides needed shade in a space too limited for tree shade. The vines are in their second year of growth, planted as 6–8 ft (2–2.5 m) vining plants. This Japanese wisteria develops its flower panicles after the foliage appears, providing color contrast between flowers and foliage. The use of deciduous vining plants for summer shade in limited areas permits the flow of desirable sunshine warmth in winter and adds interesting vine patterns. On the foreground posts are *Clematis* vines. Through careful selection of clematis varieties, flower color is provided from spring through fall. Mississippi State, Mississippi.

MANAGEMENT Japanese wisteria (*Wisteria floribunda*) is a high-maintenance vine requiring frequent pruning to keep it in bounds. Prune after it flowers in late spring, again in early summer, and as needed. If the wisteria does not bloom, it may be getting too much nourishment and bypassing its reproductive stage. Stop fertilizing, if this is the case, and root prune 5–7 ft (1.5–2 m) from the trunks in late winter to stress the plant and stimulate bloom. Mulch trunk to create a mowing edge and to protect from mower damage. Mulch around the *Clematis* vines in early spring and late summer. Prune to judiciously thin the vines every two to three years once they are well established. When to prune clematis vines depends on when they flower and whether they flower on old or new wood or both. For new-wood flowers, prune in early spring before growth begins. For old-wood varieties, prune right after flowering. For *Clematis* that flower on both new and old wood, do light corrective pruning in fall or early spring. Pinching tips will stimulate low branching. In summer, the tulips (*Tulipa*) and pansies (*Viola*) could be replaced with *Begonias* for colorful foliage and flowers. Apply organic mulch to the summer annuals and fertilize every three to four weeks with a liquid food. Water with a drip system weekly.

88. Deciduous vines provide shade in summer and, being void of foliage in winter, permit the flow of warming sunlight when it is desirable. In this high-density apartment complex, the colorful, summer-flowering coral vines provide a feeling of privacy and soften hard construction. The creeping fig vine gives year-round wall insulation, useful in energy conservation. The use of Asian jasmine ground cover and a low, pruned hedge control pedestrian circulation to street access. Houston, Texas.

MANAGEMENT In late fall, prune to judiciously thin the coral vine (*Antigonon leptopus*) on the porch to maintain within the space. In winter, thin the Asian jasmine (*Trachelospermum asiaticum*) ground cover. Add a loose organic mulch to the jasmine and other planting areas to conserve moisture. The evergreen creeeping fig (*Ficus pumila*) vine on the masonry wall needs general thinning in late winter and midsummer. Also remove creeping fig vines 12 in (30 cm) away from wood shutters and trim to avoid potential damage to materials. In late winter, remove interior dead wood from the hedge shrubs (*Ligustrum*). Shear to maintain shape and size. During the growing season, about every three to four weeks, shear the hedges at the curb to maintain a low form. Edge ground cover away from walks. During extended drought of three weeks, apply 1 in (3 cm) of water by drip irrigation.

89. The small-scale crape myrtle trees on the south facade of a house provide shade from the late summer sun in the southwest. The trees soften the roof line and provide a transition from roof to ground. The low liriope ground cover remains below windows and unifies the planting composition. Palmetto plants provide interesting foliage patterns in the ground cover and white flowers in summer. On the extreme right is a tree-form holly, providing an evergreen, vertical definition of space. Starkville, Mississippi.

MANAGEMENT Prune crape myrtle (*Lagerstroemia fauriei*) trees in late winter to remove dead wood, to improve air circulation to help prevent diseases, to enhance branch pattern effect, and to prevent possible damage to house structure. Mulch tree trunks for protection from mower and ease of mowing. Trim or mow ground cover (*Liriope muscari* 'Majestic') to 2 in (5 cm) height in late winter if damaged by cold. Mulch. The slow-growing palmetto (*Sabal minor*) requires minimum management when suitably placed, only an occasional thinning might be required to maintain in space. The holly (*Ilex cornuta* 'Needlepoint') is an overgrown shrub treated as a tree-form. Prune back top in late winter to keep clear of house and roof. Remove any sucker growth developing on trunk in early summer. This five-year-old planting no longer requires a fertilization program. Mow centipede grass (*Eremochloa ophiuroides*) lawn sixteen or more times during growing season, edge every fourth time. Apply complete fertilizer if appearance indicates need. Centipede grass, hardy in USDA Zone 7b to the coastal areas, requires below-average lawn maintenance. This turfgrass may grow in the northern limit of UDSA Zone 7, but usually does not tolerate low temperatures.

90. Afternoon heat gain is reduced because of the trees planted to block western sun exposure on this midwestern residence. Fast-growing silver maple trees were closely planted near the house to serve as an immediate sun control measure. Beyond, slower growing and more strongly wooded oaks were planted to take the place of the silver maples, 8–10 years after planting. For immediate sun control, the maples were initially planted twice as close together as shown in this picture. After five years, every other silver maple tree was removed to prevent crowding and still yield effective sun control. Alto Pass, Illinois.

MANAGEMENT Water the silver maple (*Acer saccharinum*) and oak (*Quercus*) trees for two years every week it does not rain during the growing season. Fertilize trees with a complete fertilizer in early spring and in the fall until they are large enough to provide effective sun control. Remove grass around the base of the trees in the spring, summer, and fall for easier mowing.

91. Evergreen trees, such as pines, hemlocks, spruce, and southern magnolia can make an ideal windbreak for winter energy conservation. Here they also provide dramatic enframement and backdrop for building structures and garden spaces. In the foreground is a prime example of a well-maintained golf green, illustrating the effectiveness of color and texture contrasts in a well-kept lawn. Highlands, North Carolina.

MANAGEMENT Periodically prune evergreen trees to remove dead wood and to permit more light under canopies. Leave fallen foliage as mulch and ground cover.

92. This rich variety of plant types and forms creates a dead air space between the plants and building, insulating the building from winter winds and summer heat, thereby reducing heating and cooling expenses. In this condominium project, all of the residences are nearly identical in appearance. Variety in the site design is achieved through a diverse mix of plant materials. Decatur, Georgia.

    MANAGEMENT Mulch beneath trees in the fall and in early summer to prevent erosion and retain moisture. Remove turfgrass in a 6 in (15 cm) wide band along the shrub and ground cover beds in the spring, summer, and fall to allow for easier mowing.

93. The grape vine serves as insulation, keeping the house cool. It also provides a needed third dimension to define the space against the flat wall. Being deciduous, it creates an interesting wall pattern in winter. The grape vine's coarse texture gives contrast to the finer texture of the climbing fig vine beneath it. The vines, *Liriope, Sedum,* and various annuals and perennials soften the concrete block walls and steps. Athens, Georgia.

MANAGEMENT Prune grape (*Vitis*) vine in late fall or winter to maintain in available space and for increased fruit production. In late fall, early summer, and when needed, prune climbing fig (*Ficus pumila*) vine to keep it clear of the wood siding above. Apply a complete fertilizer to all plants in early spring and summer. Water twice weekly in growing season or as needed.

94. A coarse-textured leatherleaf mahonia shrub is planted at the far end under the eaves. Relating to its foliage texture is a mass of coarse-textured cast-iron plants, faced with fine-textured liriope for contrast. Note the brick mowing strip which helps to maintain the edges of the St. Augustine grass lawn and the ground cover. This twenty-five year old microclimate planting stands the test of time with minimum maintenance. Gulfport, Mississippi.

MANAGEMENT Water with a drip system every two weeks or as needed during the growing season and every four to five weeks in other seasons. Prune to restrain height of the leatherleaf mahonia (*Mahonia bealei*). Also, every 2–3 years in early spring, after it flowers and fruits, prune one-fourth of its stems to 12–18 in (30–46 cm) above grade. This will promote new vertical growth. In late winter, remove any discolored or dead foliage from the cast-iron plants (*Aspidistra elatior*). Apply organic mulch to the entire area, sifting it down through the plants to the ground. If the *Liriope* has received winter damage, prune by mowing down to 2 in (5 cm) in late winter before growth starts. If needed for color and health, fertilize lawn grass (*Stenotaphrum secundatum*) in early spring. Mow twenty or more times a season, edge every third time.

95. The shaped privet hedge acts as a backdrop for the seasonal color bed, showing off the massed flowering plants—white-flowered shasta daisies, yellow Mexican marigold-mint, rose-pink Mexican evening primrose, and European purple loosestrife. Notice the ground-level concrete bed liner separating the mulched flower bed from adjacent turf. The enclosure provided by the bed liner enhances the flower bed's visual unity. St. Louis, Missouri.

MANAGEMENT Place composted mulch on the bed in late winter, early summer, and fall. A 3–4 in (8–10 cm) layer of composted mulch will also help the flower bed to retain moisture and reduce weeding. Spent flower blossoms need to be picked every week for maximum blooming. Divide and replant perennials every three or four years. This composition features masses of shasta daisies (*Chrysanthemum maximum*), Mexican marigold-mint (*Tagetes lucida*), Mexican evening primrose (*Oenothera berlandieri*), and purple loosestrife (*Lythrum salicaria*). Shear the privet (*Ligustrum*) hedge to maintain its geometric form in late spring, summer, and late summer.

96. The camellias provide an evergreen backdrop for this turn-of-the-century gazebo. The clumps of cast-iron plants help define space in the gazebo as well as adding human scale and comfort. Baton Rouge, Louisiana.

MANAGEMENT Take yearly pH tests around the camellias (*Camellia japonica*) to maintain an acidic soil. Apply composted mulch around camellias in late winter, early summer, and in the fall to provide nutrients and hold moisture. Divide cast-iron plants (*Aspidistra elatior*) every three years for maximum growth.

97. Global boxwood plants frame the iron gate and repeat beyond as low sheared hedges, leading viewers to the elegant form of a pecan tree. The Bermuda grass lawn also helps accentuate the winter pattern of the pecan tree. Leland, Mississippi.

MANAGEMENT Every five to eight years in late winter, prune the pecan (*Carya illinoensis*) tree to remove dead wood and to permit interior air circulation to help prevent diseases. Prune the boxwood (*Buxus microphylla*) shrubs annually in late winter, to remove interior dead wood and maintain desired size. Additional shearing may be needed for size control during the growing season. Mulch shrubs in early spring with organic material. Apply a complete fertilizer to the Bermuda grass (*Cynodon dactylon*) lawn in early spring, if needed. Mow twenty or more times a growing season, edge every third time. During extended drought of three weeks, apply 1 in (3 cm) of water. To maintain a lawn under the gate is difficult, due to compaction, and often it is better to pave such areas. In this illustration, using brick paving would repeat the edging material of the lawn and add to design unity.

98. The enframement of this house's facade is provided by an enclosure mass of azaleas and liriope, a baffle of crape myrtle trees, and a live oak. The use of St. Augustine grass lawn on both sides of the azaleas and path unifies the areas. The vertical line of the oak asymmetrically balances the horizontal line of crape myrtle trees and azaleas. For unity of house and street area, a crape myrtle tree is repeated at the left of the front door. The coarse-textured, dark green pattern of a sago palm above a low mass of azaleas provides entry emphasis. The front path is extended to make a proportioned transition from path to street. New Orleans, Lousiana.

MANAGEMENT In late winter, prune crape myrtle (*Lagerstroemia indica*) and live oak (*Quercus virginiana*) trees to remove dead and excessive wood, to maintain openness, to improve air circulation to help prevent diseases, and to enhance the branch pattern. Cut back *Liriope* before growth begins in spring. Prune azaleas (*Rhododendron*) after flowering in spring to remove dead wood and to control size. Drip irrigate the oak next to the curb and weekly during the growing season, due to limited soil area. In late winter, remove any sago palm (*Cycas revoluta*) foliage damaged by the cold. Mulch azaleas, oak, and palm. In late spring, fertilize lawn grass (*Stenotaphrum secundatum*) if needed. Mow twenty or more times in growing season, edge every third time. In prolonged drought of three weeks, apply 1 in (3 cm) of water by drip irrigation.

99. Trees to enframe and provide the loggia with a backdrop are essential to establish balance and proportion in this space. The Chinese wisteria vine on the loggia repeats the green foliage of the live oak trees and softens the structural outline. The placement of the three groupings of potted annuals around the pool, with the potted tree standard at each end, provides a transition from the structure to the brick floor, defines the floor space, and provides seasonal attractions. The green lawn allows a softening effect to the hard construction floor materials, provides additional contrasting color, and serves as a directional guide to the loggia, the focal point. New Orleans, Louisiana.

MANAGEMENT Prune to remove dead wood from the Chinese wisteria (*Wisteria sinensis*) vine after flowering in the spring. Prune as needed for control and to maintain size throughout the active growing season. Tie any dangling stems to the arbor frame and mulch the root area with an organic material. Apply a complete fertilizer in early spring and summer to the potted tree standards and water daily during the growing season. Fertilize potted annuals with a liquid plant food every two weeks. Irrigate containers every day during the warm season. Fertilize lawn, here a Bermuda grass (*Cynodon*) lawn, as needed. During extended drought of three weeks, apply 1 in (3 cm) of water. Mow twenty or more times a season, edge every third time. In winter, every five to eight years, prune background oak (*Quercus virginiana*) trees. Prune trees to remove dead wood, improve air circulation to help prevent diseases, and enhance branch pattern.

100. The reflection of a garden in a placid pool of water can inspire a very moving experience. The naturally wooded bank is underplanted with spring-flowering daffodil bulbs, their flowers reflecting dots of color onto the water surface. The tall, vertical tree trunks separate the house space from the pond and give a greater sense of depth. This type of infrequent scene often inspires creativity and reflection. West Bend, Wisconsin.

MANAGEMENT Remove invasive vines and shrubs from under the trees in the wooded area in early and late summer. Allow foliage of underplanted daffodil bulbs (*Narcissus*) to die back naturally. Allow leaves to collect under trees to create a healthy, natural mulch bed which reduces invasion of weeds and feeds the bulbs naturally.

101. Although we don't often see plants specifically used for this function, in this situation the landscape adjacent to the building becomes an interesting reflection. While water reflects a horizontal image, window glass can reflect a vertical image. By duplicating what is beyond, the entire building is enhanced. St. Louis, Missouri.

MANAGEMENT Keep the reflective glass surfaces clean.

102. The creeping fig vine patterns on the light-colored brick wall and the coarse-textured shrubs create a focal point for the entry area. The form of the variegated aucuba shrubs, in front to the left, relates well to the narrow planter and the shady conditions under the roof eaves. The liriope ground cover remains below the height of the window and is also suitable to the growing conditions in this microclimate. The Chinese holly shrubs on the right repeat the coarse texture of the aucubas, contributing to design unity. Starkville, Mississippi.

MANAGEMENT In late winter, late spring, and midsummer, prune creeping fig (*Ficus pumila*) vine to maintain visibility of the brick wall, to emphasize the vine pattern, and to keep vine from damaging the wood trim. In winter, prune aucuba (*Aucuba japonica* 'Variegata') to maintain size and open foliage pattern effect. Prune Chinese hollies (*Ilex cornuta* 'Rotunda') to maintain size. If winter-damaged, prune *Liriope* to 2 in (5 cm) before new growth commences. Because of the dry soil in the microclimate, mulch all planting areas with organic material and water weekly in warm weather. Mow lawn twenty or more times during a growing season, edge every third time.

103. Patterns of the deciduous Boston ivy vine define the expanse of a masonry wall and serve a functional purpose as a wall cooler in summer. A special design attraction of this vine is that foliage projects outward from the wall, creating a third dimension and casting shadow patterns. Although the vine to the left is dead from unknown causes, it at least displays the attractive winter pattern effect of this normally long-living vine. In cool climates this vine develops brilliant red fall foliage. Boston ivy is better suited to large wall expanses, otherwise keeping it under control becomes a continuous maintenance problem. Salzburg, Austria.

MANAGEMENT On a large wall expanse, Boston ivy (*Parthenocissus tricuspidata*) vine management is limited to removal of fallen foliage after frost. Mulch roots with an organic material. This vine will attach itself to almost any material. It should not be planted on wood structures due to the damage its rootlets may cause. Boston ivy is easy to establish, fast-growing, and vigorous once established.

104. Branch and foliage shadow patterns of live oak trees unify the paving surfaces and low-growing plants. The oaks also provide an effective enclosure for this symmetrical entry drive design. New Orleans, Louisiana.

MANAGEMENT Prune live oak (*Quercus virginiana*) trees every five to eight years in winter. Remove dead wood, increase interior air circulation to help prevent diseases, and prune to enhance the branch pattern. In early spring, apply a complete fertilizer to the low-growing mondo grass (*Ophiopogon japonicus*) ground cover. Sift mulch down among plants. If cold-damaged, in early spring before growth begins mow to 1 in (3 cm) high. The centipede grass (*Eremochloa ophiuroides*) lawn will require a complete fertilizer annually in early spring due to competition from the large trees. Water the lawn during prolonged drought. Mow fifteen or more times during the growing season and edge every third time.

105. These crape myrtle trees have been shaped as beautiful specimen plants at the entry to this country home. The trees also enframe the symmetrically balanced entry and provide an outstanding seasonal effect. Note their wintertime bark color, smooth texture, twisting branches, and how the branching pattern repeats the pattern in the nearby windows. The mounding evergreen shrubs contrast with and accent the crape myrtles and provide transition from house to ground level. Starkville, Mississippi.

MANAGEMENT Prune the crape myrtles (*Lagerstroemia indica*) in late winter to keep their sculptural shape. Mulch the evergreen boxwood (*Buxus*) shrubs on either side of the entry and the holly (*Ilex cornuta*) shrubs beneath the windows in the fall. Shape the shrubs in late winter and again in early and late summer.

106. This symmetrical planting creates a bold view in this brick courtyard. In this example, plants are used purely for sculptural reasons. The plant forms are varied and include erect junipers, arching Canadian hemlocks, ball-like boxwoods, and free-form dwarf yaupon hollies. The potted plant on the left provides transition from the raised planter to the courtyard. Atlanta, Georgia.

MANAGEMENT Shape evergreens in late winter and early summer to achieve the size and proportion desired. This composition includes juniper (*Juniperus*), hemlock (*Tsuga canadensis*), shaped boxwood (*Buxus*), and yaupon holly (*Ilex vomitoria* 'Stokes'). Take yearly soil pH and nutrient samples in any raised bed planting to keep abreast of soil conditions. Mulch with compost in late winter and again in the fall to help retain moisture and provide nutrients. Change seasonal, annual pot plantings in spring, and again in fall if conditions permit. Water raised bed plantings each week as required.

107. The sculptural quality of the eastern redcedar establishes it as a terminal accent from the entry walk. A background planting of evergreen glossy privet, screening an adjacent residence, also enhances the beauty of the light-colored cedar bark. The St. Augustine grass lawn leading around behind the tree leads one to imagine what may be concealed behind. Baton Rouge, Louisiana.

MANAGEMENT Periodically remove dead redcedar (*Juniperus virginiana*) limbs for enhancement of the branch pattern effect as a focal point. Due to the heavy shade and competition from tree roots, establishment and maintenance of a lawn grass, such as the St. Augustine (*Stenotaphrum secundatum*) used here, is difficult. A hardy, trailing evergreen ground cover, such as bigleaf periwinkle (*Vinca major*), is more suitable. Apply a complete fertilizer to a ground cover planting in early spring and sift a lightweight mulch material down among the stems. During any prolonged drought of three weeks, apply 1 in (3 cm) of water by drip irrigation to the ground cover and glossy privet (*Ligustrum lucidum*). Once established, the redcedar tolerates low moisture conditions.

108. Spruce pine trees provide a feeling of sculptured lines, defining and canopying the limited space against a fence. The trees extend the vertical lines of the fence and brick wall. A ground cover of native ferns adds seasonal effects. In the background beyond the wall a Japanese maple provides foliage pattern and additional sculptural quality with its branches. New Orleans, Louisiana.

MANAGEMENT Periodically prune spruce pines (*Pinus glabra*) to enhance the sculptural quality of the branch pattern. Remove dead limbs from pine every two to three years. Gather pine straw from the pavement in the fall to use as a mulch. Apply a complete fertilizer to the ferns in early spring and mulch to help conserve moisture in the limited soil area. Remove dead or injured fronds by cutting them back to the ground after plant is established. Drip irrigate the ferns as needed during prolonged drought. In late winter, prune the maple (*Acer palmatum*) to retain its form and size and to increase circulation of air.

109. The distraction of a dull parking area in this upscale condominium project is reduced by the use of shrubs, raised planters, and brick curbing. The landscape architects did such a masterful job blending parking space and materials into the overall site design that gaping voids and distractions are minimized. Chicago, Illinois.

MANAGEMENT Prune the juniper (*Juniperus*) shrubs in late winter and again in early summer to keep their informal form and size. Mow the lawn twenty times a season. Trim grass away from all edges every third time it is mowed. Fertilize the lawn for health and color as needed. Trim the wintercreeper (*Euonymus fortunei*) ground cover away from the raised planter edges in late spring, summer, and early fall.

110. Trees and shrubs in this apartment community provide varied interest while softening and reducing the impact of three-hundred visually identical units. While the plants contribute variety to the overall composition, they also create interesting spaces and provide a transition from the parking areas to the buildings. Annual and perennial beds provide much needed color variety to the landscape. Roswell, Georgia.

MANAGEMENT Prune the American sweet gum (*Liquidambar styraciflua*) and southern waxmyrtle (*Myrica cerifera*) trees, and juniper (*Juniperus*) and Chinese holly (*Ilex cornuta*) shrubs as needed in late winter and early summer. Mulch all planted areas in early spring and in the fall. Dead-head annual marigold (*Tagetes*) flowers every week throughout the growing season. Remove grass and weeds from mulch beds in the spring, summer, and early fall.

111. The large, bold steps to this famous craftsman-style house are subordinated and blended into the landscape by the use of creeping fig vine. This blending of house and garden illustrates an important design principle espoused during the Arts and Crafts movement (1890–1920). Pasadena, California.

MANAGEMENT Shear the evergreen creeping fig vine (*Ficus pumila*) back to the brick face in late winter, early summer, and again in late summer to retain its uniformly flat form.

112. Refurbishing 1800s homes in New Orleans often involves creating parking areas that front established landscape spaces. To harmonize this parking area with the home landscape, a dark slate paving stone was selected and shrubs and ground cover were planted along the edges. The pavement color and coarse texture and the variety of plants used help to minimize the impact of a potentially distracting parking area. The line of tall, Japanese yew shrubs on the right serves as a baffle to mask the neighboring residence and direct the user down a narrow walk to a side entry. New Orleans, Louisiana.

MANAGEMENT Cut the liriope (*Liriope muscari*) ground cover back to 2 in (5 cm) in late winter to make way for new growth. Prune the Japanese yew (*Podocarpus macrophyllus* var. *maki*) shrubs as needed in late winter and again in early summer. Prune the evergreen azaleas (*Rhododendron*) near the house after blooming, in a naturalistic manner as needed. Mulch with compost in late spring, early summer, and fall to retain moisture and provide nutrients. Place one cup of cottonseed meal around each azalea after blooming, for nitrogen needs. Plant Madagascar periwinkle (*Catharanthus roseus*) and *Impatiens* in late spring after frost for summer color. Remove dead plants in late fall and compost.

113. The clematis vine provides a colorful pattern of green foliage and purple summer blossoms on the wood lamp post in the foreground. Alongside the steps on the left globed-shaped, evergreen boxwood form a transition that softens the geometry of the steps. English ivy clothes the brick pillars while its green foliage repeats other foliage in the space. The tall, slender holly plant between the walk and house moderates the white wall structure and roof line. It acts as transition from roof to the walk and people on it, relates it to the pedestrian walk space, and provides shade. New Bern, North Carolina.

MANAGEMENT Every two to three years, prune to judiciously thin *Clematis* vines to maintain size. Pruning to enhance flowering is specific to clematis type. See discussion in Management, photo 87. Prune boxwood (*Buxus sempervirens*) shrub forms to remove dead wood and to retain within the limited space. Cut English ivy (*Hedera helix*) back as needed to maintain new growth and constrain vines. Mulch vines and shrubs with organic material to conserve moisture in restricted soil areas. Fertilize all plants in early spring, and water weekly during prolonged drought. Water container boxwood (*Buxus*) twice weekly or as needed. Apply a complete fertilizer in early spring and summer.

114. Japanese privet shrubs are pruned as small tree-forms, interrupting the wall and roof line of the structures, providing a canopy to relate the space to human scale, and establishing a sculptural quality. The lower-growing holly shrub mass on the left, enclosing a space with a solitary tree form and English ivy ground cover, serves as a directional guide toward the house entries. Other low shrub masses of the same height help to unify the total composition. The contrast of mondo grass ground cover and the holly ferns on the right creates a desirable focal point at the beginning of the path. The extension of the path to the street provides an effective design transition from narrow path to wide street. Baton Rouge, Louisiana.

MANAGEMENT In late winter and midsummer, prune side branches of Japanese privet (*Ligustrum japonicum*) shrubs to maintain open sculptural quality and canopy. Remove interior dead wood of holly (*Ilex*) shrub borders in late winter. Shear shrubs in early spring and as needed during the growing season. Remove any dead fronds from holly ferns (*Cyrtomium falcatum*) in early spring. Prune mondo grass (*Ophiopogon japonicus*) to 1 in (3 cm) in early spring if cold damaged. Cut back English ivy (*Hedera helix*) as needed to restrain growth. Mulch all plantings with organic material sifted down among stems. During extended drought of three weeks, apply 1 in (3 cm) of water by drip irrigation.

115. The structural ruins pictured here are part of the historic Afton Villa, where a garden area has recently been developed. The visual appeal of historic structure ruins, or rock walls with soil-filled joints, is here enhanced with plantings. Such planting areas are distinct microclimates requiring plants tolerant of low moisture. The light green goldmoss sedum in the wall is one found in historic southern gardens and tolerates drought in sun or shade. The light-colored flowering plant at the wall base is oxalis, another antebellum (pre-Civil War) plant tolerant of limited growing conditions. The potted boxwood defines the space. St. Francisville, Louisiana.

MANAGEMENT   Fertilize goldmoss sedum (*Sedum acre*) and *Oxalis* wall plants with liquid plant food every two weeks. Irrigate wall plants and potted boxwood (*Buxus microphylla* var. *japonica*) every two days during the warm season. Fertilize potted plant in early spring and again in midsummer. Mulch. Prune potted plant in late winter and shape as needed during growing season to remove dead wood and maintain size.

116. The bark of the birch tree in the background functions as accent due to its lighter color and because it is located on the centerline of the deck and foreground walk. Its location defines the vertical space and creates a feeling of depth against the fence. The smaller hawthorn tree on the left and the Japanese spurge ground cover provide balance and enclosure for the deck. The hawthorn provides seasonal white flowers in spring, a lovely winter branch pattern, and red berries. Milwaukee, Wisconsin.

MANAGEMENT Prune birch (*Betula*) and hawthorn (*Crataegus*) trees in late winter to maintain size, increase air circulation to help prevent diseases, and enhance the branch pattern. Fertilize with a complete fertilizer in early spring if needed. Once plants are established, fertilize only when foliage indicates a need. Mulch all planting areas with an organic material. Mow lawn twenty or more times a growing season, and edge every third time. Water the Japanese spurge (*Pachysandra terminalis*) ground cover often and deeply while plants are getting established. Water regularly throughout the growing season.

117. The oakleaf hydrangeas accent and enclose the entry space. The coarse texture of the hydrangeas imparts a lively, friendly, and welcoming feeling. The repetition of white gives a sense of coolness to the entry space of this Deep South residence. Starkville, Mississippi.

MANAGEMENT Cut the oakleaf hydrangea (*Hydrangea quercifolia*) back after it blooms to retain its size. Fertilize the shrub with compost in early spring and again in late fall. Cut off any bloom spikes in late winter before the plant produces new growth. Feed the annuals in the concrete planter with a liquid fertilizer every two weeks. Because of the small size of the planters and their exposure to the hot western sun, water plants every two or three days as needed.

118. The enclosing lattice fence and plantings are located to center attention on an existing live oak. The light-colored, fine-textured St. Augustine grass provides contrast for the darker, more coarsely textured plantings. This narrow lot appears larger by concealing the property line (left) and part of the house (right). Baton Rouge, Louisiana.

MANAGEMENT Prune the oak (*Quercus virginiana*) tree every five to eight years in winter. Prune to remove dead wood, to open interior for increased circulation of air as a help in preventing diseases, and to enhance the branch pattern. Prune shrubs to maintain size in late winter. Also remove any dead or diseased wood and rubbing branches. Once established, shrubs are fertilized only as foliage color indicates the need. Fertilize St. Augustine grass (*Stenotaphrum secundatum*) lawn in early spring, if needed. During prolonged drought of three weeks, apply 1 in (3 cm) of water to lawn. Mow twenty or more times each growing season, edge every third time.

119. The color and pattern of the espaliered forsythia is accent against the flat, natural wood fence. It remains a focal point as its green foliage turns yellow in fall and drops to leave an attractive light-colored pattern of stems. The ground cover is a sprawling euonymus vine, giving a rich green foliage base for the forsythia. The curvilinear stems of the staghorn sumac define the space. Note the gravel under the fence and between the stepping stones to reduce maintenance. Chicago, Illinois.

MANAGEMENT Prune the *Forsythia* after it flowers to maintain size. Prune again after new wood hardens in summer. Thin center of plant to provide espaliered effect. Old or weak *Forsythia* canes can be cut back to the ground after flowering once the plant is established. Prune *Euonymus* ground cover in early spring and summer and as needed to maintain density.

120. Naturalized bulbs in pine straw mulch provide color contrasts by their flower and foliage. The color of treated natural wood seems most effective in naturalized plantings. Pine Mountain, Georgia.

MANAGEMENT Fertilize bulbous plants (*Narcissus*) as they appear above the ground. Especially after flowering, foliage acts to produce and store food in the bulb for the next year. Remove foliage only after it yellows. Every four or five years, dig and divide bulbs as foliage turns yellow. Replant in late fall.

121. The beauty inherent in this fall scene is doubled by the reflection of it in the water. The light-toned bark color of the tree trunks creates striking contrasts to the darker tones of foliage and water. The red-berried plant on the right is possumhaw holly which has attractive light gray bark as well as colorful berries. Learning to appreciate the winter effects of the color of bark, frosted turfgrass, and dried seed pods, as well as the patterns of leafless trees, can add months to garden pleasure. Starkville, Mississippi.

MANAGEMENT Fertilize sloping St. Augustine grass (*Stenotaphrum secundatum*) lawn in early spring, mow twenty or more times during the growing season, and edge every third time. Apply 1 in (3 cm) of water during extended drought. Every five to eight years, prune trees to remove dead wood, to open interior for better air circulation to help prevent diseases, and to enhance the winter branch pattern effect. Thin suckers developing on possumhaw (*Ilex decidua*) to retard thicket development. Leave fallen foliage beneath trees in naturalistic area as mulch to conserve moisture and provide an attractive appearance. Remove dead plant foliage at water's edge in early spring.

122. Against the green background of the loblolly pines, the winter foliage of a solitary American beech provides color and texture contrasts. The beech foliage, the tones of various tree barks, the frosted St. Augustine grass, and the bare tree branches provide a harmonious winter color, line, and shadow pattern composition. Starkville, Mississippi.

  MANAGEMENT Prune loblolly pines (*Pinus taeda*) and American beech (*Fagus grandifolia*) tree every five to eight years. Remove dead wood, thin limbs to permit interior air circulation to help prevent diseases, and prune to enhance branch pattern. Fertilize St. Augustine grass (*Stenotaphrum secundatum*) lawn in early spring, if needed. During extended drought of three weeks, apply 1 in (3 cm) of water. Mow twenty or more times a growing season, edge every third time.

123. Winter berries of the firethorn provide long-lasting color in the landscape. Shown here is a firethorn shrub trained as an espalier on an arbor. It provides a mass of white spring flowers, evergreen foliage, and colorful berries in the fall. Berries do not drop readily, usually lasting until eaten by birds in late winter. Warm-colored berries and dried seeds and seed pods add enduring, winter seasonal garden effects. Jackson, Mississippi.

MANAGEMENT Fertilize fruit-producing plants, such as the firethorn (*Pyracantha*) pictured here, with potash in the spring to stimulate fruit production. Mulch to conserve moisture and to protect plant base from mower damage if sited in a lawn area. Prune to remove dead wood, to permit better interior air circulation, to help prevent diseases, and to enhance branch pattern.

124. The summer-flowering oakleaf hydrangeas provide cool, white color and patterns for the warm season, warm pink to yellow fall foliage, and attractive dried flowers in winter. This shrub mass balances the brick pillar and serves as a transition to the lawn, as well as functioning as a welcoming presence to the driveway. Flowering dogwood trees and the lawn area provide contrasting greens as background. Birmingham, Alabama.

MANAGEMENT Fertilize and mulch the hydrangeas (*Hydrangea quercifolia*) in early spring. Prune after summer flowering if needed to control size. Mulch dogwoods (*Cornus florida*) in early spring, and prune to remove any dead branches. Mow lawn twenty or more times per growing season, edge every third time. During extended drought of three weeks, apply 1 in (3 cm) of water by drip irrigation to all plantings.

a.

b.

125 a, b, c, d. Although a formal perennial garden is not suitable for every situation, the potential for year-round seasonal drama enhances every garden whether formal or informal. Here the color and form of the sculpture establishes a permanent presence, linking and highlighting all seasons. This series of photos is provided to emphasize seasonal changes and delightful garden potentials throughout the year. A major point is to consider all four seasons for garden planting designs, basing considerations on climate and the obvious or not-so-obvious seasonal changes and requirements of the plants.

The first photo (a) is the spring season—the single-flowering dogwood on the left has already peaked and, on the upper level, the double-flowering dogwood will peak at the same time as the German irises in the lower garden. The iris planting area around the sculpture is enclosed by two types of boxwood, a low edging or border type with global boxwoods accentuating the steps. The next photo (b) illustrates valuable summer shade and shadow in the early summer. Color highlight is provided by climbing roses on the wrought iron contrasting with the dark green creeping fig vine. Fall (c) is the season of changing foliage colors, leaf raking, and emerging structures and patterns of limbs and branches of deciduous trees and shrubs. Winter (d) can be the most beautiful, and in many regions, the most long-lasting season. Intri-

c.

d.

cate branch patterns are outlined against the sky and fall as shadows on the contrasting color of the Bermuda grass lawn. If a garden is aesthetically pleasing in its winter minimalism, it can be judged a successful design composition throughout the year. Athens, Georgia.

SPRING MANAGEMENT Divide specific perennials and replant. Dead-head other perennials and weed. Plant summer- and fall-flowering bulbs. Apply a balanced fertilizer to Bermuda grass (*Cynodon*) lawn, if needed. Begin mowing lawn as needed.

SUMMER MANAGEMENT Mow lawn weekly and edge every third time. In drought of three weeks, provide lawn 1 in (3 cm) of water. Drip irrigate perennials weekly. Dead-head perennials about once a week or more. Weed. Stake tall perennials. Watch for insects and diseases, particularly on roses (*Rosa*), and be ready to treat severe outbreaks if required. Shear boxwood (*Buxus suffruticosa*) edging and global (*B. sempervirens*) specimens for neat appearance, as needed throughout the summer. After new growth hardens, prune pear (*Pyrus*) tree against building wall to maintain formal espalier. Tip prune crape myrtle (*Lagerstroemia indica*) trees for more blossoms on new wood. Prune creeping fig (*Ficus pumila*) vine to keep it in bounds. Every three to four years, after foliage turns yellow, dig spring-flowering bulbs (here *Iris × germanica* is used) for replanting. When bulbs fail to flower or plants produce smaller flowers they may need dividing. In late season, replenish perennial mulch for nutrients and climate protection.

FALL MANAGEMENT Weed and dead-head perennials as needed. Raise mower blade and mow lawn less frequently. Water lawn and perennials, as needed. For winter protection, apply fertilizer void of nitrogen, such as 0–20–20, to all plantings until plants are well established. Rake and compost fallen tree leaves. In late fall after the soil cools, replant bulbs dug up in the summer and any new spring-flowering bulbs.

WINTER MANAGEMENT In this season most plants appear totally dormant, but there is underground plant activity and, therefore, in prolonged drought, water the garden. Every five to eight years, prune dogwood (*Cornus florida*), pear, and crape myrtle trees to remove dead wood and to increase air circulation to help prevent diseases. Prune shrubs to remove dead wood, shape, and maintain in space in late winter before growth begins.

126. The Romans were the first to perfect the art of topiary, the pruning of shrubs into decorative shapes, due to a favorable climate and cultural development. Great Dixter Gardens, East Sussex, England.

127. The knot garden was introduced into Europe in the 15th century from the Middle East. Illustrated are ones being redeveloped in front of the Old Palace, 1497. Hatfield House and Gardens, Hertfordshire, England.

128. The pleached allée provides shelter from frequent showers in England and protection from the sun in the Mediterranean area. Its use was originally in limited spaces in medieval walled castles and cities. Herb gardens for food and medicines developed as a result of medieval political action. Flowering *Laburnum* is illustrated in Queen's Garden. Royal Botanic Gardens, Kew, England.

129. Spanish garden enclosures provide shade, privacy, and human-scale spaces. Sevilla, Spain.

130. Contrasts of lines and light and dark, enclosed and open spaces, and limited use of water are typical design influences originating from the culture of the medieval Arabs and climate of Spain. Generalife Garden, Grenada, Spain.

131. The cool, evergreen color of Italian cypress (*Cupressus sempervirens*) trees, water, and non-living ground covers reflect climatic influences on design. Garden of Lindaraja, Alhambra, Grenada, Spain.

132. The use of retaining walls on the steep topography of Italy makes space available for gardens and active water features in the Renaissance era. Villa d'Este, Tivoli, Italy.

133. In medieval Spain, a *glorieta*, a wood- or plant-enclc pavilion at the garden walk intersection provided clim shelter and a social area. Grenada, Spain.

134. A warm, dry climate, and formal court life favor the use of evergreen *Citrus* trees, white sculptures, and terra cotta urns for color rather than flowers in formal gardens. Medici Palace, Florence, Italy.

135. The *parterre de broderie* garden in the French Grand Style design was located to be viewed from above on raised walks and from the chateau. Political and social factors influenced the development of these large-scale, formal gardens. Vaux le Vicomte, Seine-et-Marne, France.

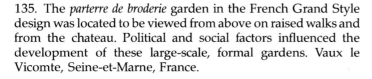

136. André Le Nôtre's Grand Style of formal, axial gardens typifies the social and political life of Louis XIV. Illustrated is the Latona Fountain on the major axis of the gardens at Versailles, France.

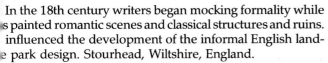

In the 18th century writers began mocking formality while ...s painted romantic scenes and classical structures and ruins. ...influenced the development of the informal English land-...e park design. Stourhead, Wiltshire, England.

138. This scene represents a typical, uninterrupted pastoral scene as designed by "Capability" Brown in the 18th century. The haha keeps livestock out of the garden without blocking the view. Petworth, West Sussex, England.

139. Tree groupings in pastures, water, and classical structures of a landscape park contrast earlier formal garden design near the house. Chatsworth, Derbyshire, England.

140. In the 18th century, probably due to their distance and untamed environment, early Americans did not copy the then-popular informal landscape park design as displayed across the Atlantic. Instead they were influenced by the traditionally formal, enclosed English Tudor and Dutch Renaissance designs. Charleston, South Carolina.

141. In colonial America, vegetable and ornamental ga: boundaries were limited by protective enclosures. Garde: techniques, such as espaliered fruit trees, that would cons space while maintaining food production or ornamental v were popularly utilized. Mt. Vernon, Virginia.

142. Large-scale axial garden designs in the southern United States were influenced by social conditions stemming from plantation life. An axial allée of live oaks (*Quercus virginiana*) enframes and draws the eye to the house. Rosedown, St. Francisville, Louisiana.

143. This composition of garden styles includes Renaiss: formal, symmetry with Roman topiary, Victorian flower c: and the 18th-century landscape park in the background. : style can be traced to major social, climatic, and political factc the time of its conception. Warwick Castle, Warwicks: England.

A lack of flower color in landscape parks in the Victorian
fluenced the introduction of bedding-out annuals to fill the
and pasture voids. Kew, England.

146. The pollarded hornbeam (*Carpinus*) trees
provide an enclosure for the lawn space and
shade for viewing the fountain in an eclectic
garden design. Dumbarton Oaks, Washington,
District of Columbia.

145. Eclecticism was rampant in the late 1800s and early 1900s
in the United States. Pollarded live oak (*Quercus virginiana*) trees
enframe the axis of a 16th-century Italian Renaissance garden
design. Villa Vizcaya, Miami, Florida.

147. An American French château, grandly enframed by
tuliptrees and sited on the central axis of an Italian Renaissance
garden, typifies the eclecticism of the wealthy in the late 1800s.
Biltmore House and Gardens, Asheville, North Carolina.

148. Soil pH can be used to indicate nutrient availability. For example, when soil pH moves well above or below pH 6.5 most nutrients become locked up and unavailable for plant use. Additionally, some plants are very definite about their requirement and will fail to perform if the soil pH is not within their needed range. (See Appendix C for a general listing of pH requirements).

Soil pH can be determined by a soil testing lab, through analysis of samples, or the gardener can conduct tests within minutes with soil pH testing kits available at gardening supply centers. This kit shows two soil types being tested and a color chart displaying different pH levels. Tests should be taken in the spring in areas of high rainfall, and in the fall in areas of low rainfall.

149. The raw materials pictured on the left will become finished compost like that on the right with a carbon to nitrogen (C:N) ratio of approximately 10:1. Through fast composting of leaves, pine straw, and lawn clippings, finished compost can be made in two to three weeks. Fast composting involves chopping through the compost as the pile is turned every three or four days, and keeping the compost covered to retain heat and moisture. The raw materials in the compost pile must have a C:N of 25:1 in order to produce a nourishment level that allows microorganisms to flourish and create finished compost rapidly. Compost is ideal for regular use around plants because it provides nutrients, and retains soil moisture. Research shows that plant diseases are reduced because of the diversity of microorganisms in the compost acting against diseases.

150. Compost can appear somewhat moldy when freshly decomposed. This compost is too moldy for immediate use, and the pile needs to be turned and covered for about one more week. Tree leaves and blades of grass should be hardly recognizable. The compost pile will cool from a hot temperature of 150°F (66°C) to 110°F (43°C) when ready to turn. Generally, when microorganisms have converted the raw materials to half their original bulk the compost is ready to be spread around the garden.

151. This grove of trees at the entrance to a residential development presents a stately, orderly impression due to the elimination of shrubs and vines on the ground plane and through extensive mulching with pine straw. By creating an uninterrupted ground plane, the tree trunks stand out like sentries at the gate. Madison, Mississippi.

MANAGEMENT Mow the turfgrass twenty times a year. Trim along the curb every third mowing. Mulch in fall and again in spring. Remove invasive plants from the mulched area in the spring, summer, and fall. Maintain gently flowing bed lines. Roller-coaster bed lines would convey a hectic feeling at odds with the planting. Through mulching this wooded area, not only is the design more diverse and interesting, but management costs are reduced by at least one-half.

152. The organic shredded bark mulch around the live oak trunk base reduces lawn mowing maintenance. This example shows that by extending the mulch out from the trunk a greater distance than actually needed, it can provide a more proportioned mulched base area for a large tree. It also adds design value to a functional material and near-absolute protection from mowers. The shade-tolerant lawn is centipede grass. New Orleans, Louisiana.

MANAGEMENT Every five to eight years, prune live oaks (*Quercus virginiana*) to remove dead wood and to increase interior air circulation to help prevent diseases, and to allow a somewhat less restricted flow of sunlight, rain, and air for the lawn. Remove fallen leaves in the spring. Replenish mulch as needed. With low light intensity and the live oaks' root competition, the centipede grass (*Eremochloa ophiuroides*) lawn will require a complete fertilizer in early spring and midsummer. Without rain each week, apply 1 in (3 cm) of water. Mow lawn sixteen or more times per growing season, edge every fourth time.

153. This residential service area for garbage container storage receives heavy pedestrian traffic. It is also located in a shaded microclimate where a lawn would be difficult to establish or maintain. The loose pea gravel, about 0.5 in (1 cm) deep, provides a pavement-like material for safe pedestrian circulation, yet permits the flow of food, moisture, and air to the root system of the Japanese evergreen oak and shrub mass. Walterboro, South Carolina.

MANAGEMENT Every five to eight years, prune the oak (*Quercus acuta*) to remove dead limbs and to increase air circulation to help reduce diseases. Remove fallen oak leaves in the spring and as needed. Feed shrubs and tree with a complete fertilizer, if needed, in late winter. Also prune shrubs to shape and to maintain size in late winter.

154. These concrete and brick mowing strips allow a mower to cut next to planting beds without having to use a string or hand trimmer each time. Trim the grass away from the mowing strips every third mowing for a neat edge. If using concrete, be sure to put in reinforcing bars to control cracking and use expansion joints to allow the material to expand and contract. If using brick, place paving brick flat on top of a steel-reinforced concrete footing. Use a mortar bed to connect the two materials. Brick mowing strips can be one or two bricks wide. If a raised-bed effect is desired, mortar the back bricks on end to the concrete footing. Joints between bricks can either be flush or butt jointed, or they can have a ⅜ in (1 cm) mortar joint that is finished flush with the brick. Like the concrete mowing strip, the concrete foundation for the brick mowing strip must have steel reinforcing bars and expansion joints for durability and long life.

155. Remove grass a minimum distance of 12 in (30 cm) from tree trunks in order to allow for easier mowing. Make the radii large enough to accommodate the size mowing equipment used in order to avoid having to return to trim lawn edges with a smaller mower. Notice the difficulty in mowing around the small tree without the tree ring. If one prefers tree branches to grow to the ground as opposed to being limbed up, mulch 12 in (30 cm) beyond the branches. Otherwise, prune limbs up to avoid being in the way of grass mowing equipment and personnel.

156. When designing earth mounds or berms that will be covered with turfgrass or other plant materials, keep in mind that berms dry out faster than level ground. If they are too steep, or mowed with too wide of a mower, scalping will occur. This picture illustrates both the drying out pattern of berms and scalping. Atlanta, Georgia.

MANAGEMENT Remove turfgrass 12 in (30 cm) from around trees for easier mowing. Mow mounds with a mower 18 in (46 cm) wide. Water mounds every week it does not rain significantly. Trim and remove turfgrass away from walks and planting beds every third mowing. For long-term reduction of landscape management costs, convert grass on mounds to a low-maintenance planting. A ground cover such as ivy (*Hedera*), liriope (*Liriope muscari*), or a low-growing juniper (*Juniperus*) are all suitable and demand less in the way of maintenance. Additionally, the ivy and juniper are drought-tolerant once established.

157. Not all grassed areas have to be mowed regularly. Landscape management zones can be created where management levels of different areas range from intense to intermittent. There are often situations in which a natural meadow or prairie landscape enhances an overall setting and results in savings from reduced mowing costs. If native grasses and wildflowers already exist, continue managing the meadow by mowing once a year before spring growth occurs and after plant seeds are naturally dispersed. If converting a grass field to a meadow, it will take a number of years for non-grass meadow plants, such as *Aster*, goldenrod (*Solidago*), and sunflowers (*Helianthus*), to establish themselves. Columbus, Mississippi.

158. Informally trained on a wire attached to the house, evergreen smilax vine enriches the loggia corner with a pattern of green foliage and cascading stems. The variegated aucuba on the far right repeats the coarse texture of the vine. Begonias planted in the urn provide a cool, summer color. The smilax, aucuba, and begonias grow well in partial shade, as demonstrated in this garden. Starkville, Mississippi.

MANAGEMENT Place an organic mulch material around the smilax (*Smilax lanceolata*) vine and aucuba (*Aucuba japonica* 'Variegata') shrub in late winter. Prune aucuba to maintain in space. In early summer, after new growth has matured or hardened, prune the evergreen smilax to remove dead stems and judiciously thin to maintain within the space. Secure remaining stems to the structure. Fertilize *Begonia* in early summer and midsummer. Irrigate twice weekly. Replace annuals with winter-hardy seasonal plants in late fall where appropriate.

159. This espaliered 'Mine-No-Yuki' cultivar of the fall-blooming evergreen camellia shrub was first attached to the brick wall twenty-five years ago as a 2–3 ft (0.5–1 m) tall plant. Today, it provides an enduring contrasting pattern of color and texture against the bare white wall and emphasizes the entry area of the house. Gulfport, Mississippi.

MANAGEMENT Mulch camellia (*Camellia sasanqua* 'Mine-No-Yuki') with organic material in late winter. After new growth has matured or hardened in summer, prune to remove dead wood and judiciously thin excessive growth to maintain interesting branch pattern against the wall. Secure the remaining branches to the wall. With a well-established espalier, such as this one, fertilize only when foliage color indicates the need. Watch for foliage scale and treat immediately if found.

160. A large sugar hackberry (*Celtis laevigata*) tree is growing on a site scheduled for grade changes. The new grade reaches the bottom of the red bricks in the tree-well protection wall around the tree. The purpose of the tree-well with radiating pipes (see next photo) is to nurse an existing tree through suffocating grade changes. It provides for the circulation of water, food, and air to the tree root system after the soil fill has buried it. The lower photograph illustrates the value of this same tree in front of the building facade twenty-one years later. The tree provides a feeling of enclosure, spatial definition, winter branch patterns and shadows, and summer shade. Mississippi State, Mississippi.

161. This illustrates the methods used in 1964 to establish a concrete foundation for the construction of a brick wall tree-well. Here it is being used around a mature American elm (*Ulmus americana*). Note that the extended concrete pipes from the wall foundation are covered with loose gravel. This permits air, water, and nutrients to percolate through to the soil below after the soil fill is added. The top 8–12 in (20–30 cm) above the gravel will be filled with topsoil to the final proposed top grade. One of the pipe lines extending out from the well must be connected to a storm drainage system or a lower elevation to accommodate excessive rainwater from the bricked tree-well. Today, 4 in (10 cm) perforated plastic pipes are more commonly used rather than short joints of concrete ones as pictured. The holes in perforated plastic pipes are placed downward on the gravel. The solid part of the pipe is placed upward to permit rainwater nearer the original grade to enter the pipe. The interior original soil grade of the bricked well may be mulched with 1 in (3 cm) of washed gravel or it may be planted with a shade-tolerant ground cover, such as bigleaf periwinkle (*Vinca major*). If a tree-well is exceptionally wide, the interior space around the trunk is sometimes decked with wood for a seating area. Mississippi State, Mississippi.

162. Some trees are quite attractive when left unpruned and limbs are allowed to grow to the ground. Often the cutting of limbs is for pedestrian circulation or view, or specific aesthetics. Trees that easily maintain their appeal as unpruned elements include most hollies, cedars, spruce, southern magnolias, and certain juniper or pine species and cultivars. An added benefit to this approach is realized with trees such as magnolias that continually drop large leaves, petals, or fruit. If branches are allowed to grow to the ground, most of the plant debris falls within the plant body, hidden by the outside leaf structure, thus reducing maintenance while enriching the soil. St. Louis, Missouri.

MANAGEMENT Holly (*Ilex*), cedars *Cedrus*, southern magnolia (*Magnolia grandiflora*), juniper (*Juniperus*), and pine (*Pine*) are examples of possible reduced-maintenance tree selections. Almost all types of these trees will do well when left unpruned at the base. To further ease management tasks, if trees are planted in turf areas, create a 12 in (30 cm) wide mulch band to allow mowing equipment to mow around the tree. Remove invading grass from the mulch area in the spring, summer, and fall.

163. Locating a tree so it will eventually have to be pruned away from power lines insures long-term management expense, hazard, and, probably, an ugly, butchered tree. The visual effect of overhead power lines can be reduced by selecting and planting low-growing trees beneath the lines. The tree baffle creates a pedestrian space separate from the street space, and it limits views of the power lines and power poles. Starkville, Mississippi.

MANAGEMENT Prune trees away from the pedestrian and automobile space. Fertilize new street trees with a slow-release, complete fertilizer for several years until they are established. New street trees need at least 1 in (3 cm) of water weekly for the first two years after planting. Apply water slowly at a rate of 5 gal (20 l) per tree, each week during the growing season.

164. This apartment developer tried to preserve as much of the natural woodlands as possible for aesthetic reasons and to reduce landscape management costs. A wide, turf walkway continues throughout the project, providing access and a contrast to the woodlands, allowing residents to stroll about the grounds comfortably. Naturally pruned evergreen shrubs have been planted near the apartment buildings to provide visual transition to the ground plane. Sandy Springs, Georgia.

MANAGEMENT Having natural woodlands is not labor free. Litter needs to be picked up every two weeks. Noxious plants such as poison ivy or poison oak (*Rhus*) and rampant vines such as Japanese honeysuckle (*Lonicera japonica*) need to be removed in spring, summer, and fall. A natural woodland is attractive if it has visual unity. When conditions get scrubby and unkept looking, unity and attractiveness are lost. Leave fallen foliage in wooded areas to accumulate naturally and return to the soil as humus. Spread fall leaves gathered from lawn areas in wooded areas. Prune the shrubs near the building in a naturalistic manner in early spring and summer.

165. Grass would not grow well on this north-facing slope and it would be difficult or hazardous to mow because of its steepness. Ground cover is a solution. As shown, a healthy, uniform ground cover on a slope gives a rich, textured, established look. Kosciusko, Mississippi.

MANAGEMENT Every other year in late winter, mow the English ivy (*Hedera helix*) back to the ground to remove woody stems and promote vigorous growth. Trim the vine away from the walkway in the spring, summer, and late summer.

166. Shrubs planted closely together and mulched correctly can create a favorable impression with minimal management. The India hawthorn shrubs at this entry to a residential development convey a mood of activity and strength, offering contrast to the surrounding lawn areas. The shrub planting directs pedestrians and vehicles to the guardhouse and deters people from cutting through. The cabbage palm trees are used as accents or exclamation points to attract attention to the guardhouse. The firethorn is used to create a pattern on the brick wall and provide seasonal variation. Seabrook Island, South Carolina.

MANAGEMENT Prune the India hawthorn (*Rhapiolepis indica*) shrubs for form and size in late winter and again in early summer. Prune the firethorn (*Pyracantha coccinea*) in late winter for form. Lightly prune this vigorous plant again in summer and late summer to retain its shape. Remove dead leaves from cabbage palms (*Sabal palmetto*) periodically, or leave them hanging for a more naturalistic look. Mulch with a shredded bark in the fall and replenish in early spring. Fertilize shrubs with a slow-release, complete plant food in the spring.

167. Establish ground cover beds around free-standing trees to create easier mowing conditions and to lower management costs. Plastic lawn edging is used around this clump of oak trees and is obscured by the liriope foliage. Also note that the large radius of the bed lines facilitates mowing. The Japanese aucuba adds variety to the overall composition and enriches the journey down the walkway to the front door. Columbus, Mississippi.

MANAGEMENT Cut the liriope (*Liriope muscari*) ground cover back in late winter to allow for new growth. Prune lower branches of oak (*Quercus*) tree to keep the trunks clean and sculptured looking. Prune the Japanese aucuba (*Aucuba japonica*) as needed for form in late winter. Mulch in the fall and replenish in early spring. Japanese aucuba cuttings can be taken year-round and make attractive and long-lived indoor table arrangements.

168. Before the landscape architect was called in, grass extended from the street to the house. Turf quality was poor beneath the trees because of the deep shade conditions. There were a number of understory trees and even the mailbox, blocking or interrupting views to the house from the street.

The solution to poor turf quality was to mulch the areas beneath the trees, creating separate lawn and mulch areas. The time required to mow the front landscape was cut in half. Then ivy was planted on 3 ft (1 m) centers in the mulch under the trees. The ivy will ensure long-term stabilization of the steep slope beneath the trees. Until the ivy vines fill in the area, the centipede grass will be overseeded with winter rye grass to avoid erosion and maintain ground color contrast in the winter. When the dark green ivy produces cover under the trees, the tan winter color of the centipede grass will offer an attractive seasonal contrast and overseeding with rye grass will no longer be necessary. All lawn edges were defined by narrow plastic lawn edging.

The visually pronounced mailbox was moved to the far side of the driveway, out of the main view of the house yet still readily accessible. A row of crape myrtles was planted, beginning along the drive from street-side to where the natural wooded area began. The crape myrtles provide a defined entry and separate the view of the drive from the view of the house. They also contribute a feeling of warmth and welcome through their color and texture and the space they create. Columbus, Mississippi.

MANAGEMENT Until established, fertilize the ivy (*Hedera*) in late winter with a complete, slow-release fertilizer. Remove weeds or grasses in the mulch beds in the spring, early summer, and late summer. Mow the grass fifteen or more times a season. Overseed with annual rye grass in fall each year. Mow the rye grass five times a season. Trim along edges every third mowing. Prune crape myrtles (*Lagerstroemia indica*) into a tree-form in the early spring of each year. Remove suckers from the base of the small trees in the spring, summer, and fall. Fertilize with a low nitrogen, high phosphorus, high potassium fertilizer in late fall.

169. The before picture (top) of the Melby home shows a lack of space definition and generally unfulfilled landscape potential. The front landscape space is part of the same space as the adjacent street. Trees in front of the house were randomly located, thus creating a chaotic series of connected spaces. There was no definition of edges to separate where one residential landscape ended and another began. The unbalanced landscape was difficult and time-consuming to maintain

Eight years later (lower photo) a balanced landscape has been created. The front space is defined and unity is the result. Randomly located trees have been removed, thus creating a more unified, attractive space in proportion with the house. Edges are defined. The viewer clearly sees the separation of the Melby landscape from the neighbor's. A clump of red maple trees, on the left side of the house, and a baffle of crape myrtle trees, on the right adjacent to the deck, create a transition from the house to the front open space. The trees also serve to accent the central part of the house and the front door. Visual unity, variety, and reduced maintenance is the result. Starkville, Mississippi.

13

Shrubs and Trees

Successful growth and appearance of shrubs and trees will follow an accurate assessment of soil and exposure conditions of the site to match plant selection. Continued success comes from proper pruning, fertilizing, watering, and mulching. Correct management of shrubs and trees greatly reduces the chances of diseases, pests, and weed growth, thus ensuring healthy plants. Healthy plants reduce management costs and increase the value of the landscape and property.

With the smaller-scale houses prevalent in urban and suburban areas, pruning may be the most important yet most abused landscape management practice. If a shrub or tree grows too large for its site it is often lopped off simply to crowd it into the space. The natural growth habit of the shrubs or trees must always be considered when pruning. Unfortunately, a great deal of time and money is spent shearing and destroying the natural shape of plants. Some people with pruning clippers or a well-oiled chainsaw in hand often lose sight of their objective.

The following list encompasses most of the valid reasons for pruning shrubs and trees. Consider when preparing to prune whether the situation warrants it. The benefits of pruning must outweigh the resultant shock to the plant. Reasons to prune include:

1. To remove broken, unhealthy, and dead wood. Such parts may harbor diseases and insects, absorb and retain heat, and be hazardous to people, pets, plants, and structures. This pruning is often done at any season.

2. To remove stems or limbs rubbing against other stems. Such movement can injure the bark, thus interrupting the flow of internal life-supporting fluids and inviting disease to the injured tissues. This is usually warranted

at any time of the year. If given a choice however, winter is best since the plant is not in active growth.

3. To stimulate growth. Some plants become leggy without pruning, and growth response as a result of pruning helps to produce a filled-out or bushy plant. Usually this is done when the plant is not in active growth, though sometimes that may be necessary. It is never done late in the growing season as a new flush of growth could be damaged by frost.

4. To maintain a plant within a desired space. This can be effective as long as it is not a total battle with the plant's habit of growth. A pruning battle leaves no victors. Again, site and size must be considered in selection. Minor clipping to allow passage to an area will not burden management. However, topping a 30 ft (9 m) tree to 15 ft (5 m) is a losing battle. The plant will normally respond by growing twice as high. Meanwhile its structure is seriously weakened and its design effect totally destroyed.

5. To maintain a desired plant shape. This may involve removing water sprouts and suckers, or to reintroduce the natural shape after environmental damage, or to maintain an espaliered form.

6. To control disease and insect problems. Removal of excess growth provides for more light and air and healthier growing conditions.

7. To increase flower production. Pruning causes new growth on which some plants flower. This is specific by plant type.

8. To increase fruit production. Also specific by plant, this type of pruning is done in late winter or summer.

9. To create unusual design effects. This is done in creating topiary forms, such as pollarding, espaliering, and pleaching. Also, prune for a more sculptural quality for night lighting and silhouette effects. Such fantasies require frequent pruning and are plant specific.

10. When transplanting. It is appropriate to prune off broken or damaged growth, either limbs or roots. Note that research now holds that it is no longer beneficial to top prune a plant to compensate for root loss.

11. To remove weak stem structure. This is normally done in spring while the plant is actively growing and capable of healing pruning woods. Examples are double crotches or forked trunks that weaken the plant's structure and need correcting.

12. To root prune in order to reduce top growth. Reducing the root system by severing reduces the rate of top growth. Root pruning is done in winter. Sometimes root pruning is part of preparing a plant for transplant.

13. To make tree forms from overgrown shrubs. Generally this is known as training to a standard. It is specific by plant type.

These thirteen points are the reasons to prune a tree or shrub. Correct pruning stimulates a plant to perform at its best, allowing a natural response to the stimulation offered by pruning. Incorrect pruning has the opposite effect, weakening plant structure and development, perhaps fatally.

Begin pruning shrubs when they are young. Waiting until shrubs are rampantly overgrown makes it difficult to prune to fit a space and maintain a natural shape. Some flowering plants, such as Japanese privet (*Ligustrum japonicum*) and shrub althea (*Hibiscus syriacus*), flower on new growth. An increase in new growth and subsequent flowering will result from pruning. Other plants, primarily deciduous ones such as *Spiraea* and *Forsythia*, flower only on old wood. Therefore, it is important to know where plants flower to avoid destroying future flowers by pruning.

A general practice for pruning spring-flowering shrubs, such as *Forsythia*, is to prune right after they flower. This allows a full growing season of new wood which will be the old wood for flowering next year. For those that bloom later, prune in the winter or dormant season. Care should be taken not to prune in late summer or fall, because it will stimulate growth. New growth is easily damaged by cold weather, as it is unable to mature or harden before frost. Evergreen shrubs that do not produce showy blossoms are pruned in late winter before growth commences.

Always prune to the natural shape of shrubs. Prune, *do not shear*, for a natural shape. Study the plant before pruning to decide which branches need control or elimination. Look for those branches which are crowded, dead, rubbing others, broken, infested with insects or diseases, or brushing a structure or the ground.

Try to visualize what the plant will look like with the missing branches. Is its natural shape being honored? Will it maintain its structural integrity? If so, then cut the branches. Be careful not to cause large holes in the shrub mass. Thin some of the older branches by pruning all the way back to the main stems, then prune others proportionately. Always cut just above the joint of a leaf or side branch where new growth will quickly develop during the growing season.

Deciduous shrubs generally grow faster than evergreen types. For fast-growing shrubs, such as *Forsythia*, annually remove approximately one-fourth to one-third of the oldest growth. For deciduous shrubs that develop numerous stems from the ground up, such as *Spiraea*, remove approximately one-fourth of the oldest stems at ground level, rather than partially pruning back from the top. This will encourage more overall growth. Flowering deciduous shrubs normally require one major pruning a year. Time of pruning depends on the plant's flowering season. The major pruning may be followed by an occasional light pruning during the growing season to control the size and maintain the natural shape of the plant.

Narrow-leaved evergreen shrubs require little pruning except for shaping and thinning and removal of unhealthy, dead, or irregularly shaped growth. Also, remember that narrow-leaved evergreens, unlike other type shrubs, do not sprout new growth on old wood if severely pruned. Broad-leaved evergreen shrubs require primarily dormant season pruning or pruning after they flower, as in the case of evergreen *Rhododendron*.

Training or shaping a shrub for the desired natural form requires concentration on plant buds, joints, or nodes that signify a growing point. Always prune back to a growing point. Never leave any wood projecting above it, as it will merely rot back to the joint. Diseases may develop in rotting wood.

A joint looks like a ring around the stem and marks the area where new growth buds originate. If a more spreading growth is desired, prune back to a bud facing outward. If a more vertical natural growth is desired, prune back to a bud facing inward.

If a plant needs thinning, to permit better air circulation and help reduce disease, cut back to a side branch or the trunk. Remove any branches which may be rubbing against other branches to prevent bark damage. Dead wood must be removed back to live wood.

Tip pruning or pinching back will make a young plant bushy. Occasionally, a couple of long shoots may grow that do not relate to the total plant mass and that interrupt its outline. Such shoot growth can be pruned back to a joint within the plant mass.

Some shrubs, such as *Nandina, Mahonia,* and barberry (*Berberis*) have no side branching. Usually new growth is limited to the upper portion of the plant. To keep this type of shrub full and bushy, pruning is needed every year or two. Prune one-fourth to one-third of the oldest vertical stems back to different heights, and prune a few of the oldest back to ground level. Remember always to prune back to a joint.

For a desirable natural shape, which suits many garden design compositions, shrubs should be pruned not sheared. Unfortunately, many landscape plants take on the appearance of meatballs or green-painted plywood boxes due to being sheared rather than pruned. If the reasons for pruning given above are considered, green meatballs and leafy plywood boxes would never enter the landscape. Remember to begin pruning when the plant is young in order for its size to relate to the space and to avoid major pruning, which often results in a visual landscape catastrophe.

Recreating an historic garden design and topiary pieces involves other considerations. If a formal appearance is required, the situation warrants being the one exception to the rule that *pruning* is more attractive on shrubs than *shearing.* Sheared plants with unnatural shapes may be desired in an historic or formal garden or in a fantasyland park. An example of the formal shape is the early American garden style using sheared boxwoods (*Buxus*) or formally sheared hedges. When pruning such a formal garden, first remove any dead or diseased wood and rubbing branches within the plant. Use pruning clippers or a lopper if necessary. If the sheared-hedge effect is desired, shear so that the bottom of the plant is slightly wider than the top to ensure adequate sunlight for foliage growth. Hedge shears are to be used for formal hedges and shapes, not to maintain the natural shape of plants.

Overgrown shrubs can become ideal small-scale trees in a limited landscape space and with low, slab-constructed houses and structures. Therefore, with proper pruning, the overgrown white elephant shrub may transform into a specimen small tree accent. In late winter and on a healthy plant, start by removing a major portion of the lateral branches from the lower two-thirds of the shrub. Thin the remaining ones in the crown or the top of the shrub. Growth sprouts will spring out along the new tree trunks, but after a year or two of diligently removing them this problem will be minimized and easily managed.

Trees are pruned similarly for many of the same reasons as shrubs, yet on a decidedly larger scale. The most common reasons to prune trees is for the removal of diseased, dead, and broken limbs, to control growth hazardous to structures, to increase density of foliage mass, as in the case of open-branching pines and other conifers, to open the interior to improve circulation of air and light, to enhance the visual beauty of the branch pattern, and to yield more effective outdoor lighting.

General guidelines suggest that in removing dead tree limbs, cut back slightly into the living wood. Also removing excessive interior growth provides for more light and air and healthier growing conditions. It can also allow a more dramatic branch pattern for winter and uplighting effects for deciduous trees. For maximum healing, limbs should be cut *almost* flush with the trunk.

Be careful not to cut into the bark collar (see Figure 13-1), the ridge around the side limb at the trunk. For better and more rapid healing of the wound after removing a limb, this bark collar should remain intact. In removing limbs, when a statement is made "to cut back to the trunk," it means to cut back only to the raised bark ridge at the trunk. The bark collar will keep the wound smaller and provide more rapid healing.

Trees may be pruned in winter or summer. During winter dormancy there will be less sap bleeding since sap is not actively flowing. It is best not to prune trees when foliage is appearing or falling to avoid excessive bleeding of sap.

Figure 13-1. Tree pruning.

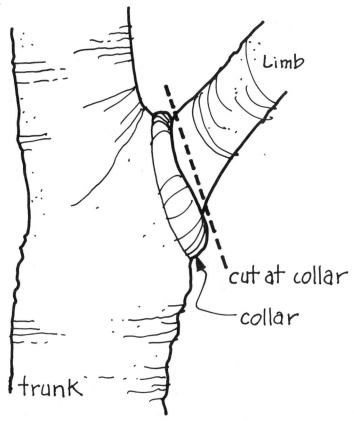

To avoid damaging the tree when cutting a large and heavy limb, first undercut approximately one-third of the limb diameter (about 6 in/15 cm) toward the trunk below the place the top cut will be made. Then, make a second cut on top a few inches or centimeters beyond the undercut. A very important third cut is made near the trunk to remove the remaining stub, being careful to leave the bark collar intact.

For removal of large branches at the trunk or from the limbs, sometimes it may be necessary to tie a rope to the limb to be removed. Loop the rope over a strong limb above the one to be removed, and lower the cut limb gently to the ground to prevent damage to other parts of the tree or nearby objects.

In addition to removing large primary limbs at the trunk, smaller branches (known as secondary branches) can be removed from large horizontal branches to allow opening to air and sunlight. These branches are pruned flush with the horizontal branch.

Any cut larger than 1 in (3 cm) may be painted with a latex paint, such as semigloss dark brown. However, this is for aesthetics only. Research indicates that painting pruning wounds may actually retard healing.

Sometimes it is desirable to prune the roots of a tree. Root pruning is done to retard tree growth in limited spaces, protect existing hard construction, conserve open space, or to maintain an espalier. Root prune in the winter. A majority of the tree's feeder roots are in the top 12–18 in (30–46 cm) of the soil. Feeder roots are located horizontally at and beyond the canopy dripline. To root prune, push a spade all the way down at different places of the dripline circling the tree. To retard, yet not halt tree growth, spade down in enough places on the circle to equal one-third the tree's circumference. This will cut approximately one-third of the root system and reduce the tree's top growth.

Root pruning is also helpful when transplanting an existing tree. A year prior to transplanting, estimate the width of the soil ball or root spread needed for successful transplanting. To estimate it, the soil ball diameter measurement will be 10–12 in (25–30 cm) for each 1 in (3 cm) of the trunk diameter. For example, a tree with a 2 in (5 cm) diameter will require a soil ball with a 20–24 in (50–60 cm) diameter. Dig alternating sections of a trench 12–18 in (30–46 cm) deep to define the edge of the soil ball to be dug the following year. These trenches, approximately one-third the canopy circumference, will alternate with non-dug, undisturbed soil. Now refill the trenches with the removed soil, pack down, and water in.

Root pruning is a practice that causes new roots to grow in the loose soil where root pruning occurs. Many new roots give a tree a better chance for survival after transplanting. The difference between this root pruning practice and root pruning to retard tree growth is that all existing roots beyond the defined circumference are removed when the tree is transplanted. In pruning to retard top growth, roots in soil areas not trenched will remain active.

Basic hand tools for pruning informal, naturally shaped shrubs include hand clippers, long-handled loppers, and possibly a small hand saw. For formally shaped shrubs and hedges, small hand clippers, for removing interior dead wood, and shears, for cutting back branches uniformly, are needed. For pruning trees, hand clippers, long-handled loppers, a small hand saw, a rope, and ladder are needed. It is important that all clippers and saws be kept sharp for easier, less damaging, and less hazardous pruning.

Further management of trees and shrubs may involve fertilization, particularly if plants are growing in lean, sandy soil. Fertilization may also be needed following environmental stress from insects, diseases, or drought. A soil sample must be taken to determine what, if any, nutrients are needed. The local county extension agent can provide instructions on how to take soil samples. Most extension services can also direct gardeners to a reliable soil testing laboratory where soil can be tested for a minor fee. Tests can be elaborate or a simple N-P-K analysis. Soil testing services are usually provided at land grant universities and independent labs. By specifying which plants one intends to grow or is growing, the testing laboratories will offer recommendations on the type and amount of fertilizer to use.

Early spring is the best time for growth stimulants for most shrubs. These are fertilizers heavy in nitrogen. Avoid the use of nitrogen after mid-August in most regions, in order that the plants can harden before the first killing frost. Otherwise, new growth may be severely damaged or killed. The fall is the time to winterize plants. Use a fertilizer with only phosphorus and potassium, elements which do not stimulate growth.

Chemical fertilizer may be broadcast among shrubs or sprayed on the foliage. If broadcast on a tight soil surface, it may be useful to scratch the surface for better penetration and less runoff due to rainfall or slope. Little or no fertilizer may be needed the first three years after planting shrubs, particularly if using a composted mulch each year.

Dr. Alex L. Shigo, a nationally recognized tree management authority from New Hampshire, recommends that deciduous trees be fertilized in early spring as the foliage appears. There are several ways to apply fertilizer for trees which the average gardener can use. They include broadcasting fertilizer at the dripline, placing dry fertilizer in holes in the soil, or spraying it on the foliage. The broadcast method is normally the most practical.

To broadcast fertilizer is to spread it with a mechanical distributor, usually non-motorized. A mechanical spreader for the broadcast method may be designed for shoulder use, or wheeled varieties are also available. Both of these spreaders have calibrations to accurately broadcast the correct amount of fertilizer. Broadcasting fertilizer by hand is not recommended for the obvious reason that accuracy is not possible. Too much fertilizer can damage plants.

For lawn trees, care must be taken not to fertilize too early in the year. Otherwise, turf growth under them may be stimulated and damaged by late cold spells. If in doubt, wait. Remember, the root system of a tree may be two to four times the tree canopy diameter. It is necessary to place the food where the feeder roots are, usually out near the canopy edge (dripline) and beyond. Trees should never be fertilized within 12 in (30 cm) of the trunk because of possible injury to the root collar and trunk base. The type and amount of fertilizer to use can be determined by a soil test.

Another method for fertilizing trees in a lawn is to establish fertilizer holes located equally around the circumference of the dripline and beyond. The holes can be made at a 60° angle with an electric soil auger, a punch bar, or a post-hole digger. Place a mixture of sand and a complete fertilizer in a 1–2 in (3–5 cm) diameter hole 12–18 in (30–46 cm) deep in the soil. The hole mixture should be 1 part sand to .5 part dry fertilizer. Use 2–4 lbs (0.9–1.8 kg) of a complete fertilizer for each inch (3 cm) of trunk diameter measured at 4.5 ft (1.4 m) above the ground. For example, an 8 in (20 cm) diameter trunk requires 16–32 lb (8–16 kg) of a complete fertilizer. Trees with less than a 6 in (15 cm) diameter require 1–2 lb (0.4–0.9 kg) fertilizer per inch (3 cm). Water and cover the fertilizer holes with soil or sand to prevent waste from splashing. This method is effective for use only in light soils through which water and the fertilizer will move freely. It is not suitable for heavy clay soils.

Young trees, depending on specific plants, can be fertilized every year after their first to encourage growth. When a desired size is reached, the application of fertilizer can be less frequent. Large trees will need little if any fertilizer.

After determining the need and method for fertilizing trees and shrubs, one is then faced with the array of fertilizers available. One popular form is the slow-release fertilizer, valuable in reducing the chance of burning plants by over fertilizing, in preventing leaching of fertilizers which cannot be rapidly absorbed by plants, and in helping reduce late frost damage to surrounding lawns in the spring. Slow-release fertilizer releases nutrients gradually over a variable period of time, anywhere from two weeks to eighteen months—depending on temperature, moisture, and microbes (minute life forms). There are three types of slow-release fertilizers—synthetic organic fertilizers, coated fertilizers, and natural, organic fertilizers.

Synthetic organic fertilizers break down in the soil to form ammonium and nitrate ions which plants can use. The absorption of these two ions is the end product of all fertilization for plants. Examples of synthetic organic fertilizers are IBDU (isobutylidene diurea) and UF (urea formaldehyde).

The coated type is a soluble fertilizer coated with a plastic material (polymer) or sulfur and the fertilizer gradually leaks out. The natural, organic type is heat treated, dried, and consists of compressed manures and compost which break down biologically and release nutrients.

Slow-release fertilizer is available as a solid or liquid. The nitrogren content can be high, usually 25% to 30%, but due to its slow release there is no danger of plants being burned. Slow-release fertilizer is available for trees, shrubs, vines, and lawns, and its product cost is approximately twice that of the quick-acting fertilizers. Information about the rate of application of slow-release fertilizers is printed on its packaging.

Mulching shrubs and trees begins with their introduction to the landscape. The time to apply an organic mulch is right after shrubs and trees are planted and the soil is settled. Mulching helps reduce management efforts: it conserves soil moisture, reduces or eliminates dreaded soil compaction, moderates soil temperature changes, eliminates soil erosion, and limits weed growth. And the addition of organic matter always improves soil structure over time.

A 12–18 in (30–46 cm) wide mulched surface around tree trunks in the open lawn can eliminate hand trimming of the turf in that area after each mowing. The mulched area also helps reduce trunk damage caused by mowers and string trimmers. Most gardeners eventually learn that improper use of string trimmers and mechanical equipment causes extensive, often fatal damage to a tree. The trimmers and equipment can cut the life line just under the bark, the thin layer of living tissues known as the cambium layer. This bark layer is vital and must be protected from damage.

According to tree expert Dr. Shigo, a suitable mulch consists of composted leaves and wood chips, because this can allow mycorrhiza to evolve. Mycorrhiza is a mutually beneficial association of root and fungus tissues living in the top 2 in (5 cm) of soil which absorb water. Other suitable mulches are shredded bark, shredded corn cobs, or pine straw, as well as those given in chapter 11.

If plant roots grow into the mulch, the mulch is too deep and should be thinned by removal. Many landscape managers maintain their mulch at 4 in (10 cm) of settled organic material.

Mulching management is needed every year, and twice a year if the mulch decomposes rapidly. In warm climates, mulches are added each year in the fall and again prior to spring growth. In colder climates, mulch is added after the ground freezes in the fall to prevent thawing and refreezing of soils which can damage plants. Remember, the mulch must be light and friable (loose) enough for air and water to flow through the mulch to the soil.

Watering in after planting shrubs and trees is a primary management practice. Watering for growth and transplanting recovery is critical. This is especially true throughout the first two years while plants are getting established. It is best to deeply water once every week during the growing season when there is not a soaking rain. Frequent light sprinklings cause roots to come to the surface seeking the limited water, making the plant roots susceptible to damage by droughts. Water during the winter even after plants are well established if the plant site is usually dry.

Drip irrigation or the simple open-hose method is preferable to sprinkler irrigation. Water soaks in more thoroughly while allowing less evaporation and runoff. Also, with drip irrigation water does not wet the foliage. Damp leaves tend to invite sunscald or leaf fungus. To reduce evaporation, irrigate in the early morning.

14

Vines, Espaliers, and Ground Covers

After lawns, vines and espaliers may require the most care. Vines and espaliers can provide very positive aesthetic enrichment to garden design or contribute functional value through possible energy conservation and privacy. In smaller-sized home landscapes, vines and espaliers can provide plant patterns, textures, colors, shade and shadows, and spatial definition in restricted space areas that are too small for shrubs or trees.

Climbing vines cling naturally to structures and surfaces mainly in one of three ways: (1) by means of rootlets attaching themselves to masonry, wood, or bark surfaces; (2) by twining around nearby objects, such as tree trunks, arbors, and other structures; or (3) by tendrils or string-like appendages wrapping around objects.

In addition to climbing vines, some shrubs, such as roses and a few twiggy plants, tend to climb and may be treated as vines. Knowledge of how a plant clings is of value in its management. Climbing vines may also be evergreen or deciduous. This influences management commitments as well, primarily because of leaf removal. Vines with rootlets, such as Boston ivy (*Parthenocissus tricuspidata*), trumpet vine (*Campsis radicans*), and English ivy (*Hedera helix*), train themselves. The major management requirement for vines with rootlets is to keep the vines under control and off certain surfaces. Structural wood, for example, can be damaged over a period of time. The rootlets accumulate dust and other organic, moisture-holding particles that eventually discolor or damage wood. If the vine is later pulled off the wood or other surfaces, its rootlets often remain attached to the surface. For that reason, vines which attach by rootlets are best for use on non-wood surfaces and surfaces that will not be painted.

Incidentally, English ivy (*Hedera helix*) will not strangle a tree. It is typically a vigorous vine, yet its threat to a tree's life is not in strangulation. However, if left uncontrolled, its weight can break limbs and its density may harbor pests, rodent populations, and diseases.

Twining vines, such as Carolina jessamine (*Gelsemium sempervirens*), some honeysuckle (*Lonicera*), and *Wisteria*, may need help in clinging to an object in an orderly manner. This type of vine may require being tied to whatever it is to climb until it begins to twine around its support naturally.

Vines with tendrils (stringlike appendages) include coral vine (*Antigonon leptopus*) and smilax (*Smilax lanceolata*). These vines will quickly attach to three-dimensional objects, though they will not attach to flat, solid masses, such as a brick wall.

All vines require periodic pruning, not shearing, to thin and to contain within a desired space. If on an arbor, trellis, or wall, remove growth extending far out from the overall vine mass or pattern. Also, thin interior growth. Dense interior growth may become extra thick and make the plant too heavy for its support. Such growth will also block the penetration of light and air needed for healthy growth.

Some vines, such as wisterias, grow rampantly. It is necessary to thin by removing some of the interior growth as well as new growth extending out beyond the total mass. Vines are like shrubs and trees in requiring interior space or voids for the circulation of air and penetration of light to help prevent diseases and to reduce mass.

For spring-flowering vines, prune after flowering. For most other vines, prune in late winter while the plant is still dormant. There are exceptions, of course. Grape (*Vitis*) vines are pruned anytime after the foliage falls and before growth begins in early spring. Muscadine (*Vitis rotundifolia*) vines are best pruned within six weeks after the first killing frost to prevent excessive sap bleeding. For highest fruit production, fruiting vines generally require annual pruning back to 6–8 in (15–20 cm) from the main vine, leaving two joints (nodes) for growth to originate on the side stem.

Except for fruiting vines, feed vines in early spring. Use a complete fertilizer of nitrogen, phosphorus, and potash, such as 13-13-13. Fruiting vines are fed in the spring, too, but with a fertilizer low in nitrogen and high in phosphorus and potash for the production of fruit.

As with all plants, vines develop more vigorously when mulched. Mulching the root area is particularly effective if there are hard construction materials nearby that absorb and reflect heat, such as masonry, asphalt, or stone.

An espalier involves a vine, shrub, or tree forced by pruning and pinning to grow flat. The plant can be trained to wires or slats, or against a wall or fence. Espaliered fruit trees, such as apple (*Malus*), peach (*Prunus*), and pear (*Pyrus*), are commonly trained to wires for crop production purposes and to define and enclose space decoratively. Espaliers provide a strong visual effect (see photos 141, 159) and require intensive management.

The espaliered plant originated in the medieval era in Europe for growing fruit trees in a limited space, and it retains that merit today. However, for home landscapes, it is most often used for the aesthetic effects of foliage pattern, texture, color, flower, or fruit in a formal or informal manner. In the United States, espaliered trees were also used for fruit production at the famous historic sites of Mt. Vernon and Williamsburg, Virginia.

To begin training an espalier, start by selecting a plant that readily branches yet will not exceed the space available despite the annual pruning required for training. For example, a southern magnolia (*Magnolia grandiflora*) is too large a plant to be espaliered even on a two-story wall. Other magnolia species may be better suited, such as star magnolia (*Magnolia stellata*).

Also, consider the rate of growth of the plant. Fast-growing deciduous flowering shrubs, such as *Forsythia*, will provide spectacular flower color and winter stem patterns and they demand intensive management. A sasanqua camellia (*Camellia sasanqua*), a Japanese holly (*Ilex crenata*), or dwarf fruit trees are all plants suitable to a moderate management effort.

After selecting the type of plant for the intended site, select a small, young plant that has horizontal side branches. These are known as the lateral branches. Usually, the shrub or tree to be espaliered is planted adjacent to a wall and tilted toward it. It may be necessary to remove some laterals from the trunk or leader on the wall side to get it to flatten against the wall. Attach the main trunk or leader of the plant to the wall with a soft material that will not cut into the bark. This material may be rubber or elastic, wrapped loosely around the stem and attached to the structure.

To pin the plant to brick or stone walls use a short, stout nail driven into the mortar joint. If the wall is concrete, drill holes and drive lead anchors into the holes. Then, attach either concrete nails or screws into the lead anchors. Tie the main trunk to the structure with as few ties as necessary to establish support. Several strong side branches (laterals) are then attached to the wall. Remove any other branches which do not naturally lean toward the wall.

Each year, to achieve the desired design effect, some branches are removed and some are attached to the wall. The best time to pin branches against the wall and to prune is after the spring growth matures or hardens in early summer. Prune and pin while branches remain soft enough to bend without breaking. Thereafter, periodic minor branch removal and pinning may be needed during the growing season to maintain a neat espaliered effect.

Caution: personal experience has illustrated that wasps often build nests in espaliered plants and vines and can be a hazard when pruning the plant in summer. Therefore, any wasps' nests should be removed the day or night before pruning and pinning.

If the espaliered effect is to be formal and symmetrical, more management is required than if informal. If the plant grows too tall for the space, top prune. Vigorous growth can also be temporarily restrained by root pruning. This is usually done by making a half circle around the plant and pushing a spade its full depth into the soil. Begin circling 4–5 ft (1.2–1.5 m) from the major trunk of the plant. After a year, if growth is still rampant, circle closer to the trunk with a spade.

Fertilizing espaliered plants is a bit more constrained than with some landscape plantings. In early spring, an espaliered plant may be fertilized with a composted mulch or a complete chemical food. A complete chemical fertilizer provides nitrogen, phosphorus, and potash, such as 13-13-13. To better control the growth and management requirements of the plant, however, limit the use of nitrogen.

Early spring is the most effective time to mulch espaliered plants for the benefits of moisture conservation and weed control. Mulch again in the fall, if the mulch has deteriorated, to moderate temperature extremes of winter. Do not mulch deeper than 4 in (10 cm), or roots may grow into the mulch, thereby increasing plant vulnerability to freezes and droughts.

A ground cover planting uses low-growing plants that usually do not exceed 18–24 in (46–61 cm) in height. Plantings are usually evergreens, though deciduous ground covers can be used. Plant selection depends on the design effect desired. Design considerations involve all the elements of visual design, plus some consideration as to fragrance possibilities and foot traffic potential. Some ground covers respond to being walked on by yielding a wonderful fragrance. Other ground covers respond to foot traffic by wilting and dying.

Some ground covers, such as English ivy (*Hedera helix*), spread by creeping and branching on the ground. It has been said about the growth of English ivy that the first year it sleeps, the second year it creeps, and the third year it leaps. Once established, it tends to spread rapidly. Other plants cover the ground by increasing the number of individual plants by underground roots called stolons. One example of a stoloniferous ground cover is creeping lily turf (*Liriope spicata*). A plant that multiples through stolons often requires more management in a limited planting area, and it is difficult to eradicate once established. Some ground covers increase in size by producing new plants in a clump, such as liriope (*Liriope muscari*). This liriope species is fairly easy to maintain in a limited space. For efficient management it is important to know how a plant grows before using it as a ground cover.

A ground cover is often used in place of lawns on steep slopes or in limited areas where mowing would be a problem or downright hazardous. It is also used as a surface material in widely spaced shrub and tree groupings to reduce weed growth and to be aesthetically pleasing by serving as a unifying element.

A ground cover can also be considered in terms of non-living materials, such as bark and gravel. The landscape beauty of a living ground cover is generally more design effective than a non-living ground cover. The range presented in colors, textures, and forms is inherently greater. However, there is a place for both. Non-living ground covers may even be a necessity in water-restricted areas. Living ground covers soften hard construction materials, reduce heat reflection and absorption, and add vitality to the design.

Establishing a ground cover planting requires fairly intensive management in the early years due to the small plant size and limited root system. However, management considerations begin with thorough soil preparation before planting can start. Check pH levels, work in organic materials, and let the area settle before planting.

Place the plants in staggered positions, like the black squares on a checkerboard. Staggering the plants helps provide quicker foliage coverage and shade for the soil, thus helping to reduce weed growth. After planting the ground cover it will need immediate watering and mulching. Use an organic mulch that is reasonably light textured and friable in order not to injure the small, somewhat fragile ground cover plants. The new planting should receive 1 in (3 cm) of water each week there is not a soaking rain during the first growing season. This amount of water will moisten the soil to a depth of 6 in (15 cm). Thereafter, irrigate only during prolonged droughts of three weeks or more.

Unless ground cover foliage is damaged by severe weather conditions, or the plants outgrow the space, seldom is any pruning necessary. If pruning is warranted, prune ground covers in early spring before growth commences. Whether pruned manually with hand clippers or electric ones, the pruned materials are removed and an organic mulch then added for moisture conservation and to supply food for growth. Removal of pruned materials is for appearance, since they are unharmonious as they deteriorate.

Some ground covers react positively to being mowed in late winter. Use a sharp mower blade set higher than for turf. Mondo grass (*Ophiopogon japonicus*), *Liriope muscari*, and Asian jasmine (*Trachelospermum asiaticum*) relate well to pruning by mowing. It is important to mow these types before growth commences, otherwise, the tips will look butchered throughout the summer. After mowing, the shorn foliage should be removed and placed in a composting bin. Add fresh organic mulch or compost.

During the growing season, some ground covers may require light pruning to keep growth away from activity areas, wall surfaces, and the lawn. Always cut back to a leaf or side shoot of trailing ground covers like English ivy, or to the ground in the case of stoloniferous ground covers like mondo grass.

A year after planting, feed ground covers with a complete (13-13-13) slow-release fertilizer in early spring. That fall, fertilize again with phosphorus and potash (0-20-20) to winterize the plants. After two or three years, when the ground cover is well established, an annual application of a friable or loose compost mulch may eliminate the need for adding any chemical fertilizer.

Mulching a ground cover for moisture conservation is most important in the early years when plants are getting established. Later, the foliage usually develops thickly enough to provide sufficient shade for weed control and soil heat relief. Mulching with compost has the benefit of providing valuable nutrients. A loose or friable mulch will sift down easily through the plant foliage to the soil. Sometimes a stone mulch helps in maintaining drainage, particularly with plants that are susceptible to root rot.

In the first two to three years of establishing a ground cover, watering and mulching regularly are essential. Once the foliage provides shade for the plant roots and soil, watering and mulching requirements lessen. For fast growth, water ground covers any week it does not rain. A drip irrigation system is ideal for slowly watering ground covers on a slope or other situation; it wets the ground, not the foliage. If watering with sprinklers, an early morning application reduces water loss due to evaporation and permits the foliage to dry before dark. Damp nighttime foliage generally invites fungus growth. Watering plants during the hot part of the day may cause foliage burn and waste water through evaporation.

15

Flowers

Flowering effects in a garden are provided by herbaceous plants (annuals, biennials, and perennials), bulbous plants, and by woody plants such as shrubs and trees and some vines. The woody plants provide the major backbone or framework of a garden design due to their year-round visibility, and they are discussed in chapter 13. Flowering vines are covered in chapter 14.

Herbaceous and bulbous plants are used in a secondary manner because of their seasonal appearance. They are best used in conjunction with woody plants, perhaps in incurves with a background of permanent woody plants. Used this way, the green background enhances the seasonal flower color. Further, as herbaceous and bulbous plants experience a rest period, background plants provide needed garden design support.

This discussion will relate to the use and management of herbaceous plants and bulbs. We will describe in general terms how they differ from one another and how to manage their varying needs. Though herbaceous plants are used in a secondary manner, this is not to imply that herbaceous plant elements are insignificant. They provide effective seasonal color and texture and usually involve more management than woody plants. Most herbaceous and bulbous plants prefer full sun, though many will survive and flower to some degree in partial shade.

Herbaceous plants are fleshy plants which die down in winter. Their role is secondary because they are not permanently visible all year. For this reason, the main garden design structure should be planned without dependence on the herbaceous plants. Use herbaceous plants only to add effective seasonal color and texture. Expect that they will require more management than woody trees and shrubs.

Annuals, biennials, and perennials are the three types of herbaceous plants. These terms refer to typical life cycles and affect plant choices. An annual is a fleshy plant produced from a seed. It produces foliage and flowers and completes its life cycle in only one year. Common bedding annuals are marigold (*Tagetes*), *Zinnia*, and *Impatiens*. A biennial is a fleshy plant produced from a seed, maturing and producing flowers only in its second year and then dying. Some foxglove (*Digitalis purpurea*) are biennial, yet for garden purposes biennials are often treated as annuals. English daisy (*Bellis perennis*) is an example of a perennial treated as an annual for winter bloom in the South.

An herbaceous perennial is a fleshy plant produced by the division of plants. The division of a perennial clump keeps the mother plant vigorous and provides new plants by the separation of the clump. Division also is used to control plant size and proportion in a design composition.

Perennials produce new foliage and flowers each year, growing from season to season. *Chrysanthemum,* daylilies (*Hemerocallis*), and summer phlox (*Phlox paniculata*) are perennial plants. Annuals, biennials, and perennials provide seasonal color in the landscape. To be most effective, these herbaceous plants require attentive management.

Fertilizing herbaceous plants is a necessary part of their management. (Bulbous plants have different requirements and will be discussed separately.) To avoid the chance of fertilizer burn, the best supplement is composted material placed around plants. Perennials and biennials require feeding in the late winter, spring, and summer, or a slight handful, about one-eighth of a cup (30 grams), of a complete fertilizer (13-13-13) per plant may be spread on the ground several times a year, and worked lightly into the soil with a forked tool. Follow this by soaking the soil with water. A low nitrogen food is best for all flowering herbaceous plants. Too much nitrogen encourages more foliage than flowers. For long-term feeding, natural slow-release fertilizers, such as cottonseed meal and well-rotted barnyard manures, perform admirably.

Some tall-growing, non-woody flowering plants tend to fall over as they grow if they are not staked. The best time to stake these plants is before they lean. Supports may be twiggy materials, such as small branches of deciduous shrubs or trees, or supports commercially produced for staking, such as wire rings or interlocking stakes. If a plant has only a few stems, each stem may be staked. If there are many stems it is usually easiest to enclose the group with stakes. If using twiggy materials, circle around the stakes with a soft string.

For peak blossom performance and display, it is essential to pick off dead flowers of all herbaceous plants. This is "dead-heading." In addition to improving the appearance of the landscape, dead-heading prevents seed production, which saps energy from the plant, and it usually encourages further flowering. When a plant begins to produce seeds, flowering stops. Dead-heading and merely pinching growth tips causes more tip growth, thus more blossoms. Dead-head weekly and twice weekly during the peak flowering season. Annuals will require the most dead-heading for flowering production and biennials may produce a second crop of blossoms as a result of this management practice. Some perennials, such as blue sage (*Salvia farinacea*), can be pruned back somewhat heavily and watered in late summer and additional blossoms will develop. On the other hand, perennials such as the lenten rose (*Helleborus orientalis*) produce attractive dried flowers and seeds which enhance seasonal garden beauty. In some cases, such as in naturalized design, little if any dead-heading is desirable in order that the plants will reseed themselves.

Most fleshy plants require substantial watering for growth and flower production. Moist yet not soggy soil encourages plant performance. To help conserve water and to protect root systems from the sun's heat, an organic mulch several inches (centimeters) deep is of value. Usually, mulching benefits start at the time of planting. The material used may be pine straw, crushed pine bark, shredded hardwood bark, or compost.

The best time to water is early in the morning before the sun's heat intensifies and water droplets can cause foliage burn. Also, if foliage becomes wet, as with sprinkler use, watering early in the day permits it to dry before night when fungus may develop on moist foliage. Soaker type irrigation provides less water loss due to evaporation, as well as causing less damage to fragile plants. Ideally, for any week without rainfall, apply 1 in (3 cm) of water by irrigation. To measure that amount, space out small cans under the irrigation spray and when they fill with 1 in (3 cm) of water, turn off the irrigation system. The soil will be moistened to an approximate depth of 6 in (15 cm), depending on soil type.

Annuals and biennials cannot be divided to multiply or increase growth. Perennials are divided to induce or maintain vigor, to control the size of the plant clump, and to yield additional plants. How often perennials should be divided depends on the individual plant species and its performance. Many require dividing only every three to four years. A few perennials grow so rapidly they may need dividing annually.

When perennials should be divided is based on their flowering season. Division is done opposite the flowering season, with winter being excluded. For example, if the plant blossoms in spring or summer, divide in the fall. If it flowers in fall, divide in early spring. Some plants can simply be pulled apart at the roots after they are dug up. Some require cutting with a sharp spade or knife to divide them as they are dug. Either way, take care to leave roots and several eyes (growth buds) on each division. Replant in prepared soil with the roots spread out. Gently place soil over the roots with the eyes slightly above the soil level. Water after planting. The soil preparation for replanting divisions is similar to that for bulbous plants and is given at the end of this chapter.

Some of the most popular spring- and summer-flowering perennials include bulbous plants. Plants generated from bulbs, tubers, corms, tuberous roots, and rhizomes together represent what are known as bulbous plants. Tulips (*Tulipa*), daffodils (*Narcissus*), lilies (*Lilium*), and hyacinths (*Hyacinthus*) develop from bulbs. *Anemone*, lily of the valley (*Convallaria majalis*), and peonies (*Paeonia*) share the pip-type rootstock. Corms are the source for *Gladiolus*, *Crocus*, and *Freesia*. Tuberous roots produce *Ranunculus* and *Dahlia*. Rhizomes produce *Canna*, *Iris*, and *Calla*.

The life cycle of bulbous plants involves the production of foliage and flowers each season and the storing of energy in bulb-like organs (the tubers, tuberous roots, corms, or rhizomes) below the soil surface. Plants then become dormant for several months. Most bulbs, such as daffodils and lilies, die down seasonally. A few are evergreen in the South, such as bearded irises (*Iris* × *germanica*). Management efforts are in fertilizing, mulching, dead-heading, watering, and division. Tender bulbous plants, such as some dahlias and *Caladium*, are typically lifted from the garden before winter.

For established bulbous plants, fertilize in the spring with a complete fertilizer (13-13-13) when the bulb tips emerge from the soil. In the fall, work bone meal lightly into the soil to provide an organic, slow-acting phosphate source for the development of strong stems. In the winter, a light sprinkling of wood ashes can add needed potash for root growth.

A composted mulch of 2–3 in (5–8 cm) will help protect bulbous plants from stresses due to summer heat and winter cold. Mulching will also conserve moisture and reduce weed growth.

The removal of flower heads after blooming is essential. This prevents the bulbous plants from sacrificing energy to produce unwanted seeds, and will enhance the garden's appearance. Immediately after flowering and dead-heading, the plant can begin storing energy for the next blooming period. The energy source comes from the plant's leaves, which allow photosynthesis. For this reason, foliage should never be removed until it yellows in late spring or early summer. Therefore, it is not advisable to plant bulbous perennials in lawn areas that require frequent mowing. Mowing may remove the foliage before it serves its function of gathering energy for the bulb.

Many bulbs are effective in perennial borders or as underplantings in ground covers, or in naturalizing an area. A naturalized area is one usually under light tree cover and has an informal, natural appearance. *Narcissus, Crocus,* and spider lily (*Lycoris*) are effective in naturalized areas among trees, as long as they get enough filtered light.

Usually there is sufficient seasonal rainfall for established spring-flowering bulbs. For summer-flowering bulbs, water as for other perennials. This means that during any week in which there is no rainfall, moisten the soil to a depth of 6 in (15 cm) with approximately 1 in (3 cm) of water. Lily bulbs require some moisture throughout the year since they are never completely dormant. In winter, water only enough to keep them from drying out. For all bulb types, additional water is needed primarily to settle the soil of new plantings.

Most bulbous plants require dividing every three to four years. Naturalized bulbs may need dividing every five to six years. Bulbous plants display the need to be divided when blossoms are smaller in size and fewer in number. As soon as the foliage yellows, bulbs can be dug for division. After digging, shake off soil and let bulbs dry in a partially shaded area on a structure above grade, such as on a table top or wire screen. After drying, they may be stored in a cool place.

Spring-flowering bulbs are planted in late fall. Summer- and fall-flowering ones can be planted in the spring. When planting bulbs remove the soil to the depth indicated in Figure 15-1 or slightly more. Gently press the bulbs into the soil to keep them erect, with the pointed end or sprout up, and refill the hole with the friable soil mix. Water the planting to settle the soil then mulch to conserve moisture and moderate summer heat and winter cold.

Usually bulbous plants are planted in masses or drifts. Therefore, the planting hole has to be wide enough to readily accommodate a number of bulbs. Spacing of the spring-flowering bulbs varies with the type and variety. Tulips (*Tulipa*) are set about 4–6

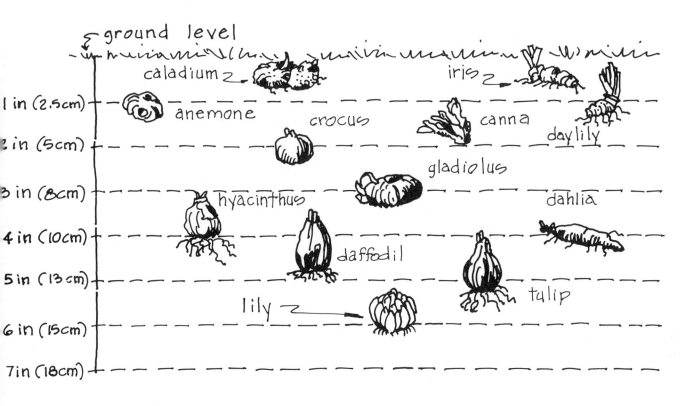

Figure 15-1. Bulb planting depths.

in (10–15 cm) apart, daffodils (*Narcissus*) 6–8 in (15–20 cm), hyacinths (*Hyacinthus*) 3–6 in (8–15 cm), *Crocus* 3–5 in (8–13 cm), Dutch and Siberian *Iris* 2–4 in (5–10 cm), and bearded iris (*Iris × germanica*) 8–10 in (20–25 cm). For summer-flowering plants, many of which are tuberous roots, the spacing is approximately: *Dahlia* 2–3 ft (0.5–1 m), lily (*Lilium*) 1.5–2.0 ft (0.5–0.6 m), *Gladiolus* 8–10 in (20–25 cm), *Canna* 10–15 in (25–38 cm) and daylily (*Hemerocallis*) 2.0–2.5 ft (0.6–0.8 m).

Planting herbaceous and bulbous plants requires specific soil preparation. For most vigorous growth, these plants demand both adequate subsurface and surface drainage. None will last long in soggy soil. Bed preparation may be accomplished in several ways depending on existing soil conditions. In well-drained soil, spread 2–4 in (5–10 cm) of organic material and cultivate it 9–12 in (23–30 cm) deep into the soil. Also add one heaping teaspoon (0.5 ml) of a high phosphorus, low nitrogen fertilizer (5–10–5) for every square foot of soil surface. For tight, heavy soils, add 0.5 in (1 cm) of mason's sand (regular construction sand used in making concrete and mortar), 2–4 in (5–10 cm) of organic matter, and one heaping teaspoon (0.5 ml) of high phosphorus/low nitrogen fertilizer for every square foot of soil surface. Mix thoroughly. Plant the herbaceous plants in the well-prepared soil, water, and mulch.

16

Regarding Pests and Diseases

Even well-planned gardens can be rapidly undone by infestation and disease. Establishing a healthy garden starts with soil preparation and appropriate plant selection. Certain plants, such as roses (*Rosa*), seem to bring their own host of potential problems. Maintaining a healthy garden is possible if a gardener learns to identify symptoms so proper precautions can be taken or proper treatment given.

Any garden plan can be damaged overnight by pests, particularly insects, transient or native, which tend to eat plants more at night than in the daytime. It is not recommended that a garden be sprayed all over in the hope of controlling or eradicating all insects. To treat the entire garden with insecticides also destroys beneficial insects that help pollinate flowers and balance other insect populations, such as the lady bug beetle and praying mantis. One way to control populations of harmful insects is to keep a garden clean, cleared of weed overgrowth and litter.

There are three categories of insects that can damage landscape plants above and below the ground level: chewers, suckers, and burrowers. To control damage one must learn to identify the source. Long-term observation will usually tell a gardener whether damage is caused by a disease or insect, or if it is mechanical. Holes in leaves may be bacterial, developing slowly and colorfully, or signs of insect feeding. Other holes could perhaps simply have been poked in a leaf. Sometimes domestic animals may contribute the plant damage, either by spraying, chewing, or crushing.

Once it is established that insect damage is the most probable cause, the damage itself provides clues to the type of insect and therefore the type of treatment needed.

Because information changes so rapidly regarding the best and safest treatments, our best advice is to become familiar with the symptoms on the plant, and then discuss treatment with the state Cooperative Extension Service agents or garden center personnel. If it is possible to collect a suspect insect, intact, quite often the Extension Service can provide positive identification.

For all pesticides, it is very important to read and follow the directions for use and storage. Basically, there are three types of pesticides: contact spray, digestive poisons, and all-purpose spray. Carefully read the label. Certain insecticides must be used when air temperatures are above 60°F (16°C) and below 80°F (27°C), whereas others can be used at any temperature. Before resorting to insecticides, determine if insects can be controlled by picking off by hand or eliminated by using insecticidal soap spray. If stronger sprays have to be used, read the entire label for safety precautions, time to spray, and the list of pests it will control. Measure the fluids or substances accurately and use extreme caution in spraying or dusting. Pesticides are toxins. In using any pesticide, remember that it can be poisonous for pests, people, and the environment, and use with extreme care.

Many chewing pests feed on plants at night. Results of their presence become very obvious in the daylight. Some chew the foliage, making holes around the edges or on the leaf surface, and some chew the blossoms. Some prefer feeding on the roots, and the damage is not visible until the plant begins to wilt. This group of feeders includes immature beetles and weevils (order Coleoptera), grasshoppers (order Orthoptera), bagworms and immature moths (order Lepidoptera), and snails and slugs (class Gastropoda). When treating foliage to control root damage, be sure to cover the underside of foliage as well as the top and the soil. For snails and slugs, use a digestive poison or a bait. Beer placed in pie pans in the garden is good bait for slugs, though it may seem wasteful to use it that way.

Sucking insects are small and difficult to see, yet the results, evident on foliage, stems, and buds, can be profound. Some, like the common aphid (order Homoptera), excrete a sticky substance on the foliage which may attract ants. Ant (order Hymenoptera) activity on plants may be a first sign of possible aphid damage. Leafhoppers (order Homoptera) feed by sucking on the underside of foliage, which results in white stippling on the upper side. Mealybugs (order Homoptera) feed in social clusters on stems and produce a white substance. Spider mites (class Acarina), visible only if nearsighted or using a magnifying glass, stipple the underside of foliage and produce a silvery web. Thrips (order Thysanoptera) feed inside flower buds, deforming them and often halting their development. Thrips eat plant foliage, too. Whiteflies (order Homoptera) feed on the underside of foliage and fly about when disturbed. Scale insects (order Homoptera) usually develop in masses, their soft bodies covered with a shell for protection. Scale insects also secrete a sticky substance attractive to ants. After the scale insects are controlled, ants can be discouraged by thoroughly washing the plant with a household liquid detergent diluted with water to remove the attractive insect secretions. All of these insects can be considered garden pests, although their presence on plants is usually not fatal. Judge the extent of harmful populations to determine what sort of control is warranted.

Soil pests spend part or all of their life cycle in the soil. They may cause soft-stemmed plants to be cut off at ground level or turfgrass roots and blades to be severed. Root-feeding pests impair the flow of water within the plant and cause the plant top to wilt, often to die. Obviously, a gardener cannot delay in taking action. These pests include cutworms (order Lepidoptera) and grubs (order Coleoptera).

The most commonly used pesticide for controlling cutworms and grubs is applied to the soil and is then taken up by the plant roots. This type of pesticide is known as a systemic since it is taken into the plant's system. Pests which feed on the plant sap are then killed. Systemic pesticides may also be applied to the foliage.

Burrowing insects (orders Diptera, Lepidoptera, and Coleoptera) can be most damaging in the larval stage, eating fruit, stems, and trunk areas, and leaving small burrow holes as evidence. Leaf miners develop from flies (order Diptera) that lay tiny eggs on the foliage surface. After hatching, the larvae burrow through the leaf. Their activity is evidenced by curved, serpentine, bleached lines on top of foliage, resulting from insect feeding and development. Burrower populations are easiest to control when the adults are mobile, laying eggs within flower petals, stems, trunk, and on foliage. Spray flowers as the last petals fall to control codling moth (order Lepidoptera).

Various beetles (order Coleoptera) are capable of feeding on stems and foliage as adults, and on roots as larvae. Sometimes both adults and larvae are foliage feeders. The elm leaf beetle, for example, causes leaf damage by both adults and larvae. Bark beetles can bore directly into a tree to create egg galleries. Spray stems and bark if small burrow holes are evident, before the eggs hatch. Check with the local extension service for identification and life cycle information. If infestation is severe, remove damaged wood, being careful to clean clippers after each cut by dipping in alcohol to sterilize and destroy any eggs remaining on the blades.

When there is adequate soil moisture yet a plant wilts, the cause may be parasitic soil nematodes (class Nematoda). Nematodes are microscopic worms that get into plant roots, causing gall-like swellings and interfering with the plant's ability to take up water through the roots. The most common nematode pest is the root-knot nematode. Once a planting develops nematode problems, there are no chemicals that can be applied to cure them. The key to avoiding nematodes is careful selection of planting stock. Avoid those with galls on roots that could signal a nematode-infected plant.

Plant diseases may develop due to elements beyond one's control, such as climate zone or weather patterns. A lack of needed nutrients, incorrect soil pH, poor soil structure, improper irrigation practices, or improper fertilization which causes a high soluble salt level and nutrient toxicity, can also favor disease outbreaks. Identification of the exact pathogen is usually beyond an individual's scope. What we can do, as caretakers and gardeners, is learn which plants are vulnerable in our area, what the symptoms are of infection, and what response is needed.

Disease may result from fungi, bacteria, or viruses. Fungi are many-celled parasites living on green plants and only some are capable of causing plant disease. They reproduce via spores carried by air and water to other plant hosts. Powdery mildew is an example of a common and stressful plant fungus. It is displayed as a white powder on succulent leaves and stems. Plant foliage can lose its ability to carry on photosynthesis, due to reduced sunlight reaching the leaf, and eventually will die if covered by too much powdery mildew. Fungal diseases are usually easier to control than bacterial diseases, and viral diseases require dramatic intervention.

Bacteria are single-celled, microscopic organisms, some of which are parasites on landscape plants. Symptoms of a bacterial plant infection include wilting, gall formations, dying buds or other tissues, or scorched foliage. An example of a common bacteria is fire blight. Common host plants are hawthorn (*Crataegus*), crabapple (*Malus*), and firethorn (*Pyracantha*). Symptoms are small, angular, reddish spots on the upper side of foliage, which worsen until eventually the foliage shrivels, turns brown, then black. Branches may subsequently blight and turn black. Normally smooth bark can crack and turn an unhealthy brownish black. Insects may casually transmit bacteria from blossom to blossom during pollination or flight. Garden tools can also pick up and transmit bacterial infection. Bacterial diseases can be treated.

Viruses are submicroscopic particles that can permanently infect a host plant. Not all plants are susceptible to devastating viral diseases. Some of the symptoms of viral diseases are yellowish, mottled, stunted foliage, and abnormally variegated foliage and flowers. A viral disease typical to *Camellia japonica* is displayed as abnormal foliage variegation. The incidence of viral infection can be reduced by controlling the insects carrying the infection. Presently there is no cure for viruses and the infected plants must be eradicated. An immediate control is to buy only virus-free plants when possible. As with pests, learn to diagnose signs of disease. Viral diseases are currently less common to plants than bacterial or fungal infections. Talk with the county extension agent or garden center personnel about control measures for specific diseases.

Plants with a fungal disease may develop yellowish or rusty spotted foliage, brown scabs on leaves, holes in the leaves in the center of diseased areas, contorted leaves, and white or black powder on the foliage and stems. Sometimes a plant suddenly wilts and dies. Sudden wilting and dying is often caused by a root-rot fungus stemming from excessive water saturating the soil, suffocating roots, and creating a perfect environment for root-destroying fungus.

There are many fungicides available today, yet one of the most permanent fungus controls is to maintain a clean garden area with well-drained soil and good air circulation within and among individual plants. Management practices also have a large impact on the extent or incidence of fungus. Water plants early in the day so they will dry before dark to avoid fungus growth. Fungus multiplies at very specific levels of heat and humidity. Moisture invites multiplication, particularly in the absence of sunlight. Also, carefully remove diseased plant parts from a garden in the fall to prevent carry-over of fungus through the winter. Excessive moisture and humidity, poor soil drainage, poor air circulation, and ground accumulation of diseased plant parts contributes much to the growth of fungus. Cleanliness and circulation, both of air and water, are essential for the reduction of garden diseases.

When it is necessary to spray because of fungus, remember to add a spreader or sticker to the mixture to help it adhere to the plant. The spreader or sticker material may be purchased at a garden store, or several squirts of a household liquid detergent can be added to the fungicide spray solution after it is mixed. Spray thoroughly over, under, through, and around the plant for best control of fungus. It requires less effort to spray only the top of foliage, but effective and economical results require a thorough coverage of the plant.

Worldwide, the most common fungal disease involves leaf spots. An example of this disorder is rose black spot, which shows up on rose leaves as a black spot with a fringed or feathery margin, sometimes surrounded by a yellow halo. Infected foliage drops. The fungus meanwhile is alive and active on fallen leaves. Careful sanitation is one of the best ways to reduce or control all incidences of black spot. Frequent removal of the fallen infected leaves will help, and they should be boxed or bagged for removal. Do not compost infected leaves.

Powdery mildew is another common garden fungus. It appears as a white, powdery coating on foliage, stems, and flower buds. Various types of powdery mildew have specific plant hosts. Powdery mildew of crape myrtle starts on young leaves as small blisters that develop into a white powder. Young foliage curls and distorts, and the crape myrtle buds often fail to flower. Two weeks after initial infection, diseased foliage and buds drop.

Cool nights and warm days with poor air circulation provide optimum growing conditions for powdery mildew. This is one reason why it is said that air circulation is essential for healthy plants. For trees or shrubs, achieving adequate air circulation may necessitate removing some of the lower branches by thinning. Also, if plants are against a masonry garden wall, it is wise to have small air holes in the bottom fourth of the wall for air circulation. For treatment of powdery mildew, begin spraying fungicides in early spring on susceptible plants. Time spraying for when new growth is beginning. For some plants, a dormant spray is appropriate. This may be applied in late winter when plants are dormant. However, avoid applying dormant fungicide sprays at extremely cold temperatures. Read and follow the directions on the container carefully.

Downy mildew is a foliage condition resulting from a parasitic fungus. Foliage symptoms are intravenous discoloration (a yellowing of the leaf area between the veins) and brown spottings, and chlorosis or yellowing. Leaf veins remain green. The downy mildew fruiting structures are masses of white developing on the underside of the leaves. Controls are the same as for powdery mildew.

Sooty mold fungus may be a problem on broad-leaved evergreens, appearing as a black, velvety coating on foliage and twigs. It usually develops in early spring and fall during cool, wet weather. The mold itself does not damage the plant. Damage arises when the sooty mold becomes too dense and blocks out light needed for plant growth. The plant responds by yellowing and becoming stunted.

Actually, sooty mold is a secondary condition coming after insects make a honeydew conducive to its growth. Therefore, sooty mold is not controlled with a fungicide. Sooty mold can be treated with an insecticide or liquid detergent spray. After getting rid of the insects, the plant may be thoroughly cleaned by spraying with a solution of water and household liquid detergent.

Stem canker may typically develop on camellias, roses, and lilies. Stem canker produces swelling and discoloration of the stem. The stem discoloration varies in color from brown to dark red. Under humid conditions, fungal growth that may have a cobwebby appearance is frequently observed along the cankered area. The cankers should be removed by pruning back to healthy stem tissues. After each cut, the clippers need to be sterilized in alcohol to prevent spreading the disease. Dispose of the infected tissues by a means other than composting.

The most prevalent of all plant diseases, embracing a host of microorganisms that may be bacterial or, more commonly, fungal, are the leaf spot diseases. Disease symptoms are exactly what is suggested—spotted discolorations within the leaf. Environmental factors, such as pesticide misuse and watering leaves on hot sunny days, may produce leaf spots. However, spots resulting from environmental disorders can usually be tracked and avoided.

Leaf spot infection is sometimes displayed as a solid color mass, spreading from the leaf margin inward. Sometimes the discoloration browns and grows. Leaf spot diseases produce brown, red, purple, or yellow spots on foliage and stems. Often, diseased spots on leaves disintegrate to become small holes in the leaf. The area surrounding the hole maintains infectious spores which spread by air and water to other foliage. Severe leaf spot causes foliage to drop, which can be a serious concern. Other leaf spots, such as those on oak trees, are usually merely unsightly. With oaks it is not a serious problem except in the case of oak leaf blister which may weaken trees over several years by early defoliation.

Root rots may affect Hinoki falsecypress, lilies, *Rhododendron*, camellias, and other garden plants. Root rot can develop with almost any plant needing good drainage that is sited in poorly drained soil. Generally this condition is favored by excess water during prolonged rainfall coupled with poor soil drainage. Under these conditions, when soil aeration is low, roots are subject to attack from these fungi and may rot. Wilting foliage can be a sign of root rot, particularly if plants in other areas show no sign of water stress. If warranted, improve the drainage in a susceptible planting area by digging and filling several post holes around the plant with a mixture of half soil and a porous mulch material such as sand or gravel.

Flower blight may be caused by a fungus or bacterium. Some camellias are subject to flower blight caused by a fungus. Tan to brownish spots develop on flower petals and the flowers fall off early. Azaleas, particularly the Kurume and Indica types, are subject to a petal blight caused by a fungus particular to *Rhododendron*. Pinpoint circular spots appear on the underside of azalea petals, enlarging rapidly, and appearing white on colored flowers and brown on white flowers. The flowers subsequently wilt and are covered with white, frosty matter that is actually masses of fungal spores. The fungus continues to develop on fallen flowers. Good control practice is to maintain cleanliness by removing the fallen flowers and bag for disposal. In January, remove all the old mulch and replace with new mulch before the plant flowers. To control this blight early in the growing season, spray the ground and the flowers with a fungicide and judiciously thin stems to provide better air circulation.

Rust in a landscape, unfortunately, is not limited to iron objects. Foliage and stems, depending on the plant species, may also develop a somewhat rusty look from fungi. There are more than 4000 species of rust fungi particular and specific to plants. Rust disease is evident when the upper side of foliage is mottled and yellowish, while yellow-orange, dotted formations appear on the underside of the foliage. The upper leaf surface displays the damage, the lower surface displays the active fungus spores. Rust spores can easily survive most winters. It is essential to clean the ground surface area of any infection. Rust is typically found on crabapples, hawthorns, roses, and many other herbaceous ornamentals. Plants may require treatment with a systemic fungicide if the infection is widespread.

Scab is a fungus capable of totally destroying the fruit of pyracantha, apples, peaches, and other plants. On fruit, scab infections first appear as crustlike spots that grow. Scab may develop on foliage, too—dark sooty blotches yellow, then brown, eventually causing infected foliage to drop prematurely. Twigs may also be infected with scab and can harbor the fungus all winter. Control requires three or four fungicide sprayings from early spring through summer. Check with local nursery personnel or extension services if scab appears prevalent and persistent and requires control in the home landscape.

Fire blight is a highly contagious bacterial disease typically infecting apple, cotoneaster, pear, and pyracantha. Symptoms differ from those of sunburn in that sunburn usually causes a bronzing discoloration. Fire blight produces a truly scorched appearance. It initially causes flowering shoots to wilt, turn black or brown, and die. Fire-blighted foliage hangs downward for a period before dropping. Twigs develop dark brown to purplish infected bark which may also show slight cracking. If the infection continues into larger limbs, dark cankers develop. The bark and dead foliage actually looks as if it has been touched by fire.

To control an existing infection, use a bactericide when the plant is half in bloom and again when in full bloom. This will limit the spread of the disease, as pollinating bees carry the bacteria from plant to plant when gathering honey. Sprays are available which will not harm the bees. Remove all diseased limbs. Between cuts, dip pruners in alcohol to reduce spread of disease. Clean around plants by removing any diseased blossoms, foliage, fruit, or wood.

17

Preservation of Existing Trees During Site Changes

Earth grading on new home and building sites indicates that apparently not everyone knows that plants, like people, require nutrients and water for survival. The life-giving elements for trees, shrubs, vines, ground covers, turfgrasses, and flowers are primarily absorbed through a plant's root system. To cover and seal off the roots of an existing tree, young or mature, with additional soil, or to remove soil and some roots when grading a new site, will often cause a tree to become unhealthy and die. Adequate protection for existing trees on a site before earth grading commences will help assure plant survival. The objective of this chapter is to emphasize careful preparation and to explain methods of tree protection on a new site. The photographs of tree-well construction are of large-scale landscapes, yet the procedure is the same for small-scale home sites.

To save a tree and to reduce future management needs when changing the soil grade under a tree canopy, an ounce of protection more than equals a pound of cure. The best time for this protection is prior to construction on a site, if possible. When adding to the existing elevation around a tree, construction of a tree-well system will help provide needed nutrients and water for the buried tree roots. When removing soil from a tree's root system area, whether before or after site construction, it is difficult to save a tree if more than one-third of the tree's roots are removed.

In raising the soil grade around a tree, the root system must be protected in order that the supply of air, water, and nutrients can continue uninterrupted. This may be achieved by building a tree-well system, which, it will be seen, is more than a wall around the trunk. This tree-well protection should be completed before construction of any other kind commences on the site.

Color photograph 160a illustrates an existing sugar hackberry tree (*Celtis laevigata*) growing on a building site which is to receive a 3 ft (1 m) soil fill. This will take the soil level to the bottom of the red bricks in the wall around the tree. The brick wall is the only visible evidence of its tree-well system. The other elements of the system include a retaining wall with perforated pipes radiating out from the wall base to slightly beyond the tree canopy dripline. Pipes are covered with loose gravel and topped with topsoil. The retaining wall is constructed at least 2 ft (0.6 m) or more away from the trunk and slightly higher than the finished soil grade. The resulting open well may be merely the 2 ft (0.6 m) allowed from the tree trunk or it may be extended to accommodate people and activities. The inside of the tree-well is usually mulched or planted with a ground cover.

The method of establishing a tree-well system is as follows. On top of the existing grade, spread 2 in (5 cm) of washed gravel from the wall to 3–5 ft (1.0–1.5 m) or more beyond the branch tips or tree canopy. From within the inside edge of the tree-well wall, extend 4 in (10 cm) perforated plastic pipe sections out to the edge of the gravel. The perforated pipes, laid out like spokes in a wheel and with holes downward, are spaced 4–6 ft (1–2 m) apart. Cover pipes with loose gravel to within 12 in (30 cm) of the finished grade. Cover the gravel with a filter fabric that will keep soil particles from washing down between the gravel. The remaining space can be filled with topsoil to the finished grade (photograph 160b).

The objective of the pipes is to maintain the flow of rainwater, air, and nutrients through the open well, pipes, and gravel to the existing root system. The tree-well wall keeps soil away from the trunk to prevent bark damage. The tree-well system remains in place forever and the tree's root system readjusts to the changes in elevation.

Two very important facts should be remembered when providing tree protection for a soil fill for grading. Firstly, the root system of an existing tree may be two to four times wider than the tree canopy. The feeding roots are near the edge of the canopy and beyond, and are within the top 2 ft (0.6 m) of the soil. Secondly, in order to accommodate excess water during prolonged rains, at least one of the perforated pipes from the well must be allowed to carry runoff. Extend it to an open, lower grade elevation or connect it to an underground storm drainage system, otherwise the buried roots will drown.

In the case of the sugar hackberry tree mentioned above, constructing the basement for the new building behind it temporarily lowered the water table around the tree so much that a provisional irrigation system had to be installed. Once construction of the basement was completed, the original water table level was restored. The water table is another important matter to remember, though it may not be a consideration on all site developments.

As a substitute material for covering the perforated pipes, broken but clean bricks from the construction site may be used instead of washed gravel. Bricks with fresh mortar on them are not usable. The lime in the mortar mixes with water, forming an acid which could harm the tree's root system. The broken brick pieces or gravel covering the pipes permit air spaces for the flow of nutrients and water to the root system, within and beyond the radiating pipes from the tree-well.

The tree in the well in color photograph 160a is the same tree as in photograph 160b, which was taken twenty-one years later. The passage of time indicates the value of preserving a tree to define the space, and the success of the tree-well system. The tree provides human-scale canopy and shade for the five-story building.

The best time to provide this tree-well system protection is prior to any site grading. Sometimes an existing but failing tree may yet be saved with a well system construction, if the soil fill has been on the root system no longer than a year. Tree performance and success depends on the type of soil used for the fill. A sandy, porous soil will not have been as damaging as a heavy, clay soil fill.

Some site grading involves soil cuts and the removal of soil around existing trees. Root protection is much more difficult to provide, particularly with a mature tree. If at all possible, it is best to avoid soil removal directly under the tree canopy and just beyond it. If there is sufficient advanced knowledge of a soil cut which will affect tree roots (at least a year) some protective measures can be taken. The tree can be fed with a complete fertilizer (13-13-13) and the branches judiciously pruned to balance with the tree roots it is estimated will have to be removed later. Ideally, the pruning and fertilizing would occur in late winter prior to grading the following summer.

In addition, a wall should be constructed out just beyond the canopy dripline, at the feeding roots. The wall will maintain the existing grade and root system above the proposed lower elevation. Even so, the chance of tree survival remains low.

Another practice is to let nature indicate the limbs to be removed after the soil cut is made. Tree roots damaged or severed during grading reduce the supply of nutrients and water to the tree, resulting in specific limbs showing unhealthy foliage growth. These limbs can be removed to compensate for the apparent root damage, and the tree fertilized. Prune and fertilize in late winter, if possible. Drip irrigate the tree any week there is no rainfall, particularly during the growing season.

The chance of a tree surviving a soil cut is less than after a soil fill, primarily because the subgrade water table is lowered along with the soil. Many roots are severed or damaged in the process. For this reason, the soil area under the tree canopy must be irrigated during prolonged dry periods. Irrigation needs will be present for the life of the tree. It would be of long-range management value to install a permanent, drip irrigation system under the tree. Do not overwater existing trees, however. Old trees are like some people, they do not take radical change well.

Also, if soil grade is to be lowered within 50 ft (15 m) of an existing mature tree, care must be taken to prevent the tree roots from drying out during excavations. By deeply lowering a nearby grade, the subgrade water table in the soil around the tree is lowered. It may be necessary to irrigate the soil under the tree canopy and for several feet beyond until the adjacent work is completed. For example, soil was excavated for a building basement within 50 ft (15 m) of the previously mentioned sugar hackberry. Until the new building's basement wall was constructed up to the original soil grade, it was necessary to irrigate the sugar hackberry twice a week at least.

An indirect problem for existing trees in a construction area is soil compaction. This can be due to vehicular or foot traffic or storing heavy materials on the ground. Depending on the type of soil, this could mean the death of the tree as air, water, and nutrients are unable to reach the root system through the compacted soil. Heavy soils compact readily, particularly if damp from rain. On construction sites, care must be taken to prevent vehicular traffic and parking under and around an existing tree canopy. Erecting barricades before construction begins may sidestep this problem. However, if soil compaction does occur there is some immediate recourse to help the tree recover. For the soil under and beyond the canopy, lightly cultivate with a tiller set no deeper than 1–2 in (3–5 cm). Feed the tree with a complete fertilizer (13-13-13) and water frequently during the year following the soil compaction. An application of organic mulch on the cultivated area will help conserve moisture, enhancing root recovery and soil structure.

18

Reducing Management: A Summary

1. Grow grass only where it readily grows. Mulch all other areas or plant with living ground covers.

2. Keep turf healthy and thick to reduce diseases and weed intrusion. To do this, first maintain it only in areas that receive enough sun. Next, take pH tests yearly to maintain the correct environment for the best nutrient level for the turf. Gardeners may have to add lime every year or two in hot, humid areas, and sulfur in arid areas typical of the West. Take soil samples to evaluate the amount of nutrients available. Nitrogen, phosphorus, and potassium, along with certain micronutrients, are critical to a healthy lawn. Their availability will help reduce maintenance. To reduce dependence on fertilizers, mow grass often with a mulching-style mower. This practice can reduce fertilizer needs by 20 to 40%.

3. In areas with many trees, create large, mulched beds around the trees to eliminate difficult and time-consuming mowing. Mulch in the fall and spring. Remove weeds from mulched beds in spring, early summer, and late summer. Pull mulch 2 in (5 cm) away from tree trunks to eliminate moisture near trunks and possible injury by insects and disease.

4. For freestanding trees in lawn areas, create easier mowing by establishing a living ground cover or mulch ring large enough to accommodate the mowing radius of the

mower. Using ground covers around trees will also emphasize the tree in the landscape design. Exercise care in using this technique so the design does not become chaotic.

5. An alternative to mulching and using ground covers around trees is to remove turf for a distance of 6–8 in (15–20 cm) around tree trunks. This allows for quick mowing around freestanding trees without injury to the tree trunk.

6. Create an easily maintained system for separating lawn areas from mulched beds. Use a ground-level brick or concrete mowing strip, or ground-level plastic or steel edging strips. The line created by the edges of the grass and mulch beds is an important visual and psychological component of the garden. Neat, clean edges give a cared-for, manicured appearance. The line effect created in the landscape will give viewers a feeling of calmness, playfulness, or strength, among other possible feelings, depending on the style of line used.

7. Remove a 6–8 in (15–20 cm) grass strip from lawn areas along the edges of buildings and around freestanding objects. This will give a neat appearance and allow a mower to cut close enough to make labor-intensive string trimming or use of an edger unnecessary.

8. Mulch beneath and beyond all shrub beds to reduce weed growth and to make it easier to mow around the shrub bed. Without mulch, a person has to mow under the shrub dripline. With mulch, there is no stopping and push–pulling of the mower to cut grass and weeds growing beneath shrubs (see Figure 18-1). In fact, a riding mower can be used to cut along the straight edges and large radii of the shrub beds, which eliminates trimming with a push mower.

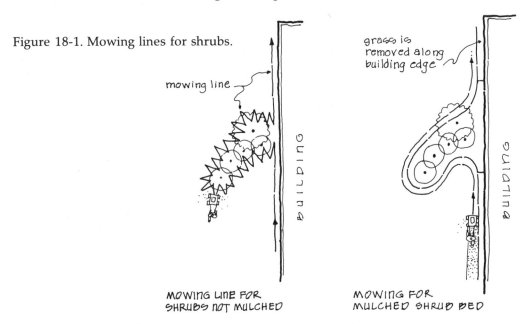

Figure 18-1. Mowing lines for shrubs.

9. Do not establish lawns where slopes exceed 33% or a 3:1 ratio. Grass on banks greater than a 3:1 slope is both unsafe to mow because of the steepness of the slope and more time-consuming to mow because of the greater care needed to prevent accidents.

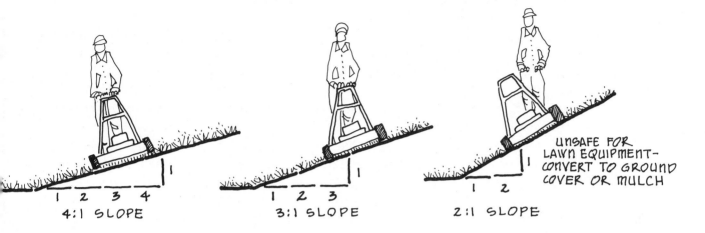

4:1 SLOPE

3:1 SLOPE

2:1 SLOPE

UNSAFE FOR LAWN EQUIPMENT—CONVERT TO GROUND COVER OR MULCH

Figure 18-2. Maximum slope ratios for lawns.

10. Separate different kinds of ground covers with a separator or barrier extending above and below ground level to stop runners or below-ground shoots from growing into one another. Wood, plastic or steel strips work well as separators. An example of the need for such barriers came when planting a large bed of liriope (*Liriope muscari*) next to an established big-leaf periwinkle (*Vinca major*) bed. This was done blithely, and a physical separation between the two beds would have been easy to install when preparing the second bed. For the past three years an hour twice a summer has been required to remove the more aggressive periwinkle from the liriope bed. A bed separator would have eliminated both the tedium and the threat to the liriope.

11. In small lawn areas with difficult access, replace turfgrass with either mulched shrubs or ground cover. This will reduce overall management time.

12. Reduce the need to water plants by hand to the barest minimum. In most areas there are prolonged dry spells that will seriously stress the garden if it does not receive supplemental water. This means either dragging hoses and watering by hand, or turning on a valve or switch and watering automatically. Hand watering is time-consuming and usually wastes precious water because soils cannot absorb water as fast as the sprinkler or impatient gardener puts it out. If watering garden areas automatically, sprinkler heads or drip irrigation are generally used. Both systems can be hooked either to a manual valve, to turn on when necessary, or to an automatic controller that turns on the irrigation via a programmable clock. It is best to water with a

sprinkler system early in the morning when water pressure is higher. Also, the sun evaporates early morning irrigation water from the plant foliage and thereby keeps plants healthier. Drip irrigation is ideal for watering trees, shrubs, and certain ornamental flowers and grasses. Sprinkler irrigation is best for turf areas and large beds of ground covers.

13. For flower beds, start by creating the best soil possible. Remember, the ideal garden soil provides plant nutrients for health and growth and has plenty of air for maximum root growth. Microorganisms flourish in the ideal garden soil. The soil will maintain a pH of 6.5 to 7 and its structure will be spongy enough to hold, yet release, water during dry periods. Mulch soil with 2 in (5 cm) of composted organic matter in late winter, summer, and fall. This will keep it in top shape and serve as insulation to keep plant roots cool in the summer and retain warmth in the winter. Mulch also reduces the evaporation of valuable moisture, thereby reducing the need to water the flower beds. Regular maintenance of the soil is one of the most effective ways to reduce maintenance of a flower collection.

14. If a person knows exactly what needs to be done and when, one is usually able to then plan and prepare for the task. This gets the work done better, faster, and at the right time. We suggest developing a chart, a landscape management plan. Make a column of the 12 months and beside each month list which landscape tasks need doing. Post it in the office, workshed, garage, or into a datebook for a continual visual reminder. This visual landscape management plan may become the friend on whom to depend for timely prompting. We find it much easier than having to deal with sad-looking plants that were neglected. For example, there is a neighbor who forgets to cut back the liriope (*Liriope muscari*) ground cover in February before it grows out. In March when remembered and mown to the ground to remove last year's growth, the tips of emerging new growth are also cut. This causes the liriope to grow out ragged, and it looks stressed for the rest of the year. Noting when to put out those tropical *Caladium* or when to put down that first light fertilization to keep the lawn most healthy can all be noted on the management plan. A good landscape management plan can serve as a memory.

15. Select trees and shrubs that fit the site ecology. Plants that are native to an area usually perform best because they can live in harmony with the local soil, weather, and seasonal moisture regimes. Avoid filling the garden with disease-prone exotics unless willing to invest extra care.

16. Select trees and shrubs that do not have to be pruned to maintain a specific size. Allow for mature plant growth and natural shape.

APPENDIXES

Instructional Outline of Text

Section I: Design

1. Process
Design process
Elements of design—line, form, space, texture, color
Principles of design—balance, unity, variety, proportion, emphasis, transition

2. Designing Space
Canopies create space
Vertical spatial definition
Defining open space
Enclosing space
Providing floors
Separating use areas
Reducing vastness
Concealment and revealment
Screening
Providing ground forms
Creating depth
Transition
Changes in perception of space
Plant growth
Mulch
Plant forms
Time

3. Engineering Considerations
Reduction of mechanical light glare
Pedestrian circulation control
Vehicular circulation control
Soil erosion control
Noise and air pollution reduction

4. Climate Control
Sun control
Windbreak
Insulation
Microclimates

5. Aesthetics
Enframement and backdrop
Reflection
Silhouette/shadow projections
Pattern
Living sculpture
Soften hard construction
Accent or focal point
Seasonal effects—foliage, flower, fruit, seed pod or capsule, and bark

6. Garden Elements: Origin and Evolution
Geographic influences
Formal, symmetrical balance and rectilinear garden design layout

American (USA) colonial gardens
(1620–1775)
Topographic influences
  Retaining walls
  Dynamic water displays
Climatic influences
  Pergolas and arbors
  Pleached allée
  Trees planted for shade
  Tree groves
  Glorieta
  Topiary
  Plant walls
  Potted plants
  Glazed pottery and tiles
  Stone pavements
  Building orientation
  Small-scale water effects
Social influences
  Street trees and parks
  Atrium/patio

Informal asymmetrical garden design
  layout
  Perennial garden
Political influences
  Espalier
  Herb garden
  Mount or mound
  Tree-framed axis
  The Grand Style
  Pollarding
Economic influences
  Plant introductions
Religious influences
  Human scale spatial enclosures
  Labyrinth/maze
  Specimen plants
The origin of contemporary American
  garden style
  Bauhaus
  The Great Depression
  The California School

Section II: Management

7. **Management Strategy**
   Balanced landscape
   Landscape management plan
   Task and time expenditure
   Management plan development

8. **Soils**
   Soil composition
   Ideal garden soil
   Monitoring the soil

9. **Fertilizers**
   Plant nutrients
   Essential plant growth elements

10. **Composting**
    Microorganisms are the key
    Recipe for successful compost
    Building a compost pile
    Signs of a successful compost pile

11. **Mulching**
    Mulch—organic and inorganic
    Advantages of using mulch
    Application of organic mulch
    Application of inorganic mulch

12. **Lawns**
    Warm-season grasses
    Cool-season grasses
    Selecting a lawn grass
    Lawn management

13. **Shrubs and Trees**
    Reasons to prune
    Pruning shrubs
    Shearing shrubs
    Tree-form shrubs
    Pruning trees
    Root pruning
    Pruning tools
    Fertilizers
    Mulching
    Watering

14. **Vines, Espaliers, and Ground Covers**
    Types of vines
      How to train and prune
      Fertilizing
      Mulching
    Espaliers
      How to train and prune

Fertilizing
Mulching
Ground covers
Establishment and pruning
Fertilizing
Mulching

15. Flowers
Herbaceous flowers
Fertilizing
Staking
Dead-heading
Mulching
Watering
Division of perennials
Bulbous plants
Fertilizing
Mulching
Dead-heading
Watering
Division
Planting herbaceous and
bulbous plants

16. Regarding Pests and Diseases
Insects
Chewing
Sucking
Soil
Burrowing
Other pests
Diseases
Fungus
Virus
Bacteria

**17. Preservation of Existing Trees During
Site Changes**
Raising the existing soil grade—tree-well
system construction
Lowering the existing soil grade
Compaction of existing soils

18. Reducing Management: A Summary

Plants and Soil pH Preferences

PLANTS PREFERRING ACID SOILS

Trees	pH range
Apple (*Malus*)	5.5–6.5
Crabapple (*Malus*)	5.0–6.5
Crape myrtle (*Lagerstroemia indica*)	5.0–6.0
False cypress (*Chamaecyparis*)	5.0–6.0
Fir (*Abies*)	5.0–6.0
Flowering dogwood (*Cornus florida*)	5.0–7.0
Holly, American (*Ilex opaca*)	5.0–6.0
Magnolia	5.0–6.0
Pin oak (*Quercus palustris*)	5.0–6.5
Pine (*Pinus*)	5.0–6.0
Southern red oak (*Quercus falcata*)	5.0–7.5
Sourwood (*Oxydendrum arboreum*)	4.0–8.0

Shrubs	pH range
Azalea (*Rhododendron*)	4.5–6.0
Camellia	4.0–5.5
Gardenia	5.0–6.0
Heather (*Calluna vulgaris*)	4.5–6.0
Holly (*Ilex*)	5.0–6.0
Huckleberry (*Gaylussacia*)	5.0–5.5

Shrubs	pH range
Hydrangea, blue-flowered	4.5–5.0

Flowers	
Coreopsis	5.5–6.5
Daffodil (*Narcissus*)	6.0–6.5
Phlox	5.0–6.0
Strawberry (*Fragoria*)	5.0–6.0

Vines	
Bittersweet (*Celastrus*)	5.5–6.5
Carolina jessamine (*Gelsemium sempervirens*)	5.0–6.0

Vegetables	
Carrot (*Daucus carota*)	5.5–6.5
Bean, lima (*Phaseolus limensis*)	5.5–6.5
Peanut (*Arachis hypogaea*)	5.0–6.0
Pepper (*Piper nigrum*)	6.0–6.5
Potato (*Solanum tuberosum*)	4.8–6.5

PLANTS PREFERRING NEUTRAL-TO-ALKALINE SOILS

Trees	pH range
American plum (*Prunus americana*)	6.0–8.0
Banana (*Musa paradisiaca sapientum*)	7.0
Beech (*Fagus*)	6.0–7.0
Buckeye (*Aesculus*)	6.0–8.0
Catalpa	6.0–8.0
Colorado spruce (*Picea pungens*)	6.0–7.0
Elm (*Ulmus*)	6.0–7.5
Empress tree (*Paulownia tomentosa*)	6.0–8.0
Gray dogwood (*Cornus racemosa*)	6.0–8.0
Hackberry (*Celtis*)	6.0–8.0
Maple (*Acer*)	6.0–7.5
Peach (*Prunus persica*)	6.5–7.0
Pear (*Pyrus*)	6.0–8.0
Possumhaw (*Ilex decidua*)	7.0–8.0
Redbud (*Cercis*)	6.0–8.0
Sumac (*Rhus*)	6.0–8.0

Shrubs	
Abelia	6.0–8.0
Barberry (*Berberis*)	6.0–8.0
Beautyberry (*Callicarpa*)	6.0–7.0
Blackberry, ornamental (*Rubus*)	6.0–8.0
Butterfly bush (*Buddleia*)	6.0–7.5
Deutzia	6.0–7.5
Thorny elaeagnus (*Elaeagnus pungens*)	6.0–8.0
Flowering quince (*Chaenomeles*)	6.0–8.0
Hibiscus	6.0–8.0
Hydrangea, pink-flowered	6.0–8.0
Lilac (*Syringa*)	6.0–7.5
Firethorn (*Pyracantha*)	6.0–8.0
Viburnum, deciduous	6.0–8.0

Flowers	
Astilbe	6.0–8.0
Begonia	6.0–8.0
Canna	6.0–8.0

Flowers	pH range
Columbine (*Aquilegia*)	6.0–8.0
Coneflower (*Rudbeckia*)	6.0–8.0
Cosmos	6.0–8.0
Daylily (*Hemerocallis*)	6.0–8.0
Dianthus	6.0–8.0
Hollyhock (*Althaea rosea*)	6.0–8.0
Nasturtium (*Tropaeolum*)	6.0–8.0
Peony (*Paeonia*)	6.0–8.0
Petunia	6.0–8.0
Shasta daisy (*Chrysanthemum*)	6.0–8.0
Zinnia	6.0–8.0

Vines	
Clematis	6.0–8.0
English ivy (*Hedera helix*)	6.0–8.0
Grape (*Vitis*)	6.0–8.0
Honeysuckle (*Lonicera*)	6.0–8.0
Morning glory (*Ipomoea*)	6.0–8.0

Vegetables	
Asparagus	6.0–7.0
Beans (*Phaseolus*)	6.0–7.5
Broccoli (*Brassica oleracea* var. *italica*)	6.0–7.0
Cabbage, cauliflower (*Brassica oleracea* var. *capitata*)	6.0–7.0
Cantaloupe (*Cucumis melo* var. *cantalupensis*)	6.0–8.0
Corn, Indian (*Zea mays*)	6.0–7.0
Cucumber (*Cucumis sativus*)	6.0–8.0
Eggplant (*Solanum melongena*)	6.0–7.0
Okra (*Hibiscus esculentus*)	6.0–8.0
Onion (*Allium*)	6.0–7.0
Peas (*Pisum sativum*)	6.0–8.0
Radish (*Raphanus sativus*)	6.0–8.0
Spinach (*Spinacia oleracea*)	6.5–7.0
Tomato (*Lycopersicon esculentum*)	6.0–7.0

Landscape Management Plan

A public landscape parallels a home landscape except usually for scale. Landscapes are comprised of land, plants, spaces, and hardscape materials that contribute, when properly arranged, to a predictable human experience. Land uses, circulation, and long-term management are considerations for all scales of landscapes.

The functional uses of plants in this turn-of-the-century courthouse landscape include design for the reduction of solar energy heat gain on the west and east building sides, creation of outdoor spaces, direction of pedestrian flow, accent of major entries, control of erosion, reduction of the need to mow grass in difficult places, and subordination of hard construction elements. Mulch is used throughout to retain soil moisture and reduce the need to weed.

This landscape management plan directs maintenance so as to ensure a quality landscape for the public to enjoy. The plan was developed in order to solicit bids from landscape contracting and landscape management companies.

Attala County Courthouse Landscape
Kosciusko, Mississippi
for the Attala County Board of Supervisors
Pete Melby, ASLA, Landscape Architect
Landscape Management Plan

Lawn
Mow as needed to remove ⅓ of the grass blade. Take a yearly pH test from each of the four quadrants of the lawn in the early spring of each year. Adjust according to the ideal pH range for the grass according to the county agent. Fertilize in March only if needed to repair damaged grass or for grass color. Otherwise, do not fertilize unless you want to do a lot of grass mowing. Observe lawn for pest and disease damage. Contact the county extension agent for further direction if problems occur.

Litter
Remove all litter and fallen limbs on grounds by Thursday or Friday weekly.

Edging
With a push style, mechanical edger with steel blades, cut grass back from all edges every third mowing. Edges include all concrete walkways and all bed edgings separating ground cover from grass.

Shrub Beds
Remove all weeds in shrub beds in May and July. Add additional shreaded bark mulch to shrub beds in October of each year to a total mulch depth of 6 in (15.2 cm).

Annual Beds
Special preparation is required on the annual beds. It is our objective to create a soil that is friable, continually high in organic matter, naturally high in soil nutrients, and has a pH of 6.5. Create a soil that drains well but has enough clay in it to hold water for three days. Add composted organic matter each February and again in June. Weed every third mowing. Fertilize with 8-8-8 granular fertilizer taking care to avoid getting the granules on plant foilage, or use an approved complete liquid fertilizer in February, June and September.

Ground Cover
Mulch liriope (Liriope muscari) with a shredded bark mulch to a settled depth of four in (10.2 cm) when planted. Supplement each fall to create a maximum of four in (10.2 cm) of mulch. Be sure to apply mulch to all spaces between plants. Mow the ground cover back to the ground in early February every other year. Collect clippings and compost them. Fertilize each February for three years after initial planting with 8-8-8 granular fertilizer. In May and July remove intrusive grasses and broadleaf plants. Apply herbicides such as Post and Image; test on a small area to ensure the safety of using on liriope. Be sure to apply carefully and when there is a no wind situation to prevent drifting of spray. The alternative to using herbicides is to hand remove all intrusive grasses and broadleaf plants.

Mature Shade Trees at Perimeter of Site
Continually examine the trees for poor and diseased branching and remove branches to allow for strong development and to prevent injuries from falling limbs. Make a list of proposed mature tree trimming needs at the beginning of each landscape management yearly contract to be considered for inclusion into the contract. Additional trimming of mature trees after the contract has been set shall be on an addendum basis to be approved by the contracting officer.

Newly Planted Trees at Perimeter of Site

Fertilize with 8-8-8 fertilizer in February each year. Apply one cup 3 ft (91.4 cm) around each tree. In November fertilize each tree with one cup of 16-0-30 scattered evenly around tree. This gives winter hardiness and protection from summer heat stress. Prune shade trees in February to maintain a single trunk. Remove all suckers at the base of the trees as they appear.

Raking

Remove all leaves, pine straw, twigs and branches by October 30 and again by December 15 from all landscape areas.

Sweet Bay Magnolias (Magnolia virginiana)

Fertilize with a cup of 8-8-8 in February. In November, fertilize with 16-0-30. Do no pruning on this accent tree.

Magnolia "Little Gem" (Magnolia grandiflora "Little Gem")

Allow branches to grow to the ground. Place shredded bark mulch in a 3 ft (91.4 cm) ring around each tree. Fertilize in February with a cup of 8-8-8. In November, fertilize with a cup of 16-0-30. Do not prune this tree.

Japanese Magnolia (Magnolia soulangiana)

Prune branches progressively up from these multitrunk clump trees as the shrubs beneath them grow taller. The ultimate form should be a clean trunk up to a 6–8 ft (1.83–2.44 m) level. It might take 7–10 years for the tree to reach this form. Fertilize with a cup of 8-8-8 in February. In November, fertilize with a cup of 16-0-30 per tree.

Manhattan Euonymus (Euonymus kiautschovica)

Fertilize with ½ cup of 8-8-8 spread 2 ft (61 cm) evenly around the base of each shrub in February. Once this shrub reaches a size of 6 ft (1.83 m) in diameter, begin to prune it back one branch at a time with hand held "parrot type" pruning shears. Stop fertilizing once the shrub reaches its mature size and needs pruning back. Carry out the pruning task by pruning the shrub in a naturalistic manner. Alternate tip pruning with pruning branches 12 in (30.5 cm) into the shrub. This will produce a shrub that has a natural look to it as opposed to a "sheared" look.

Japanese Boxwood (Buxus microphylla)

This fast growing shrub needs little attention except for pruning. Once the shrub reaches 3 ft (91.4 cm) in diameter, prune in a naturlistic manner with parrot-type pruning shears in April and June.

Azaleas (Azalea spp.)

Fertilize azaleas with two cups of cottonseed meal placed around each shrub in May. Test the soil pH every two years in the spring to ensure the pH is below 6.5. If above 6.5, spread iron sulphate around each plant according to package instructions. Be sure to keep off concrete walkway as it will stain the concrete a rust color. Maintain an organic mulch around azaleas to a depth of 4 in (10.2 cm).

Elephant Ears (Alocasia spp.)

Cut foilage back after the first killing frost. Mulch 12 in (30.5 cm) deep over these tropical rhizomes in November each year.

Banana Trees (Musa paradisiaca sapientum)

Cut foilage back to the ground after the plant is killed back by frost. Mulch 12 in (30.5 cm) deep, 3 ft (91.4 cm) diameter around the base of the tree to protect the cold sensitive, root system.

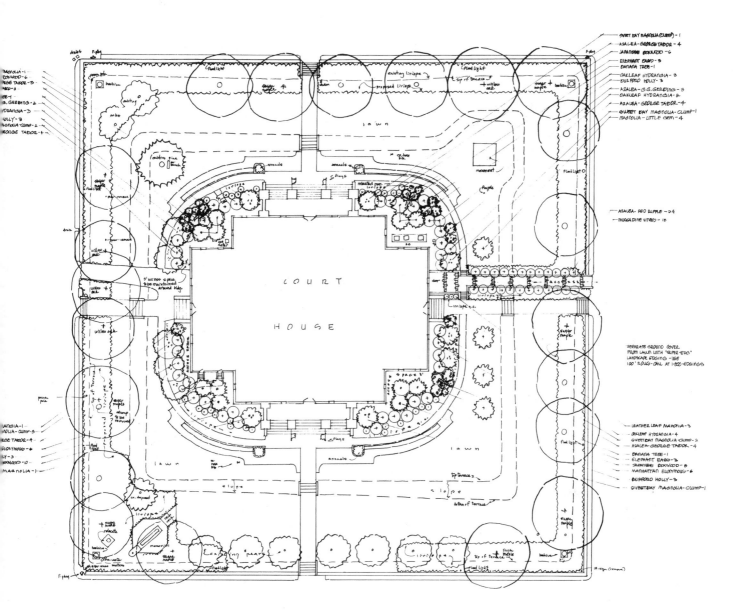

Oakleaf Hydrangea (Hydrangea quercifolia)

This plant must have good drainage around its roots to survive. Once the plant reaches 5 ft (1.52 m) diameter, prune in a naturalistic manner immediately following flowering. Fertilize with one cup of 8-8-8 in February each year.

Leatherleaf Mahonia (Mahonia bealei)

These freeform shrubs will need little attention until they reach a height of 4 ft (1.22 m). At that time, cut the longest cane back to the ground in February. Do this yearly.

Muscadines (Vitis rotundifolia)

Prune muscadines back to two buds between Jan 15–Feb 15. Remove all pruned material from the site. Initially train the vines to follow trellis. Keep trunk clean for 4 ft (1.22 m) from the ground, then let branches grow, while keeping one main branch.

In future years prune after frost in the fall or late winter, all new growth to be pruned back to two buds and thinned as necessary. Consult the county extension agent for details of pruning. Fertilize yearly in February with 1 cup 8-8-8 per vine. scattered around the base.

Fire Ant Control
Place ant control material such as Orthene or approved natural organic substance on ant mounds in April, June and August each year. Repeat procedure every two weeks if the mound is not killed.

Irrigation
All trees, shrubs and ground cover will be irrigated with drip irrigation. Evaluate all irrigation every two weeks to ensure plants are not being overwatered. Begin operating the drip system twice a week for three hours during the hottest and driest part of the summer. Operate the spray system for the liriope ground cover separately from the trees and shrubs. Water once a week for 30 minutes during the hottest and driest part of the summer. Reduce operation of the spray heads if there is runoff. This plant is rather drought tolerant once established. Do all irrigating in the early morning hours.

Glossary

Acid soil. Soils with a pH below 7; common in areas of plentiful rainfall. *See also* pH.

Aerobic bacteria. Bacteria that need oxygen to survive; present in the breakdown of organic matter into compost.

Agronomist. One who works with the science and economics of crop production.

Alkaline soil. Soils measuring above pH 7 are considered sweet or alkaline; tend to develop in semiarid and arid regions, and in areas where water and lime rock mix to create a free-lime or soluble lime situation.

Allée. Axial landscape space enclosed by walls, colonnades, or trees. Ancient Roman origin.

Ammonium nitrate. A synthetic, granular, fast-release fertilizer that is approximately 33% nitrogen.

Ammonium sulfate. A synthetic, granular, fast-release fertilizer that is approximately 21% nitrogen.

Anaerobic bacteria. Bacteria that do not need oxygen to exist; present in compost piles that need more frequent turning or aeration; evidenced by a strong, disagreeable odor from compost pile.

Angle of repose. The angle at which soil will rest naturally without further sloughing off.

Atrium. Originally a house kitchen with a recessed fire pit centered under a roof opening, later becoming house reception room with pool in center under roof opening, potted plants, and frescoes of outdoor scenes. Ancient Roman origin.

Azulejo. Colorful, glazed tile for veneering walls, steps, and stone benches. Moorish origin.

Bacteria. Unicellular microorganisms occurring in a wide variety of forms either as free-living organisms or parasites and having a range of biochemical, sometimes pathogenic, properties.

Bactericide. A chemical compound that kills bacteria. *See also* pesticide.

Baffle. Plants that form partial enclosure with limited views and pedestrian circulation.

Balanced landscape. A landscape that is in harmony with nature; one that works with the soils, slopes, sun, shade, and moisture resulting in healthy plants and soils that require the least amount of attention and resources to thrive.

Balustrade. A garden stone banister used along the edge of steps and at the top of walls. Italian Renaissance origin.

Bark collar. A ridged area near tree trunk surrounding a lateral limb.

Bedding-out. Plants used in garden areas devoted to seasonal annuals, usually containing brilliant color contrasts. Victorian origin.

Berm. A soil mound.

Boron. A naturally occurring element used by plants in very small amounts. Chemical symbol B.

Bosco (Italian), *bosquet* (French), bosk (American English). Planted tree grove that enframes an axis or walk, provides canopy and shade, and contains smaller gardens within. Italian Renaissance origin.

Bud. Plant growth point, a developing shoot, stem, or flower.

Bulb. An underground stem or root primarily used by some plants for food storage and reproduction.

Calcite. A naturally occurring mineral commonly found in sedimentary rocks.

Calcium. A chemical element used in plant cell walls; found in limestone and chalk. Used in various forms to raise the pH of garden soils. Chemical symbol Ca.

Calcium sulphate. *See* gypsum.

Cambium. A single-cell layer of formative tissue just under bark of woody plants.

Candles. Casual term referring to the growth points of a branch, such as the new tip growth on a pine.

Canker. Dead tissue on a plant twig or branch caused by a pathogen; usually seen as an open wound surrounded by callus.

Carbon-to-Nitrogen Ratio (C:N). A ratio used in blending protein and carbohydrate material; a C:N of 10 will ideally suit the needs of microorganisms decaying a compost pile.

Chelated iron. A water soluble form of iron especially useful under alkaline soil conditions.

Chlorine. An essential trace element used by some plants; is rarely deficient in soils. Chemical symbol Cl.

Chlorosis. Typically a condition in plants caused when a mineral necessary for plant health is deficient and the green leaves yellow or pale. Plants suffering from chlorosis are chlorotic.

Colonnade. A series of equally spaced columns. Ancient Greek origin.

Compost. Organic material, either plant or animal, that has undergone a decaying process.

Contact spray. An insecticide effective on contact.

Copper. A micronutrient used by plants; essential in the transformation of nitrogen into plant food. Chemical symbol Cu.

cm. Abbreviation for centimeter; three centimeters equals approximately one inch.

Concept plan. Proposed land use areas located on the site plan; usually illustrated as bubbles or diagrams labeled with activity or function.

Conifer. Woody plant with needle-like foliage and cone-like fruit. Examples: firs, pines, and yews.

Corm. An underground bulbous plant stem active in reproduction and food storage; the fleshy tissues are not arranged in layers as in a true bulb.

Cul-de-sac. A street that is closed at one end, the closed end is usually curved and includes space for vehicles to turn around.

Dead-head. The act of removing dead flowers from herbaceous plants to prevent seed production and to neaten appearance.

Deciduous. Generally refers to trees, shrubs, and vines without winter foliage.

Division. Vegetative plant propagation using plant clumps, roots, bulbs, or tubers capable of generating a new plant.

Dolomite. A secondary mineral found in sedimentary rocks; primarily composed of magnesium carbonate. Dolomite limestone is a commonly used form of lime in gardens.

Drip irrigation. The application of water to the ground drop-by-drop near the plant root zone.

Dripline. Tree canopy edge circling the trunk; most feeding roots are located within and beyond the dripline area.

Eclectic design. Mixing and blending copied historic styles. Example: Biltmore House and Gardens, Asheville, North Carolina.

Ecosystem. The interrelated community of plants and animals together with the environment.

Elements of design. The components or building blocks of a design. Examples: line, form, space, texture, and color.

Epsom salts. A white, crystalline magnesium sulfate salt, sometimes used to alleviate a magnesium deficiency.

Espalier. A plant, usually a tree or shrub, pruned and trained to grow flat against a vertical plane.

Evapotranspiration. A term used in defining the amount of loss due to water evaporation from the soil and the transpiration of water from plant leaves.

Evergreen. Plant type that retains living foliage throughout the year; may be broad-leaved or narrow-leaved (conifers) types.

Exotic plant. A foreign plant, not indigenous or native to area.

Eyes. Plant growth buds.

Fertilizer, balanced or complete. A plant food mixture containing the three essential elements—nitrogen (N), phosphorus (P), and potassium (K).

Fertilizer burn. Foliage injury caused by fertilizer; symptoms include a bronzing discoloration or spotty browning. Occurs when dry fertilizer remains on plant leaves, drawing water out of the leaves, or if fertilizer is overapplied to the soil where granules attract and hold soil water. Both situations cause leaf stress and burn due to the lack of water.

Focal point. A design term referring to a feature in an outdoor space or on a two-dimensional plane that attracts, holds a person's attention, and provides a place to which the eye continually returns.

Fresco. The art of decorative painting on moist plaster walls. Ancient Egyptian origin.

Frond. Compound leaf of a fern or palm.

Frost pocket. Usually an area at the bottom of a hill where frost settles; any microclimate that experiences frost when surrounding areas do not.

Functional planting design. The aesthetical arrangement of plants to perform tasks in the landscape, such as creating outdoor rooms, blocking winds, and reducing sun heat gain.

Fungicide. A material used to destroy fungi. *See also* pesticide.

Glorieta. A Moorish pavilion or plant-enclosed space at a garden's central intersection of paths or axes. Arabian origin.

Grading. Modification of the ground surface by cuts and/or fills of earth.

Ground forms. Three-dimensional forms on the ground plane that serve to define the garden floor visually.

Gypsum. A mineral commonly found in sedimentary rocks and containing sulfur and calcium; frequently used in amending clay soils.

Haha. A recessed landscape wall to control grazing livestock while providing uninterrupted views beyond. English origin.

Heat gain. The rise in air temperature in a space or building caused by solar rays.

Herbaceous perennial. Fleshy, non-woody plants that die back after the growing season.

Herbicide. A chemical used to destroy plants. *See also* pesticide.

Human scale. A condition whereby space and objects in the space relate to the size of the human figure. When a landscape includes human scale it is usually comfortable for a human being to be present or nearby.

Humus. Decayed leaves, twigs, and other organic matter; usually present naturally on the forest floor; finished compost.

IBDU. Abbreviation for isobutylidene diurea, a slow-release nitrogen source that is water soluble and contains approximately 31% nitrogen.

Insecticide. An agent used to kill insects. *See also* pesticide.

Inorganic mulch. A natural or manmade material that usually will not deteriorate over a period of time, serving a functional and/or aesthetic purpose on the ground surface. Examples: stones or sheet plastic.

Iron. A plant micronutrient available in most soils which assists in the formation of chlorophyll. Chemical symbol Fe. *See also* chelated.

Iron sulfate. A powdered form of iron added to soil to increase available iron.

Isobutylidene diurea. *See* IBDU.

Knot garden. Low, clipped herbaceous plants grown in curvilinear patterns or knots; herbs and flowers planted in resulting spaces. Medieval origin.

Labyrinth. In garden use, a network of intricate walkways enclosed by high hedges; a maze. Originally inspired by floor design patterns of medieval cathedrals.

Landscape architect. A professional practitioner of the art and science of designing the landscape for the use and enjoyment of people. In most states this practice is restricted by law to licensed professionals.

Landscape Architectural Design Process. Specific procedure used to evolve an aesthetic design that is in harmony with the land and reflects the needs of the client.

Landscape management. Applying an understanding of the land and investment needs while providing direction for growth, health, and appearance.

Landscape Management Plan. A specific set of directions for controlling the growth, appearance, and health of a landscape; also used to anticipate future needs.

Leach. To lose soluble matter such as plant nutrients from the root zone of plants due to water washing through the soil.

Loggia. A roofed open gallery or covered terrace.

m. Abbreviation for meter. One meter equals 100 centimeters, approximately 3.3 feet.

Macronutrient. A mineral element used in relatively large quantities by plants. Examples: nitrogen, phosphorus, potassium, sulfur, carbon, hydrogen, and oxygen.

Magnesium. A secondary plant nutrient generally available in soils and used in the formation of chlorophyll. Chemical symbol Mg.

Manganese. A plant micronutrient commonly abundant in soils with a pH between 5 and 6.5. Chemical symbol Mn.

Master Plan. The final site design showing all forms, facilities, spaces, and elements proposed for the site.

Microclimate. A smaller climate zone differing from the larger one due to specific environmental factors. The soil area under roof eaves is drier and receives less light and qualifies as a microclimate.

Microfauna. Microscopic animals; usually present and active during the decomposition of organic matter.

Microflora. Microscopic plant forms; usually present and active during the decomposition of organic matter.

Micronutrient. An element used in relatively small quantities by plants; sometimes referred to as trace elements or minor elements. Examples: iron, copper, manganese, molybdenum, and zinc.

Microorganism. Microscopic animal or plant essential to breaking down organic matter by consuming it.

Milorganite. A brand name for dried and processed sewage sludge.

Molybdenum. A plant micronutrient abundant in alkaline soils, sometimes to the point of toxicity; scarcely available in soils with a pH below 5.5. Chemical symbol Mo.

Monochromatic. Of only one color; frequently used in garden design by creating a green garden, a white garden, etc.

Monoculture. Growing one type of plant in an area, such as a lawn.

Monostand. A planting with only one variety of plant; a lawn of only one type of grass is a monostand.

Mulch. An organic or inorganic material placed on top of the soil for functional and aesthetic purposes. *See also* inorganic mulch, organic mulch.

Nitrate of soda. A fast-release, water soluble nitrogen fertilizer with approximately 10% nitrogen content.

Nitrogen. A macronutrient essential for vigorous growth of leaves and shoots; a primary building block of plant life. Chemical symbol N.

Organic mulch. A natural material that readily breaks down over a period of time and serves a functional and aesthetic purpose in the landscape. Examples: shredded bark, straw, leaves, and various hulls.

Orientation. The relationship to cardinal or compass points; in landscape design frequently useful in promoting energy conservation. As a landscape design premise the significance of orientation was first exploited in ancient Greece.

Parterre garden. Compartmentalized designs of low, clipped evergreen plants often interrupted by flowers; usually to be viewed from above. French Renaissance origin.

Pathogen. An entity that can initiate disease, typically a virus, bacterium, or fungus.

Pergola. A garden structure supported by pillars and used with climbing plants or vines; usually constructed over a walkway. Ancient Egyptian origin.

Pesticide. A substance used to control populations of insects or other plant and animal life considered to be garden pests.

Peristyle. Open court enclosed with a roofed arcade that is supported by columns. Ancient Greek origin.

pH. Symbol representing a method used to determine how acid, neutral, or alkaline a soil or water sample is; determined through testing its hydrogen ion concentration.

pH scale. A scale from 0–14 used to indicate acidity (pH 0–6.9), neutrality (pH 7.0), and alkalinity (pH 7.1–14) of water or soil; the pH scale used for soil typically ranges from 3–11.

Phosphorus. A macronutrient used by plants for root and bud growth, fruit ripening, and winter hardiness. Chemical symbol P.

Photosynthesis. The manufacture of carbohydrates by the green part of a plant with the aid of carbon dioxide, light, and water.

Pleached allée. A walkway enclosed on the sides by trees or shrubs, their interlacing limbs forming arches above. Medieval origin.

Pleaching. To plait, braid, or interlace plant branches as in an arbor.

Pollard. A tree with branches near the trunk pruned in a geometric design; also, a tree topped to encourage a flush of new crown growth. Originated during the French Renaissance to enframe garden axes.

Potassium. A plant macronutrient affecting the production of sugars in leaves, root growth, resistance to insect or disease attacks, and necessary to fruiting plants in encouraging the ripening process. Chemical symbol K.

Potassium nitrate. A fast-release potassium and nitrogen fertilizer that contains approximately 44% potassium and 13% nitrogen.

Principles of design. The fundamental codes used in arranging and integrating the elements of design. Balance, unity, variety, proportion, emphasis, and transition each represent a principle of design. *See also* elements of design.

Revetment. A facing of wood, stone, or concrete on a sloped bank to protect the bank from erosion.

Rhizome. Underground food storage plant part, also useful in propagation; actually an underground stem.

Root zone. The extent of feeder and anchoring roots emanating from a plant. The horizontal root zone of trees can extend two to three times beyond the radius of the tree canopy; vertical depths normally range from near surface to 6 ft (2 m).

Runnel. As a garden element, a narrow, shallow, hard-surfaced channel for flowing water. Moorish origin.

Rust. A reddish brown powdery discoloration of plant foliage or stems; usually a sign of fungus.

Shaduf. An irrigation device consisting of a post with a container strapped to a pivotal pole; used to lift water from irrigation ditches to gardens. Ancient Egyptian origin.

Sewage sludge. The treated and dried solid matter from sewage treatment plants used as a complete garden fertilizer.

Site analysis. The process of determining and evaluating the assets and liabilities of a site.

Sodium. A plant micronutrient and alkaline chemical element; naturally abundant in combined form. Chemical symbol Na.

Sodium borate. A sodium salt derived from boric acid; as borax soap it provides a way to apply boron to plants.

Soil grade. The ground level, natural or man-made. *See also* grading.

Soil permeability. A soil characteristic indicating the rate at which water and water-soluble nutrients move through the soil. Example: sandy soil has high permeability.

Spatial definition. In landscape design, establishing or defining landscape spaces; the creation of outdoor garden rooms.

Spore. Reproductive unit of fungi consisting of one or more cells.

Spreader-sticker. A material added to a spray solution to allow wider coverage on plant parts; typically an oil.

Sulfur. A macronutrient and a prime component necessary to the chlorophyll-making process; often used in garden soils to lower the pH. Chemical symbol S.

Systemic. Generally used in referring to a type of pesticide that acts by being taken into a plant's system.

Thatch. A layer of dead and living stems and grass blades developing between the soil surface and green grass blades.

Transition. A principle of design referring to the movement from one color, texture, line, form, or space to another.

Tuber. Underground food storage plant part, also useful in propagation.

UF. Abbreviation for urea formaldehyde, a slow-release nitrogen fertilizer containing approximately 38% nitrogen.

Urea. A water soluble, fast-release nitrogen fertilizer containing approximately 45% nitrogen.

Water table. The level below which the ground is saturated with water.

Zinc. A micronutrient used by plants in growth and seed formation; present in nearly all soils. Chemical symbol Zn.

For Further Reading

We would like to suggest the following books for those interested in pursuing the topics discussed. There are also many fine journals and local or national organizations that provide particularly current information for a field that seems to change daily. The United States is truly evolving into a gardening country. This interest is reflected in research grants, a proliferation of select gardening groups, and an abundance of information. We hope you continue to realize a balance with the environment.

LANDSCAPE DESIGN: GENERAL

Booth, Norman K. and James E. Hiss. 1991. *Residential Landscape Architecture, Design Process for the Private Residence.* Englewood Cliffs, N.J.: Prentice Hall.

Brookes, John. 1984. *The Garden Book.* London: Dorling Kindersley Limited.

Church, Thomas D., Grace Hall, and Michael Laurie. 1983. *Gardens Are For People.* 2nd ed. New York: McGraw-Hill.

Eckbo, Garrett. 1956. *Art of Home Landscaping.* New York: F. W. Dodge.

Garden and Landscape Staff of Southern Living Magazine. 1992. *Southern Living Courtyards to Country Gardens.* Birmingham, Ala.: Oxmoor House.

Laurie, Michael. 1976. *An Introduction to Landscape Architecture.* 2nd Edition. New York: American Elsevier Publishing.

Simonds, John Ormsbee, 1983. *Landscape Architecture. A Manual of Site Planning and Design.* 2nd ed. New York: McGraw-Hill.

LANDSCAPE DESIGN: HISTORICAL

Berrall, Julia S. 1966. *The Garden. An Illustrated History.* New York: The Viking Press.

Coats, Alice M., with notes by Dr. John L. Crech. 1992. *Garden Shrubs and Their Histories.* New York: Simon & Schuster.

Fairchild, David, assisted by Elizabeth and Alfred Kay. 1938. *The World Was My Garden. Travels of a Plant Explorer.* New York: Charles Scribner's Sons.

Griswold, Mac, and Eleanor Weller. 1991. *The Golden Age of American Gardens. Proud Owners. Private Estates. 1890–1940.* New York: Harry N. Abrams.

Hobhouse, Penelope. 1988. *Garden Style.* Boston: Little, Brown,

Jellicoe, Geoffrey, and Susan Jellicoe. 1975. *The Landscape of Man. Shaping the Environment from Prehistory to the Present Day.* New York: The Viking Press.

Jellicoe, Geoffrey, Susan Jellicoe, Patrick Goode, and Michael Lancaster. 1986. *The Oxford Companion to Gardens.* Oxford: Oxford University Press.

Newton, Norman T. 1971. *Design on the Land. The Development of Landscape Architecture.* Cambridge, Mass.: The Belknap Press of Harvard University.

Robinson, William. 1933. *The English Flower Garden.* 15th Edition. Reprint. New York: The Amaryllis Press, 1984.

Tishler, William H., editor, 1989. *American Landscape Architecture. Designers and Places.* Washington, D.C.: The Preservation Press.

ECOLOGY

Diekelmann, John, and Robert Schuster. 1982. *Natural Landscaping.* New York: McGraw-Hill.

Odom, Eugene P. 1959. *Fundamentals of Ecology.* 2nd ed. Philadelphia: Saunders.

McHarg, Ian L. 1969. *Design With Nature.* Garden City, N.Y.: Natural History Press.

Mitsch, William J., and James G. Gosselink. 1993. *Wetlands.* 2nd ed. New York: Van Nostrand Reinhold.

PLANT MATERIALS

Armitage, Allan M. 1989. *Herbaceous Perennial Plants. A Treatise on Their Identification, Culture, and Garden Attributes.* Athens, Ga.: Varsity Press.

Bailey, Liberty Hyde, and Ethel Joe Bailey. 1976. *Hortus Third.* New York: Macmillan.

Bryan, John E. 1989. *Bulbs.* 2 vols. Portland, Ore.: Timber Press.

Capon, Brian. 1990. *Botany for Gardeners: An Introduction and Guide.* Portland, Ore.: Timber Press.

Castleman, Michael. 1991. *The Healing Herbs.* Emmaus, Pa.: Rodale Press.

Dirr, Michael A. 1990. *Manual of Woody Landscape Plants.* Rev. ed. Champaign, Ill.: Stipes.

Heriteau, Jacqueline, with H. Marc Cathey. 1990. *The National Arboretum Book of Outstanding Plants.* New York: Simon & Schuster.

Hudak, Joseph. 1993. *Gardening With Perennials Month by Month.* 2nd ed. Portland, Ore.: Timber Press.

Jekyll, Gertrude. 1908. *Color Schemes for the Flower Garden.* Reprint. Salem, N.H.: The Ayer Company, 1983.

Johnson, Lady Bird, and Carlton B. Lees. 1988. *Wildflowers Across America.* New York: Abbeville Press.

Martin, Edward C., Jr. 1983. *Landscape Plants in Design. A Photographic Guide.* New York: Van Nostrand Reinhold.

Mitsch, William J. and James G. Gosselink. 1989. *American Horticulture Society Encyclopedia of Garden Plants.* New York: Macmillan.

Odenwald, Neil G., and James Turner. 1987. *Southern Plants. Identification, Selection, and Use in Landscape Design.* Baton Rouge, La.: Claitors Publishing Division.

Welch, William C. 1989. *Perennial Garden Color For Texas and the South.* Dallas, Tex.: Taylor.

Wyman, Donald. 1990. *Trees for American Gardens.* New York: Macmillan.

PLANTING DESIGN

Carpenter, Philip L., and Theodore D. Walker. *Plants in the Landscape.* 2nd ed. 1989. San Francisco: W. H. Freeman.

Druse, Ken. 1989. *The Natural Garden.* New York: Clarkson N. Potter.

Grant, John A., and Carol L. Grant. 1983. *Garden Design Illustrated.* Portland, Ore.: Timber Press.

Hobhouse, Penelope. 1985. *Color in Your Garden.* Boston: Little, Brown.

Nelson, William R. 1985. *Planting Design. A Manual of Theory and Practice.* 2nd ed. Champaign, Ill.: Stipes.

Robinette, Gary O. 1972. *Plants/People/and Environmental Quality.* Washington, D.C.: U.S. Government Printing Office.

Walker, Theodore D. 1991. *Planting Design.* 2nd ed. New York: Van Nostrand Reinhold.

LANDSCAPE MANAGEMENT

Brady, C. Nyle. 1989. *The Nature and Properties of Soils.* New York: Macmillan.

Beard, B. James. 1973. *Turfgrass: Science and Culture.* Englewood Cliffs, N.J.: Prentice Hall.

Bush-Brown, James, and Louise Bush-Brown. 1980. *American's Garden Book.* New York: Macmillan.

Garden and Landscape Staff of Southern Living Magazine. 1981. *Southern Living Gardening Guide.* Birmingham, Ala.: Oxmoor House.

Harris, Richard W. 1992. *Arboriculture, Integrated Management of Landscapes Trees, Shrubs, and Vines.* Englewood Cliffs, N.J.: Prentice Hall.

Melby, Pete. 1988. *Simplified Irrigation Design.* New York: Van Nostrand Reinhold.

Shigo, Alex L. 1991. *Modern Arboriculture. A System Approach to the Care of Trees and Their Associates.* Durnham, N.H.: Shigo & Trees, Associates.

Shigo, Alex L. 1989. *Tree Pruning, A Worldwide Photo Guide.* 1989. Durnham, N.H.: Shigo & Trees, Associates.

Sunset Western Garden Book. 2nd ed. 1992. Menlo Park, Calif.: Lane.

Wyman, Donald. 1987. *Wymans Gardening Encyclopedia.* Updated ed. New York: Macmillan.

PLANT DISORDERS

Although there are many fine books written on plant diseases and insect damage, one of the most appropriate sources may be the local land grant university. Annual publications, usually one for diseases and one for insects, are commonly published in cooperation with the extension services. The advantage is that these references are specific for a particular area. Other valuable references include—

Agricos, George N. 1988. *Plant Pathology.* 3rd ed. San Diego, Calif.: Academic Press.

Arnett, Ross H., Jr., and Richard L. Jacques, Jr. 1981. *Simon & Schuster's Guide to Insects.* New York: Simon & Schuster.

Carr, Anna. 1983. *Rodale's Color Handbook of Garden Insects.* 2nd ed. Emmaus, Pa.: Rodale Press.

Wescott, Cynthia. 1971. *Plant Disease Handbook, Third Edition.* New York: Van Nostrand Reinhold.

Index

Bold page numbers denote in-text illustrations. *Italicized* numbers refer to color plates.